A Complex Exile

A Complex Exile
Homelessness and Social Exclusion in Canada

Erin Dej

UBCPress · Vancouver · Toronto

© UBC Press 2020

All rights reserved. No part of this publication may be reproduced, stored in a retrieval system, or transmitted, in any form or by any means, without prior written permission of the publisher, or, in Canada, in the case of photocopying or other reprographic copying, a licence from Access Copyright, www.accesscopyright.ca.

29 28 27 26 25 24 23 22 21 20   5 4 3 2 1

Printed in Canada on FSC-certified ancient-forest-free paper (100% post-consumer recycled) that is processed chlorine- and acid-free.

Library and Archives Canada Cataloguing in Publication

Title: A complex exile : homelessness and social exclusion in Canada / Erin Dej.
Names: Dej, Erin, author.
Description: Includes bibliographical references.
Identifiers: Canadiana (print) 20200288970 | Canadiana (ebook) 20200289055 | ISBN 9780774865111 (hardcover) | ISBN 9780774865128 (paperback) | ISBN 9780774865135 (PDF) | ISBN 9780774865142 (EPUB) | ISBN 9780774865159 (Kindle)
Subjects: LCSH: Homelessness—Canada. | LCSH: Homeless persons—Services for—Canada. | LCSH: Homeless persons—Care—Canada. | LCSH: Homelessness—Government policy—Canada. | LCSH: Marginality, Social—Canada.
Classification: LCC HV4509 .D45 2020 | DDC 362.5/9280971—dc23

Canadä

UBC Press gratefully acknowledges the financial support for our publishing program of the Government of Canada (through the Canada Book Fund), the Canada Council for the Arts, and the British Columbia Arts Council.

This book has been published with the help of a grant from the Canadian Federation for the Humanities and Social Sciences, through the Awards to Scholarly Publications Program, using funds provided by the Social Sciences and Humanities Research Council of Canada.

Printed and bound in Canada by Friesens
Set in Segoe and Warnock Pro by Apex CoVantage, LLC
Copy editor: Caitlin Gordon-Walker
Proofreader: Alison Strobel
Indexer: Judy Dunlop
Cover designer: Alexa Love

UBC Press
The University of British Columbia
2029 West Mall
Vancouver, BC V6T 1Z2
www.ubcpress.ca

This book is dedicated to the bingo crew – for the laughs, the hugs, the tears, and the Timmies cards. Thank you for including me.

Contents

Acknowledgments / ix

1 Exploring Exclusion among People Experiencing Homelessness / 1

2 The Pillars of Exclusion: Homelessness, Mental Illness, and Criminalization in Canada / 27

3 Managing in Place: The Shelter as Neoliberal Total Institution / 50

4 Identity Management: Identity Making in the Context of Marginalization / 82

5 Taking the Blame: Responsibilizing Homelessness / 115

6 The Homeless Mental Health Consumer: Managing Exclusion through Redeemability / 145

7 Moving toward Inclusion / 182

Notes / 197

References / 203

Index / 225

Acknowledgments

This book has travelled with me across institutions, cities, and personal and career milestones. Consequently, the contents are influenced by the people I met along the way who have been nothing short of generous, encouraging, and supportive. Most importantly, Al, Chico, Christine, Courtney, Daniel, Doug, Gaston, Gerry, Giles, Greg, J. J., Jamie, Jon, Joseph, Julien, Karla, Katie, Lenny, Louise, Mac, Mark, Mary, Matilda, Max, Mia, Mick, Milan, Mustang, Otto, Ron, Ronan, Seamus, Shadow, Sheela, Toby, Tom, Vince, and Wanda offered their stories, perceptions, hopes, and struggles. They are the essence of this book, and I hope I have shared their lives with the same nuance and openness that they showed me. I am grateful to the organizations who allowed me to conduct research in and around their spaces. Their passion and dedication to people who use their services is obvious. Ottawa's homelessness sector and community were quick to show me how to think about resilience, courage, and fortitude within sometimes impossible constraints and challenges. In particular, the Alliance to End Homelessness Ottawa, under the guidance of Mike Bulthuis and later Kristen Holinsky, gave me the space to pursue advocacy opportunities that inform all the work I do. Terrie Meehan is a champion I don't deserve. A heartfelt thanks to Claude Lurette who read the book in its entirety and provided his support for its direction.

This work began in the hallowed halls of the Department of Criminology at the University of Ottawa. I had the benefit of being surrounded by faculty and staff who provided a place to explore, learn, and grow. Ross Hastings, Isabelle Perreault, and Prashan Ranasinghe offered feedback at various points throughout the writing process and strengthened the analytic nature of the work. Sylvie Frigon and Dawn Moore mentored me and had enormous influence over the shape of this work. Jennifer Kilty was the ultimate doctoral supervisor and friend, reading countless drafts, providing intellectual wisdom, pushing me when I needed it, and giving me an unadulterated example of how to be a badass feminist scholar. This book never would have come to fruition without her. I also had the good fortune to spend time and grow alongside peers whom I have come to admire in so many ways: Ben Roebuck, João Velloso, Jennifer Fraser, Shannon Stewart, Lisa Monchalin, Mike Kirk, Laura Dunbar, Christopher Greco, and especially Adina Ilea. They commiserated with me, challenged me, and provided insight in my early thinking of this work and I am indebted to them.

During my time at the Canadian Observatory on Homelessness (COH), based out of York University, I had first-hand experience of what homelessness advocacy looks like and how research can be a tool to mobilize change. It was thanks to the COH that I learned that responding to homelessness could be done differently. Stephen Gaetz graciously read drafts of this book and provided helpful learnings on how its themes fit within the Canadian landscape. Allyson Marsolais worked her magic to provide me the time and energy I needed to complete the book while opening up new opportunities for me to see homelessness research in action. Samantha Vite and Nadia Ali kindly provided feedback on an early version of Chapter 2 and Nadia came to my rescue to help cross the t's and dot the i's in this book's eleventh hour. Thank you. I was and continue to be inspired by many of the people who passed through the COH's doors, including Jesse Thistle, Jesse Donaldson, Steph Vasko, Niveen Saleh, and Ashley Ward. A special thanks to John Ecker and Kaitlin Schwan whose friendship has changed my career and life for the better.

I have the privilege of working in the Department of Criminology at Wilfrid Laurier University, where I have been supported to do critical research, thanks in large part to our Dean, Lauren Eisler. With encouraging hallway chats when they see me frazzled, tea trips, and sitting down to offer wise advice when I need it most, I am lucky to work with such marvellous colleagues. A special thank you to Carrie Sanders, whose mentorship and firm belief that I could write this book have been a game changer.

I am indebted to the folks at UBC Press who have made this dream a reality. Randy Schmidt has been with me every step of the way, guiding me through the thorny process of academic book publication and teaching me how to write a book. Thank you to Caitlin Gordon-Walker for such careful copy editing and Alexa Love for the captivating cover. I would like to thank the two reviewers who so thoroughly and attentively provided their feedback. The book is stronger, and hopefully more impactful, because of their astute suggestions.

Finally, I would like to thank my family for seeing me through the long days and even longer nights to make this book happen. To my parents, Tom and Carol Donohue, who have provided assistance in innumerable ways, I am forever grateful. To my family Adam, Stephanie, Colum, Rachelle, Cassandra, Garrett, Sona, Martin, Adriana, Johnny, Hanna, Abby, Cameron, Ally, Riley, and Harlow for keeping me grounded and for being understanding when I needed to go away and write my book. To Marian and Penelope – my world – thank you for being the strength I needed when I didn't have any left. And yes, Penelope, you can have your own copy.

A Complex Exile

1

Exploring Exclusion among People Experiencing Homelessness

Walking through the hallway of an emergency shelter one frosty February afternoon in Ottawa, I came across a poster on the noticeboard. In bullet points, it listed questions about issues that residents might be facing: "Were they having trouble sleeping?" "Did they lack motivation?" "Were they irritable?" "If so," the poster read, they "may suffer from depression and should seek an assessment from the visiting psychiatric nurse." This was one of my first visits to a homeless-serving agency, and I was shocked at the medicalized understanding of distress. What I perceived to be rational reactions to the difficult and oftentimes degrading circumstances of being homeless were being reconstructed as sickness. What happens when the only lens we have to look through to examine and react to marginalization – that of individual deficiency – is unable to capture the social context within which pathology, criminalization, and social exclusion are situated? In this book, I engage with this question, uncovering the ways that structural and systemic parameters limit our understanding of experiences of homelessness and reinforce the social exclusion of already vulnerable people. I also examine how people who are homeless take action to navigate this terrain.

Despite decades of advocacy, research, and frontline intervention, Canada's most vulnerable populations have seen little improvement in their collective circumstances. Arguably, things have gotten worse. Homelessness has reached epidemic proportions with almost a quarter of a million people a year finding themselves on the street in Canada (Gaetz et al., 2016).

Involuntary psychiatric hospital admissions increase yearly. Those in contact with police, as well as immigrants, are at greatest risk of homelessness, regardless of other characteristics (Lebenbaum et al., 2018). The remand rate has exploded by 355 percent over the last forty years so that there are more people in provincial jails awaiting trial while legally innocent than those found guilty of committing a crime.[1] Meanwhile, the federal prison population grew by almost 18 percent between 2005 and 2015, with Black and Indigenous prisoners being overrepresented, especially Indigenous and racialized women. A third of Canada's federal prison population is Indigenous, and although Indigenous women make up 5 percent of the national female population, they represent 42 percent of incarcerated women (Office of the Correctional Investigator, 2020). Census data reveals that Indigenous Peoples are among the poorest people in Canada while the wealth gap continues to grow across the country (Yalnizyan, 2010).

Each of these exclusionary statuses share common elements. First, racialized minorities and Indigenous Peoples are vastly overrepresented in virtually every area of social control and marginalization. They are targeted and surveilled by police and child protection agencies and are vastly overrepresented in the homeless population. In the case of Indigenous Peoples, systemic inequity and discrimination are a consequence of historical, intergenerational, and contemporary colonization practices such as those experienced through residential schools; the Sixties Scoop; the disproportionate violence and murder against Indigenous women and girls and systemic racism in the policing and prosecution of such crimes; the Indigenization of Canada's carceral systems; and settler-colonial institutions, policies, and actions both large and small. There is also a long history of Black oppression in Canada that underpins the material and cultural disadvantages Black people currently face. From Canada's historically anti-Black *Immigration Act*; the exploitation of Black temporary workers; the increasingly racialized wealth gap; and discrimination in education, employment, and access to housing and services, to the criminalization of Black bodies, people of colour experience exceptionally high rates of poverty and marginalization because of anti-Black racism that permeates the country (Maynard, 2017).

The disciplinary regimes that construct and perpetuate exclusion do so in some obvious, and some less obvious, ways. It is clear how segregation punishes and harms prisoners who are in distress. It is evident how people living in poverty are reduced to living in ghettoized neighbourhoods. It should be apparent to everyone residing in Canada that all levels of government are violating Indigenous Peoples' human rights in regard to accessing clean water, standard health care, and basic educational infrastructure. But exclusion is also perpetuated in other, more insidious ways – the person experiencing homelessness[2] who is forbidden from using the coffee shop bathroom; the man on probation whose "red zone" (areas of the city that are restricted as part of a bail or probation order) includes his doctor's office (Sylvestre et al., 2017); the single mother who is penalized for not filling out the social assistance application form correctly. Exclusion works in a variety of ways to differentiate and Other certain kinds of people from the mainstream social body.

Another technique for ensnaring people in a cycle of perpetual exclusion is to pathologize those who face socio-structural oppression and discrimination. Pathologization – treating something as a medical anomaly – dilutes complex historical, cultural, and social conditions in favour of individual deficits to be addressed by targeting personal failings (Rimke, 2016). Pathologization re-narrates people's emotional and behavioural reactions to inequity and disadvantage as being irrational cognitive patterns, uncontrollable mood swings, and a warped sense of self and the world around them. Mental illness diagnoses and the broader mental health system are key tools used to exclude those who react to and/or resist social injustice. Pathologization downplays people's distress[3] by failing to recognize and respond to the trauma that the modern social world creates.

The mad movement – the activist-oriented, user-led successor of the anti-psychiatry movement of the 1960s and '70s (Burstow, 2005) – problematizes distressed people's marginalization and challenges the use of mental illness as a medicalized concept, providing alternative understandings of distress and its treatment, such as advocating for peer-support services. When I began this research project, I immersed myself in the anti-psychiatry and mad movement literatures. Inspired by leading authors in the movement (Burstow, 2004, 2005; Laing, 1960, 1967; McLean, 2000; Sedgwick, 1982; Shimrat, 1997; Szasz, 1974, 1989), I began to think critically about how the mental health system can be used as a tool to exclude those who do not meet dominant conceptions of normality. This literature highlights the ways that psy-disciplines – psychiatry, psychology, and other disciplines related to these areas – use medical discourse to make moral and political judgments. In adopting this critical stance, I do not discount the distress many people experiencing homelessness face; rather, it is a testament to the way socio-structural conditions are rendered invisible by the biomedical model.

With these thoughts in mind, I began my research looking for transgressive acts that defied pathologizing discourses and practices. I was looking for instances where people experiencing homelessness refused medication, sought alternative modes of recovery, and questioned psy-experts. But as I spent more time in homeless-serving agencies and getting to know people who used homeless-oriented services, it became clear to me that something more complex was going on. I had to be careful not to romanticize all actions that differed from the norm as forms of resistance (Munn & Bruckert, 2010; Pollack, 2005). The people I spent time with who were homeless had a much more variegated relationship with the mental health system, those in positions of power, and their own sense of self than I had anticipated.

Despite the medical paradigm and psy-language (used and promoted by the psy-disciplines) proliferating within the homelessness sector, it became clear to me in my time in these spaces that blatantly coercive governing strategies, such as involuntary psychiatric hospitalization or forced medication compliance, are rarely used. More commonly, popular mental health interventions encourage residents to seek out their own care rather than impose treatment on them. This reality is a more complex and nuanced understanding of the mental health system and its multifarious forms of governance (diagnoses, psychotropic medication, in- and outpatient addiction treatment, case management, group therapy, provisions for basic care [encouraging/forcing hygienic practices], and involuntary hospitalization) than that described by much of the psy-literature and its critics. Diagnoses, treatments, programming, and surveillance that make up mental health practices are complex and introduce questions about how people experiencing homelessness negotiate and reconcile with the mental health system, its manifest and latent objectives, and how the system acts to regulate and manage those deemed "abnormal." In my search for answers to these questions, I came to uncover how those experiencing homelessness make sense of their mental health identity and the spaces and institutions that they frequent. I also uncovered how the mental health system can have the unintended effect of reinforcing, rather than ameliorating, social exclusion for those already marginalized.

The Project

The findings presented in this book are based on my years of immersion in spaces frequented by and among people experiencing homelessness in Ottawa, Canada. The research uses a combined social-constructionist and symbolic-interactionist paradigm that provides a critical orientation to deconstruct discourses, so as to reveal the power relations that produce them (Rose, 1998). Social constructionism views knowledge as being mediated by social, cultural, and temporal conditions. Truth claims are not rooted in a particular reality but are social processes situated within power imbalances that afford some knowledge dominance over others. Symbolic interactionism studies how people make meaning of their lives based on social interaction. Meaning-making is a social, cultural, and political process rooted in connections between people and between people and institutions (Becker, 1963; Blumer, 1969). Combining social constructionism and symbolic interactionism allows epistemological questions on the nature of homelessness and mental illness and their governance to be formed in and through an investigation of the day-to-day lives of the research participants (Hacking, 2004). I chose the methods used in this study – interviews, participant observation, and a focus group – to seek out subjugated knowledges and privilege the experiences and world views of people who are homeless. The methodological framework provides an opportunity to reveal the connections between individual experiences of marginalization and the broader social forces that impact those lived realities.

Before conducting this research, I was very much an outsider to the homeless population in Ottawa (Adler & Adler, 1987; Kaler & Beres, 2010) and continue to be in some important ways, having never experienced homelessness or institutionalization myself. In the year leading up to data collection, I volunteered in two of Ottawa's homeless shelters and one church-based soup kitchen. I took on a number of roles by serving meals in all three locations, by participating in evening socials and activity nights, and by simply spending time in the common areas of the shelters and church. I attended special events such as Christmas parties, summer barbecues, and music nights. I was often seen around the halls of these organizations four to five days a week. It took a long time to gain respect and build trust and rapport with people experiencing homelessness. There is a high turnover rate for volunteers and staff alike in homeless-serving organizations, with many people volunteering only until they reach their required number of community service hours. Similarly, those who are applying to various police forces may only volunteer during the active recruitment phase. I was able to distinguish myself from these volunteers primarily by remaining in the field for longer than a few months. But it also became apparent that I was genuinely interested in getting to know the people in the community and had frequent, candid conversations about the nature of volunteering and the paternalistic attitude some volunteers project in their attempt to "do good."[4] Indeed, the acceptance I felt in the community came from G., a soft-spoken man with whom I had always been friendly but had not had long interactions. He caught me by surprise one day when he brought me a poem he had written and framed. The poem was a beautiful rhyme about the time I spent in the shelter, with the last lines reading: "For to listen much more than to read / From a heart who believes in its cause."

Most of my encounters with people using these spaces were casual. We chatted about sports, the weather, and current events. Some interactions were especially meaningful: I did the crossword with Seamus every Friday for two years; William tried (in vain) to teach me how to paint; Jasmyn kept me company while I did dishes as she talked about her struggles with religion and men. After some time spent bearing witness to the lives of the people around me (Caron, 2014) and simply being in the community, it became evident to myself and to others that I had "taken a side" (Becker, 1967). As a result, I deepened my resolve for social justice with respect to homelessness and, over time, I transitioned from being a "peripheral member researcher" to an "active member researcher" (Adler & Adler, 1987). I have gained "acceptable incompetent" status (Lofland et al., 2006), where I am generally forgiven for not knowing certain terms and references, and people are willing to teach me rather than dismiss me as an ignorant stranger.

After a year spent getting to know the landscape of homelessness in Ottawa, I received ethics approval from the Research Ethics Board of the University of Ottawa and began data collection in two emergency shelters. The Board approved all three of my methods, and I adhered to all of the appropriate recruitment and consent protocols necessary for conducting research with marginalized groups.

Crossroads[5] is a large men's emergency shelter with over two hundred beds and many social, housing, and health services. Residents can spend time in the main lobby and lounge and have access to the dining room, staff offices, and services at various points during the day. Besides regularly being over capacity, Crossroads provides services for many people who stay at other shelters or who are precariously housed, making it an important hub for the homeless population. The second shelter, Haven, contains separate women's and men's shelters within the same overall building as well as several supportive housing developments. I spent my time in the women's section of the shelter. Haven also has just over two hundred beds and provides specialized services for those who are most deeply entrenched in street life, using a harm-reduction philosophy whereby strategies and programs seek to minimize the health risks and social harms of particular behaviours (i.e., drug use, sex work, etc.) rather than expect abstinence. Because of its harm-reduction orientation, Haven has a reputation for being rougher and more insecure than some of the other shelters in the city but is also a place with fewer barriers to service where people can stay when they are not welcome elsewhere. The core of both shelters are the frontline offices, where staff sit behind glass walls so they can watch CCTV footage of almost every corner of the buildings. Both shelters are highly regulated spaces with lots of staff presence during the day (much less so in the evening hours) and where safety and security are prioritized.

Between my time spent at Crossroads and Haven, I conducted 296 hours of participant observation, taking field notes after each volunteer shift. Field notes were a rich source of data and a way for me to reflect on my position within the field, as I often included my own thoughts, emotions, and concerns (Hannem, 2014). Conducting participant observation allowed me to witness how the agencies and actors involved in mental health care and the homelessness sector engage with residents and service users. It also provided me with insider knowledge about how the shelters function, the routines and rules of shelter residents, and how individuals experiencing homelessness form and maintain relationships between themselves, staff, and other members of the homeless population.

I conducted forty-four interviews with men and women experiencing homelessness, thirty-eight of which were used in the research.[6] Overall, I spoke with a relatively diverse subset of the homeless population in Ottawa, providing a variety of responses and perspectives. Further demographic information is listed in Table 1.

TABLE 1
Interview demographics

Demographic	Result	
Average age	37	
Gender	71% men	28% women
Race	73% white 8% Black	16% Indigenous
Sexual orientation	75% straight	25% LGBTQ2S+
Identified mental illness	84%	
Taken psychotropic medication	73%	
Identified addiction	89%	
Interaction with the criminal justice system	79%	

I recruited interview participants first through a poster put up in the shelters and later through snowball sampling as a result of my initial recruitment efforts. I conducted interviews in locations that were comfortable for participants, such as a private room in the shelter, on a park bench, or at a coffee shop. Interview participants received $25 remuneration in advance of the interview that had no bearing on the quality of their responses or their willingness to complete the interview. The semi-structured interviews lasted an average of forty-five minutes, with some lasting over two hours, and were digitally recorded with participant permission. The interviews focused on participants' experiences of homelessness; health and mental well-being; using the mental health system, including taking/refusing psychotropic medication and programming; how their status as homeless impacts their mental health; and thoughts on treatment.

Finally, I conducted a focus group with professionals and para-professionals who work in the homelessness sector. Professionals are people with education and qualifications from formalized programs and are usually backed by a professional association (e.g., the Canadian Medical Association). Often professionals have decision-making authority. Para-professionals are those who work in the field but do not have these kinds of official credentials. Para-professionals may work on the front line and organize and run programming. The focus group was made up of five key informants ranging from community service providers to individuals involved in shelter management. I used the focus group to gain information on how mental health is managed in shelters and in the community, as well as the most common mental health diagnoses and medications prescribed, and to discuss the range of mental health services offered to people experiencing homelessness. In this way, the focus group supplemented and contextualized the narratives provided by those experiencing homelessness; it did not test the truth claims made in the interviews. Following data collection, I conducted one additional interview with a mental health nurse as a "member checking" interview (Fontana & Frey, 2000) to receive clarification on some of the lingering questions I had after the interviews were complete.

Once I reached theoretical saturation[7] I left the field to the extent that I no longer collected data but I continued to volunteer at both shelters for another eight months and remained a volunteer at one of the shelters for several years. I conducted a critical discourse analysis that allowed me to situate individual narratives within broader systematic and institutional power relations. Critical discourse analysis uses texts (including individual narratives) to bring to light ideological formations as they exist within dominant social structures. Critical discourse analysis distinguishes itself from other practices, such as content analysis, by making explicit the power dynamics at play in the texts (Fairclough, 1985; van Dijk, 1993), thus fitting well within the social constructionist framework. Grounded in the participants' voices, the research explicates how people experiencing homelessness use mental health resources and other techniques to manage their status as always-already excluded.

The Argument

In this book I make two interrelated arguments. Both address how various systems manage homelessness and govern the homeless population, and the unintended consequences of maintaining the status quo. The first argument is that over the past thirty years, Canada's emergency response to the growing homelessness crisis from all levels of government created a homelessness industrial complex that individualizes the causes and experiences of homelessness and has the effect of perpetuating social exclusion. The second argument is that, given the realities of this social exclusion, many people experiencing homelessness vie for "redeemable" status, one that carries opportunities and obligations, but which remains entrenched within exclusionary discourses.

The Homelessness Industrial Complex
I use the term *homelessness industrial complex* to describe a series of sectors, institutions, public systems, community organizations, policies, practices, and funding structures designed to manage and maintain, rather than end, homelessness. I derive this concept from the "non-profit industrial complex," defined as: "A set of symbiotic relationships that link together political and financial technologies of state and owning class control with surveillance over public political intercourse" (Rodríguez, 2007, p. 21). The non-profit industrial complex points to the ways that state governance techniques and funding models constrain agencies and groups into narrow, program-specific categories that breed competitiveness and inflexibility in an effort to ensure organizational viability. These restrictions have the effect of silencing advocacy related to broader social questions, even though staff are often keenly aware of the structural issues at play in the lives of the people they serve. In so doing, the non-profit industrial complex absorbs and transforms activism into social services that at best work to reform, rather than dismantle, institutional and social arrangements (Rodríguez, 2007; Smith,

2007; Wilson Gilmore, 2007). This is obvious in the case of the "prison industrial complex," a related concept describing the business of prisons and the ways private corporations profit off the maintenance and expansion of the carceral population (Davis, 1998). Numerous studies reveal that while service providers working with criminalized people find creative ways to offer support, in many cases their work bolsters the criminal justice system and its underlying inequalities (Quirouette, 2018; Tomczak & Thompson, 2019). For example, Dobchuk-Land (2017) reveals that community-based policing initiatives are rooted in managing the urban Indigenous population in Winnipeg, rather than revitalizing that community. In the homelessness sector specifically, funding constraints encourage service providers to engage in advocacy, but in ways that align with government departmental interests (Mosley, 2012). As a concept, the homelessness industrial complex allows us to pay attention to the unique ways homeless-serving agencies are bureaucratized and how responsibility is downloaded by the state onto the homelessness sector to "do something" about homelessness. "Doing something" is often conceived by local politicians and the public as rendering homelessness less visible to the housed public.

It is not easy to unravel the concept of the homelessness industrial complex. It points to the ways that many well-intentioned, compassionate, and vocal supporters of those who are homeless, myself included, work within structures, systems, institutions, programs, and policies that are sustainable only as long as homelessness and/or the ongoing marginalization of people living precariously is maintained. Funding parameters, evaluation strategies, political buy-in, and marketable fundraising campaigns limit the kinds of narratives that the sector can use and the services they can offer, regardless of how much people working within this complex seek to make a difference for the homeless population.

The homelessness industrial complex relies on the pathologization of homelessness as a key strategy to manage what are positioned as personal and individual failings. The structural roots of homelessness – poverty, capitalism, colonialism, racism, sexism, and other forms of discrimination – are ignored or left at the periphery, while the industry builds its knowledge and capacity around managing the individual. The mental health system acts as a cornerstone for this work. Along with, and often connected to, calls for access to affordable housing, providing mental health care (usually limited to psychotropic medication) is positioned as *the* solution to the homelessness problem. This is not to say that people experiencing homelessness may not benefit from mental health care; rather, I argue that it is a problem to situate the mental health system as a panacea for the homelessness crisis. Throughout this book, I articulate the ways that these individualizing modes of governance operating within the homelessness industrial complex can actually reinforce social exclusion and contribute to the ongoing marginalization of people who have experienced homelessness. They have the effect of limiting our gaze to what is wrong with the person, rather than allowing us to look at how social, economic, and cultural structures are designed to create permanent precarity and instability.

Redeemability
My second argument is that people experiencing homelessness manage social exclusion in unique ways, including through their interactions with the mental health system. With minimal social and financial capital, those experiencing homelessness seek out, accept, or resist mentally ill identities and treatments in ways that impact their level of autonomy and access to interventions of their choosing. I situate this argument within the dialectics of exclusion (Young, 1999) that analyze the processes of accentuating marginality and difference so as to create and amplify Otherness. As described in detail below, scholars such as Bauman, Castel, Rose, Spitzer, and Young have sought to position exclusion along a continuum. Adopting this framework, this book traces the varying degrees of exclusion experienced by people who are homeless and the ways that certain kinds of exclusion are deemed preferable to others. Expanding from Rose's (2000) conceptual tools, I use the term *redeemability* as a status and identity marker that many people who are homeless strive to achieve. Redeemability connotes a level of accountability and willingness to adopt the values, norms, and behaviours that are promoted by the mental health, addiction, and homeless-serving sectors, while continuing to face social exclusion in a variety of ways. Having redeemable status in the eyes of psy-professionals and service providers, as well as their peers and themselves, means that people are deemed worthy of privileges and resources offered by homeless-serving agencies. Providers of those services have a mandate to support people to become members of included society – defined loosely as the mainstream world of housed people (where wealthy, white, cis, heteronormative, able-bodied men dominate), who are not asked to move along when standing on the sidewalk, who are not stopped by police for being intoxicated in public, and whose daily schedules are not dictated by social services.

It is worth noting at this point that exclusion (and inclusion) is not static, either as a concept or in its lived experience. Exclusion and inclusion vary depending on the spaces and communities someone moves within, the layers of privilege or oppression someone embodies, and the appetite for social and cultural diversity that exists in a particular neighbourhood or state. People experiencing homelessness, while physically and symbolically excluded in many ways, shift between varying degrees of inclusion and exclusion. There is rarely a fixed moment when someone becomes officially "included." For example, in their attempt to create a definition of what amounts to an "end" to homelessness in a given city, Turner et al. (2017) revealed that some people who exit shelters and secure housing continue to identify as homeless given the precarity of their living situation, continued impoverishment, and social isolation. Conversely, many people experiencing homelessness feel included in important ways, through formal employment (i.e., with day-labour contracts or jobs in construction, restaurants, etc.) or informal employment (i.e., drug dealing, sex work, etc.), and many, although not all, have at least one significant and meaningful relationship to a parent, sibling, or children, despite living on the margins.

Redeemability, then, points to the variations along the inclusion-exclusion continuum, in particular to the possibility of achieving a high level of integration within otherwise exclusionary institutions, systems, communities, and relationships. Redeemability highlights the tactics people use to navigate the homelessness industrial complex and the ways autonomy and freedom intersect with disciplinary technologies so that people experiencing homelessness are positioned as responsible for managing their trajectory along the continuum.

Key Messages

These arguments embody two overarching messages that I wish to communicate through this book. The first is that social exclusion, in all its iterations, has a profoundly negative effect on a person's housing, homelessness, and well-being. While rooflessness is undoubtedly the primary concern with regard to homelessness, there are subtle forms of exclusion that have grave consequences for someone's sense of self and material conditions. Without broader social inclusion and belonging, many people who have experienced homelessness will continue to face seemingly insurmountable barriers to a sense of true inclusion. The result can be a deep sense of hopelessness that stifles personal resiliency, creates the feeling that inclusion is impossible to attain, and makes striving for redeemability (and submitting to the necessary governing techniques to achieve that status) appear to be the only viable solution to surviving homelessness. This sense of hopelessness, a lack of social support and access to services, and struggles with distress make maintaining permanent housing exceptionally difficult, resulting in cycles in and out of homelessness.

The second objective of this book is to take the position that we must permanently change the way we respond to homelessness. Focusing primarily on individual deficits limits innovation and radical social transformation. While substantial structural change seems too utopian or "pie in the sky" for many, failing to recognize and address systemic drivers of homelessness inevitably leaves individual factors as the only explanatory tool for homelessness as a social phenomenon. These individualized responses responsibilize people for their homelessness and often provide narrow mechanisms for addressing personal faults (especially using the mental health system) with little to no room for autonomy, choice, or alternative conceptualizations of what it means to be homeless, mentally ill, disabled, addicted, etc. This book draws attention to the ways that collective responses to homelessness must be rooted in structural understandings of homelessness and that these structural underpinnings perpetuate exclusion and undermine efforts to reduce homelessness.

Framing Homelessness

Freedom
The historical and cultural moment in which one lives moulds how we move about the world, determines who constrains us and how, and shapes the relationships between the state, community, and private citizens. Here I am referring to governmentality, a Foucauldian term that studies how government is practised – that is, who can govern, what governing looks like, who or what is being governed, and how we govern ourselves (Dean, 1996; Gordon, 1991). Governmentality scholars examine "regimes of truth" – knowledge creation that frames the way we think about a subject (Garland, 1990). For example, homelessness and the policies, institutions, and services created to respond to it act as a kind of regime of truth. Homelessness is defined and constituted by various discourses related to property ownership, economic forces, houselessness as an identity marker, and cultural stigma. Homelessness is generally believed to be a *true* concept and state of being that calls for particular actions based on this truth – individualized, short-term, and historically dehumanizing responses built within the pre-existing capitalist market. Governmentality studies parse out how regimes of truth make up the discourses and techniques that shape the way we act on ourselves.

Foucault (1991) reminds us that power is not a possession; power moves through and around us, between state actors, professional experts, cultural icons, families, and ourselves. Modern power relations are made up of networks of actors who share (or translate) information, ideas, and values across sites and work to convince us to adopt social norms and govern ourselves, rather than force us to act a certain way through the threat of punishment (Garland, 1997; Miller & Rose, 2008). Individual subjects develop and maintain power relations by embracing discourses and technologies that shape our world views, moral compasses, behaviours, and interactions with others (Nettleton, 1997).

Autonomy – the ability to govern oneself without external constraint, domination, or coercion – is at the heart of self-governing technologies (Reindal, 1999). Despite its connotation with uninhibitedness, autonomy is laden with power dynamics that we exercise on ourselves and others. We are governed through our freedom. Rose (1999) is clear that this does not mean that freedom isn't *real* but that the notion of freedom is historically, culturally, and socially constituted and is given meaning through the techniques and practices we attach to it. Freedom does not simply remove constraints in a passive sense; it requires us to act (Dumm, 1996). We are expected to adopt technologies of the self to assess, work on, and control ourselves. This can mean anything from making litterless lunches to watching motivational TED talks, counting our steps each day, going on a yoga retreat, seeing a therapist, or taking psychotropic medication. Individuals must develop a relationship with the self to gain authority over their desires, impulses, behaviours, and cognitive patterns. To be free means to judge and act on ourselves to facilitate improvement. Freedom comes with obligations to conduct ourselves rationally and accept personal responsibility for all facets of our lives (Rose, 1999). As I describe throughout this book, a common narrative among individuals participating in self-help programs is one of accepting complete personal blame for their social circumstances. In these stories, personal power is seen as the primary mechanism for escaping homelessness, and referencing past victimization or social inequity is understood as an unhealthy avoidance strategy. Freedom, then, is a mixed blessing – the freedom to choose who you want to be is accompanied by the responsibility to choose correctly (Bauman, 1988). Failure to live up to the obligations of freedom, and to do so in a socially acceptable way, leads to a loss of that freedom. This is especially the case when self-responsibilization strategies are thrust on populations that have few resources that would enable them to live up to normative ideals. There, the distinction between freedom and coercion becomes blurred.

An analysis of practices of freedom would be incomplete without looking at the other side of the coin – disciplinary strategies. Discipline is a method of control targeting the body, mind, and behaviours in subtle ways, by manipulating time and space, and most importantly, creating the docile body that is observable, malleable, and transformable (Foucault, 1977). The bodies of those experiencing homelessness are rendered docile, for example, through anti-poverty legislation that criminalizes sleeping in public, panhandling, loitering, or causing a disturbance (Sylvestre, 2010a). Disciplinary forces are omnipresent for marginalized people who are assumed to be unable to self-govern (this lack of responsibility is unfairly thought to be the cause of their homelessness). The homelessness industrial complex is designed as a disciplinary space both for the sake of physical safety and security (Ranasinghe, 2017) and to provide structures and routines that are meant to act as building blocks for successful independent living, despite imposing limitations on residents' decision-making capacities. Disciplinary strategies are successful when those being surveilled and managed internalize a dominant society's values and act on themselves accordingly, as well as disseminating the values in the community.

Governing technologies can rely on disciplinary and self-governance elements simultaneously. Initiatives, policies, and interventions used to manage those experiencing homelessness are based on the idea that people who are homeless cannot adequately govern themselves (often because they do not have the financial and social resources to do so and because they face widespread discrimination and oppression) and so require discipline until such time as they are deemed capable of self-governance. We must keep in mind that institutional practices and techniques to assess someone's ability or potential to self-govern often exist within and reinforce class-based, racial, gendered, colonial, heteronormative, and ableist divisions (Chan et al., 2005; Jiwani, 2001; Razack, 2015).[8] Marginalized people are held to the same standards of self-actualization and self-improvement as those who are more privileged but they are meant to achieve these goals differently and with different degrees of freedom (Castel, 1988). As explored in detail in Chapter 6, the "good" neoliberal citizen exerts their individual freedom by purchasing advice, expertise, and goods from whomever they wish. For those who do not have the means to act as a consumer, disciplinary regimes impose authority figures (i.e., case manager, counsellor, probation officer, etc.) and programs on them. Their inability to participate in the consumerist project suggests a need for an external figure to make decisions for them until they are ready to handle the obligations of freedom (Rose, 1996, 1999). Many people, including those experiencing homelessness and those labelled mentally ill, are restricted from the "regime of choice" regarding which sorts of programs and experts they want to engage with or avoid. In the section that follows I consider how people experiencing homelessness navigate the mental health system given their constrained freedom, often by positioning themselves as redeemable along the continuum of exclusion.

Exclusion

People experiencing homelessness have faced exclusion throughout history, from the maligned vagabond to disdained skid row inhabitants. However, the conditions of exclusion contain unique features in the late-modern, neoliberal regime, where those experiencing homelessness are expected to take responsibility for, and use self-governing practices to improve their economic and social status. Young (1999) argues that people who are excluded are trapped in a series of circumstances that leave them in a state of desperation, and as I will argue throughout the book, hopelessness. Young describes the contemporary paradigm where excluded persons are regarded as complicit in their own exclusion: a corollary to the expectation that individuals should engage in their own governance. Many individuals internalize the rejection and dehumanization they experience, which can lead to them embodying the social processes of exclusion and excluding others in similarly marginal positions, creating further divisions. Through gentrification, policing practices, and defensive architecture,[9] public spaces are increasingly denied to those experiencing homelessness (Hermer & Mosher, 2002) so that many refrain from visiting shopping malls, busy urban streets, and public parks to avoid visible rejection, thus pre-emptively excluding themselves from these public spaces. This is part of the larger responsibilization project that will be described throughout this book, most notably in Chapter 5.

While it is undeniable that people experiencing homelessness face corporeal, social, spatial, and economic exclusion, the inclusion/exclusion binary represents a false dichotomy and fails to capture the material experiences of many marginalized people who find themselves included and excluded in various ways. I am especially reluctant to designate those experiencing homelessness as occupying a singularly excluded existence since they are already stereotyped within numerous unrealistic and harmful dichotomies: sane/insane, rational/irrational, good/bad, and productive/unproductive, among others. Powerful institutions and actors, such as the criminal justice system, adopt these classifications and further exclude already marginalized populations and so we must interrogate how the dichotomies advance institutional and state objectives. The notion of redeemability allows us to pay attention to the varied ways people experience, lean into, and/or reject exclusionary discourses and practices in any given time, location, or social context.

Thinking about exclusion along a continuum captures how exclusionary and inclusionary practices play out for people experiencing homelessness. Rather than seeing it as a process of strictly inclusion or exclusion, Young (1999) describes modern exclusion as a "sifting process" (p. 65), where people gradually experience more severe modes of exclusion (from eligibility criteria that prevent enrolment in a private school down to criminal record checks that deny access to housing) as they move toward what he terms "the underclass." As I explore various ways of conceptualizing exclusion, we must keep in mind that these are symbolic categorizations that do not necessarily reflect personal experiences; rather, they are designated onto people by those in positions of power and privilege. Those experiencing homelessness are sometimes characterized in the literature as the underclass, or "anti-citizens":

> Outside the communities of inclusion exists an array of micro-sectors, micro-cultures of non-citizens, failed citizens, anti-citizens, consisting of those who are unable or unwilling to enterprise their lives or manage their own risk, incapable of exercising responsible self-government, attached either to no moral community or to a community of anti-morality. (Rose, 1999, p. 259)

Rose describes anti-citizens as a group of long-term welfare recipients, street criminals, alcoholics, drug dealers, single mothers, and deinstitutionalized psychiatric patients. Rose and others (Huey, 2012; Young, 1999) specifically list the drug user, the criminal, and the homeless person as typifying those living "outside of society." I would add that many of those identified as mentally ill are also often subsumed in this marginalized category. Simply being without an address hinders numerous inclusionary activities, such as applying for jobs, spending time with family and friends, and engaging in self-chosen leisure activities. Moreover, interconnected institutional practices, policies, and resources reproduce social relations that exclude people experiencing homelessness across institutions and spaces. For example, over-policing already ghettoized neighbourhoods reinforces the stereotype that those living in poverty (disproportionately people of colour and Indigenous Peoples) engage in more criminal activity than those living in neighbourhoods without heavy surveillance (Nichols & Braimoh, 2018). Exclusion exists structurally and at the personal level and is a process that distances people from positive social encounters and relationships, culminating in feelings and experiences that dehumanize, degrade, and deny active participation in social life (Silver & Miller, 2002).

It is clear that social exclusion – its practices, strategies, material experiences, and consequences – is not homogenous; thinking of exclusion simply as the end point of a continuum does not get us very far toward understanding the experience of exclusion. Spitzer (1975) famously coined the terms "social junk" and "social dynamite" to distinguish between the statuses ascribed to people on the basis of their perceived level of threat. Social junk is defined

> from the point of view of the dominant class, [as] a costly yet relatively harmless burden to society. The discreditability of social junk resides in the failure, inability or refusal of this group to participate in the roles supportive of capitalist society. Social junk is most likely to come to official attention when informal resources have been exhausted or when the magnitude of the problem becomes significant enough to create a basis for "public concern." Since the threat presented by social junk is passive, growing out of its inability to compete and its withdrawal from the prevailing social order, controls are usually designed to regulate and contain rather than eliminate and suppress the problem. (Spitzer, 1975, p. 645)

Many members of the homeless population fall into the social junk category from the point of view of society's dominant classes. This is particularly true of older homeless adults, people with disabilities, and many of those who are taken up by the mental health system. Yet, as others have noted (Elbogen & Johnson, 2009), those experiencing homelessness and those identified as mentally ill are often considered to be volatile and threatening and thus not nearly as benign as the social junk category suggests. Those who perceive these groups as a threat would perhaps find the social dynamite designation more fitting:

> The essential quality of deviance managed as social dynamite is its potential actively to call into question established relationships, especially relations

of production and domination. Generally, therefore, social dynamite tends to be more youthful, alienated and politically volatile than social junk. The control of social dynamite is usually premised on an assumption that the problem is acute in nature, requiring a rapid and focused expenditure of control resources. This is in contrast to the handling of social junk frequently based on a belief that the problem is chronic and best controlled through broad reactive, rather than intensive and selective measures. Correspondingly, social dynamite is normally processed through the legal system with its capacity for active intervention, while social junk is frequently (but not always) administered by the agencies and agents of the therapeutic and welfare state. (Spitzer, 1975, pp. 645–646)

The social dynamite category is closely connected with the disciplinary tools commonly used on those experiencing homelessness and in distress, particularly the heavy reliance on the criminal justice system as a technique of exclusion. However, social dynamite refers to an acute state of risk more than one of chronic exclusion. Spitzer (1975) suggests that a population can be dealt with alternatively as social junk *or* social dynamite, or as both simultaneously. The combination of the two is expressed through the myriad of social control strategies used on the homeless population and those identified as mentally ill; however, Spitzer stops short of explaining how the two ascribed identities coexist. The coalescence of disciplinary schemes and techniques of the self is pivotal to understanding how individuals experiencing homelessness negotiate the mental health system and their sense of self, and position themselves in the homelessness industrial complex.

Other scholars use models similar to Spitzer's to describe variations in social control strategies. I am influenced by the model formulated by Rose (2000) for theorizing redeemability in this book. Rose distinguishes the ways people deemed "anti-citizens" by those in positions of power are managed based on distinctions made between those who are considered "redeemable" and those who are considered "impossible." He defines the irredeemable or "monstrous" individuals as those who lack any civility and who are made out to be permanently fragmented. They are the anti-social, the predator, and the paedophile. Criminologists have used similar terms such as "unempowerable" (Hannah-Moffat, 2000a, 2000b) and "unsalveagable" (Desjarlais, 1997) to describe the level of exclusion facing women prisoners, for example. Control strategies for this population follow an actuarial risk management logic focused on containing future harm rather than rehabilitation. Most of the research participants in this study would not be identified as the heinous criminals Rose describes, although many of them have been incarcerated in jails, prisons,[10] and psychiatric institutions at some point in their lives. The majority of those who cycle in and out of correctional facilities and homeless shelters are not likely considered high risk and are rarely under continuous state surveillance, but they do face other, less formal modes of risk assessment, regulation, and what I call *surveillance at a distance* from social services (Moore, 2011; Quirouette, 2016). Given the high rates of people experiencing homelessness who have been arrested or incarcerated (John Howard Society of Toronto, 2010; To et al., 2016), most people making up the homeless population in Canada could be described as the "semi-permanent quasi-criminal population" (Rose, 2000, p. 336) who are not impossible, but who find themselves caught up in a series of ad hoc techniques of social control. The *redeemable*, then, are those excluded people who are expected to take responsibility for their behaviours and engage in self-governance rather than rely on external modes of surveillance. Recognizing the excluded population as existing along a continuum of redeemability nuances how exclusionary practices play out and makes sense of competing actuarial and welfare-based strategies that coexist as part of the broader schemes for governing marginalized people. The excluded meet with both inclusionary and exclusionary practices, negotiating with these strategies to mediate their status along the continuum that stretches from being fully redeemed and included to complete irredeemability.

I have made the case that exclusion is not a static identity marker and that people experiencing homelessness will encounter various kinds of governing strategies that have the effect of moving them along the inclusion-exclusion continuum. Given the heterogeneity of the homeless population, it is inaccurate to pinpoint people experiencing homelessness as strictly excluded or "irredeemable" but so too would it be a disservice to the challenges and barriers they face not to address the ways governing technologies perpetuate exclusion and marginalization. Throughout my time in the shelters, it became clear to me that there are a range of strategies, tools, and techniques used to manage people who are homeless, many of which are cemented in the idea of moving people toward an included status.

At the Intersection of Inclusion and Exclusion

Although all signs suggest that those experiencing homelessness are positioned as an excluded group, we still find examples of inclusionary governance. I argue that not only can inclusionary strategies lead to further exclusion, as witnessed for example in Canada's drug treatment courts (Moore & Hirai, 2014), but also that exclusionary strategies can create micro-sites of inclusion where marginalized groups form a unique sense of community. The promise of inclusion rests on individualized understandings of, and responses to, marginalization. This often means minimizing or outright rejecting historical, socio-structural, and economic factors that perpetuate poverty, colonization, racism, sexism, ableism, heterosexism, transphobia, and other forms of discrimination. These strategies encourage people to come to terms with their own oppression and manage it as best they can rather than resist or denounce structural inequity (Goddard & Myers, 2017). Lauren Berlant's (2011) notion of "cruel optimism" is a useful explanatory tool here. Cruel optimism occurs "when the object that draws your attachment actively impedes the aim that brought you to it initially" (p. 1). Inclusionary techniques require that the excluded group buy into the norms, habits, values, and ways of being of the included social world without the means to live up to these standards.

    The act of internalizing inclusive discourses and practices while experiencing homelessness often serves to reinforce an excluded status. As described throughout the book, people experiencing homelessness are expected to maintain a strict schedule, manage complicated and inconsistent bureaucratic regulations, deal with the threat of violence and victimization calmly, participate enthusiastically in programming, and maintain a positive attitude, all while experiencing the degrading and dehumanizing conditions of homelessness. The very nature of their exclusion, typically stemming from a lack of financial resources and social ties, further entrenches their marginalized status when they are unable to live up to the standards for inclusion. Not only this, but embracing these technologies, for example self-help programs, education and work placement opportunities, and goal-oriented leisure activities (such as running or cooking groups), creates the appearance that they agree with the premise of these programs – namely the individualization and depoliticization of their exclusion. In Ahmed's (2012) analysis of inclusion, she argues that people seeking inclusion become subjects who must abide by the terms of that status. In this case many people experiencing homelessness internalize the values perpetuated by mainstream society and see their failure to become included as a personal failing rather than the result of structural barriers. If social inclusion fails, as it all too often does, these programs have the effect of permanently attaching individuals to the excluded circuit and in turn making their status as redeem*able* a permanent fixture rather than a transitive state.

The reality that relatively few people deeply entrenched in homelessness become members of included society begs the question of why so many people experiencing homelessness embrace inclusionary tactics. I offer two possibilities for why marginalized individuals voluntarily participate in inclusionary technologies that are organized by community-based organizations (besides when they are mandated to do so by bail conditions, probation orders, or shelter regulations). I suggest that the notion of hope and the desire to be the *included among the excluded* work in tandem with other potential factors (such as alleviating boredom) to explain why many excluded individuals embrace the unsubstantiated promises of inclusion.

Hope
Rose (2007) defines hope as part of the broader risk management project that seeks to manipulate the present in order to achieve a desirable future: "In a world imbued with a drive to master the future and still clinging to an ambivalent belief in progress, hope draws our gaze to a horizon on which things are imagined that we expect with desire, or desire with expectation" (p. 135). Hope is more than a subjective feeling; it plays an important role in shaping our choices and behaviours. While homeless shelters are thought of as spaces of hopelessness (Huey, 2012; Huff, 2008), inclusive strategies invite excluded people to reframe their futures by changing their present thoughts and behaviours. Regardless of housing status, hope provides people with a sense of purpose and the energy to pursue big goals. For people experiencing homelessness specifically, hope provides a framework to cope with the challenges of navigating complex social systems as well as hostility and dehumanization. Hope acts as a catalyst for individuals to make sense of, and see potential in, their futures. This is realized through ambitions to complete school, find well-paying and meaningful employment, and achieve the emotional stability to reconnect with family. Unfortunately, the resources required to successfully complete high school or post-secondary education, the dearth of well-paying, stable jobs, and complex and potentially volatile family dynamics can undermine the prospects of full inclusion. This is not to suggest that these pursuits are not worthwhile, but to acknowledge that they rarely amount to the kind of social inclusion promised or implied by these programs. In this sense, hope can be conceptualized as cruel (Berlant, 2011) or as contributing to a sense of personal failure and worthlessness (Partis, 2003) for not being able to achieve full social inclusion.

People who beat the odds and become included members of society are held up as pillars of neoliberal governance regimes and as examples that show how personal fortitude and determination are what others need to pull themselves out of homelessness. Rose and Novas's (2005) "political economy of hope" explicates the connection between a sense of hope and self-governing logics. Referencing individual participation in awareness campaigns, fundraising, and finding treatments/cures for medical conditions, the political economy of hope also points to the ways in which individuals are expected to be active players in their own well-being rather than passive recipients of wellness. The term also highlights the economic role hope plays in producing wealth for the health, wellness, and lifestyle sectors. Using a support group found on Prozac.com as an example, Rose and Novas detail the website's rhetoric that depression is manageable so long as patients adopt their own personal recovery narratives that includes taking psychopharmaceuticals. The homelessness industrial complex has a vested interest in maintaining the political economy of hope so that their programs remain full, funding is renewed, and members of the excluded community are kept busy and docile. Fostering a sense of hope maintains a steady stream of people interested in various programs and initiatives where outcomes are much more moderate than them becoming included members of society. This is not to suggest that people who administer programs are trying to deceive the homeless population. Rather, it speaks to the fiscal, social, and ideological constraints on effecting change beyond that which can be accomplished through individualized technologies and to the lack of political will and social appetite to attend to the structural and systemic causes of homelessness. The political economy of hope points to the ways in which people voluntarily participate in self-responsibilization and self-discipline with few expectations that they will receive the rights and privileges that would typically flow from adopting these ideologies, namely financial security, independence, and respect. These programs and resources provided through the homeless industrial complex placate the guilt of included society members who feel compelled to do something for those experiencing homelessness, but who are overwhelmed by the magnitude of the crisis or are unwilling to call for, and participate in, radical social change to address the root causes of inequity. The political economy of hope cultivates a climate where the excluded are expected to act out inclusive discourses without being included in a material way.

Inclusion among the Excluded

We should not assume that those experiencing homelessness and/or identified as mentally ill who strive for inclusion are simply being duped into a false sense of hope. There are strategic and practical reasons why those who are excluded might take up inclusive discourses. I argue that participating in inclusionary programs is a tool to become, and remain, included among the excluded population. If, as I have detailed, the exclusionary category exists along a continuum of perceived redeemability, it stands to reason that many marginalized people will seek out ways to be identified as redeemable. To be designated as redeemable is to be thought of as worthwhile, which comes with certain privileges. Whether those facing exclusion adopt the inclusive rhetoric earnestly or carry out a performance in order to reap certain benefits is unclear and not all that important. As Moore (2007a) articulates in her analysis of resistance in drug treatment courts, some participants play the addict identity role and follow the rules of the program to keep favour with the court in the hope that they will avoid incarceration. As I explore in the chapters that follow, there are high stakes involved in achieving the redeemable status that significantly influence the quality of life of those experiencing homelessness – factors such as being given the best rooms in a shelter, access to restricted spaces, opportunities for leisure activities, increased autonomy, and some privacy. These resources come from being singled out as worthy and can only be maintained if those identified as redeemable submit to the rules and basic responsibilization strategies set out by psy-experts, program administrators, and service providers.

Those who do not achieve or cannot sustain the redeemable status fall toward the other end of the spectrum, iredeemability. Recalling Spitzer (1975), those categorized as social dynamite are considered especially risky individuals who are not "deserving" of inclusive programs but are simply managed to minimize risk, often through incapacitation. Many people experiencing homelessness and/or who are identified as mentally ill participate in inclusionary practices to prevent people from giving up on them because that would make them even more vulnerable to incarceration in a jail, prison, or psychiatric hospital. Those who actively participate in programming are looked on more favourably by experts and para-professionals as fulfilling their role as marginal but responsibilized subjects. For example, staff may turn a blind eye to someone whom they regard as redeemable who enters the shelter intoxicated, whereas those who are considered irredeemable may be barred or expelled from the shelter. Likewise, staff may hesitate to contact police if a fight breaks out if they know they can appeal to the individual's sense of reason. Those categorized as irredeemable are thought to be inherently unreasonable, thus requiring targeted environments, such as a correctional facility, to manage them. While the redeemable are not immune to the criminal justice system's pervasive reach, it is but one form of discipline, often manifesting as hostile police interactions, ticketing, and short stays in detention centres. For the irredeemable, the criminal justice system becomes a primary containment strategy. The ways people experiencing homelessness understand and work to situate themselves along the redeemable-irredeemable continuum is a theme I follow throughout this book.

Organization of the Book

I will unpack the themes explored above – freedom, exclusion, hope, and redeemability – in the remainder of this book. I have organized the chapters to build the argument that the homelessness industrial complex ultimately reinforces, rather than eliminates, social exclusion and that inclusionary programs and discourses concerning self-responsibilization and self-governance that promote redeemability also perpetuate Otherness. At the same time, more coercive disciplinary techniques are never far away for those who find themselves closer to the irredeemable end of the spectrum. To make this argument, in Chapter 2 I provide an overview of the phenomenon we are encountering – namely the overlapping relationship between homelessness, mental illness, and the criminal justice system. This chapter provides a solid foundation for understanding the context within which people experiencing homelessness face exclusion.

Chapter 3 studies the emergency shelter, a key institution in the homelessness industrial complex, as a paradoxical site of care and insecurity. Shelters are places where technologies of freedom and discipline align to form what I argue is the contemporary, neoliberal iteration of Goffman's (1961) total institution. The high brick walls and barbed wire fences of traditional total institutions, such as the prison and psychiatric hospital, are not always necessary for exclusion. Rather, the chapter points to the ways people experiencing homelessness manage the homelessness industrial complex, where techniques of self-governance and freedom position shelter residents as having the autonomy and desire to subject themselves to near constant surveillance and adhere to strict rules and schedules.

Without a doubt, emergency shelters have an enormous impact on how people experiencing homelessness perceive and perform their personal identity. The ways people adopt, manage, and resist the mentally ill identity in particular provide evidence of how they negotiate the redeemable status. In Chapter 4, I analyze the diverse ways people perform the homeless and mentally ill identities within the context of experiencing various kinds of exclusion. The chapter reveals how people can be active participants in their own identity construction and how they negotiate their exclusion.

In Chapter 5, I probe what responsibilization discourses entail for those embedded within the homelessness sector and mental health system, and how they contribute to the quest for redeemability. Despite widespread acceptance of mental illness as a biomedical and therefore individualized problem, many people experiencing homelessness blame themselves for their status as homeless, mentally ill, addicted, and/or criminalized. Indeed, mental health and social service interventions encourage people to hold themselves accountable for their exclusion as a tool to move toward inclusion. This chapter furthers the argument that it is problematic to fixate on the mental health system in its current iteration as the primary response to the root causes of homelessness.

Chapter 6 acts as the culmination of the arguments put forth in the preceding chapters. Here I contend that many people facing homelessness model themselves as mental health consumers to establish their redeemability. Many hope that by performing techniques of self-regulation they will display their worthiness for social inclusion. Although the homelessness industrial complex is built to encourage this perspective, adopting the mental health consumer role implies accepting the pathologization and individualization of social problems, thus cementing one's status as permanently redeem*able* but never redeem*ed* and ultimately included. Still, there are symbolic and practical advantages to being included among the excluded. Meanwhile, some individuals are identified by shelter staff, professionals, and their peers as unable or unwilling to take responsibility for their marginal status and are thus categorized as irredeemable.

Finally, I use Chapter 7 to make sense of the ways seemingly benevolent programs and actions can inadvertently further entrench social exclusion. I also take the opportunity to highlight that people experiencing homelessness are not passive recipients of techniques of exclusion; instead, they make spaces and communities that give them a sense of inclusion in an otherwise exclusionary world. Finally, I offer reflections on a way forward. The homelessness sector is rapidly changing in Canada and internationally and the narratives found in this research call on us to be bold in seeking out ways to develop meaningful social inclusion if we want to prevent and end homelessness.

2

The Pillars of Exclusion: Homelessness, Mental Illness, and Criminalization in Canada

Homeless, mentally ill, and criminalized – three social categories with varying histories, grounded in distinct intellectual paradigms, and utilizing different modes of governing – but whose role in creating and sustaining an excluded and marginalized class overlap. These phenomena are rarely described for what they are – socially constituted subjectivities whose foundations are moulded through structurally, scholarly, politically, and publicly mediated discourses. How we understand homelessness in the twenty-first century is temporally, culturally, geographically, and socially specific; the fact that not having a home is an identity marker (the creation of the "homeless person") is not innate, natural, or scientific. Where categories may on occasion prove useful, it is equally important to poke and prod at them and uncover their chronology, the assumptions that propel them, and the truths that are suppressed by the dominant narratives that construct them. This book acts as a proverbial poking stick, curiously and persistently nudging and jostling at these markers of exclusion to uncover what lies beneath.

Homelessness, mental illness, and criminalization are mainstays of social science scholarship; however, they are often taken for granted, assumed to be value-neutral, objective variables. This chapter takes on a grossly undervalued aspect of scholarship in this field – namely a critical assessment of conceptions of homelessness, mental illness and criminalization, as well as their foregrounding within discourses that privilege the medical model and the individualization of distress and marginality. The pages that follow provide a detailed and interdisciplinary review of homelessness and mental illness literatures, as well as their connection to studies on addiction and criminalization. Highlighting the often understated connections between the homelessness industrial complex, the recovery industry (Travis, 2009), and the mental health and criminal justice systems calls for a nuanced analysis of the social control of marginalized people.

Homelessness

Defining and Measuring Homelessness
Thinking critically about social categories requires an understanding of the classifications themselves. In 2017, the Canadian Observatory on Homelessness released a revised *Canadian Definition of Homelessness*. The definition is well regarded in Canada and adopted by several federal and provincial government ministries:

> Homelessness describes the situation of an individual, family or community without stable, safe, permanent, appropriate housing, or the immediate prospect, means and ability of acquiring it. It is the result of systemic or societal barriers, a lack of affordable and appropriate housing, the individual/household's financial, mental, cognitive, behavioural or physical challenges, and/or racism and discrimination. Most people do not choose to be homeless, and the experience is generally negative, unpleasant, unhealthy, unsafe, stressful and distressing. (Gaetz, Barr, et al., 2017, p. 1)

The definition includes a typology of homelessness: unsheltered; emergency sheltered; provisionally accommodated; and at risk of homelessness. The definition captures the range of living spaces, structures, and housing situations that are unsafe, unsuitable, and unstable.

Also in 2017, the Canadian Observatory on Homelessness released the *Definition of Indigenous Homelessness in Canada*. This groundbreaking work, overseen by Resident Scholar on Indigenous Homelessness Jesse Thistle, injected much-needed Indigenous knowledges and teachings into the parameters of the homelessness definition. For Indigenous Peoples, homelessness is not about a lack of shelter or a habitation; it is more profoundly about a loss of "All My Relations" – that is, one's relationships with the land, people, language, traditions, and culture:

> Indigenous homelessness is a human condition that describes First Nations, Métis and Inuit individuals, families or communities lacking stable, permanent,

appropriate housing, or the immediate prospect, means or ability to acquire such housing. Unlike the common colonialist definition of homelessness, Indigenous homelessness is not defined as lacking a structure of habitation; rather, it is more fully described and understood through a composite lens of Indigenous worldviews. These include: individuals, families and communities isolated from their relationships to land, water, place, family, kin, each other, animals, cultures, languages and identities. Importantly, Indigenous Peoples experiencing these kinds of homelessness cannot culturally, spiritually, emotionally or physically reconnect with their Indigeneity or lost relationships. (Thistle, 2017, p. 6)

Combining these definitions sets out the scope and scale of what constitutes homelessness.

There is a homelessness crisis in Canada and in most parts of the world. Just how many people face this crisis is a point of contention. While there are significant methodological challenges to enumerating homelessness,[1] a conservative estimate is that 235,000 people experience homelessness in Canada each year, with 35,000 people facing homelessness on any given night. Women account for approximately 30 percent of the homeless population and people who identify as transgender make up 1 percent, although this is an exceptionally low estimate because women and gender-diverse people are much more likely to be among the hidden homeless who are rarely counted. Youth make up about 20 percent of the homeless population (Gaetz et al., 2013). The data on the rate of homelessness among Indigenous Peoples is extremely limited but estimates from major urban centres reveal that Indigenous Peoples make up between 20 and 50 percent of the homeless population while accounting for only 5 percent of the general population (Belanger et al., 2013). In Saskatchewan, for example, almost 80 percent of the homeless population is Indigenous. Bearing in mind the lack of safe, suitable, and appropriate housing on many reserves and in the North, it is a gross understatement to say that Indigenous Peoples are overrepresented in the homeless population.

A deeper dive into the data reveals that the long-standing vagabond trope does not hold up. At least 85 percent of individuals who experience homelessness are "transitionally homeless." This means that they experience homelessness for a very short time (usually less than one month), can secure housing using minimal resources, and are not likely to experience homelessness again (Aubry et al., 2013). The vast majority of people experience homelessness because of a personal crisis (house fire, job loss, family breakdown) and/or because of a lack of affordable housing throughout Canada (Gaetz et al., 2014; Suttor, 2016). The caricature version of a hobo riding the rails does a disservice to the reality of those facing housing challenges. People experiencing homelessness are not an anomaly but are living evidence of the growing wealth gap in the global North. Over 13 percent of urban Canadian households are in core housing need, meaning they spend more than 30 percent of their income on housing (Canada Mortgage and Housing Corporation, 2019) and 18 percent of renter households are in extreme core housing need, where they spend more than 50 percent of their income on rent (Londerville & Steele, 2014). Over 800,000 people in Canada use food banks every month, with increased need each year (Food Banks Canada, 2016), especially during the COVID-19 pandemic. A growing number of households are one pay cheque away from losing their housing, disrupting the myth that people experiencing homelessness are somehow a distinct group of others.

The stereotype of homelessness as a state of consistently living on the street prevails because despite accounting for only 15 percent of the homeless population, people who are chronically homeless are highly visible in public spaces. Chronic homelessness refers to people who have experienced homelessness for six months (180 days) over the past year or recurrent homelessness cumulatively reaching eighteen months over the past three years. Although they make up such a small portion of the homeless population, those who are chronically homeless use half of the shelter resources (Aubry et al., 2013). Those who are chronically homeless are often the focus of research, including in this project, where 66 percent of participants met the criteria for chronic homelessness. Those who become mired in the homelessness industrial complex can face distress, substance use challenges, violence, and discrimination.

Ottawa, Canada, the site for this research, faces the same homelessness and housing crisis as much of the rest of the country. In 2017, 7,530 people used shelter beds, an increase of 5 percent from the year before (City of Ottawa, 2018b). Consistent with national statistics, Ottawa has a relatively small number of people who are chronically homeless, but they tend to stay on the street or in shelters for more than three and a half years (Alliance to End Homelessness Ottawa, 2015). First Nations, Métis, and Inuit people make up 2.5 percent of Ottawa's overall population, but account for 24 percent of those surveyed in Ottawa's point-in-time count and 36 percent of unsheltered homeless (City of Ottawa, 2018a).

These statistics provide a glimpse of the complexity of the homelessness crisis in Canada. The numbers reveal an important but only partial piece of the story. To understand who makes up the homeless population and how exclusion permeates their lives, we must understand how this crisis was made – because homelessness as we know it was created and is maintained by a network of political and economic systems, institutions, and actors, as well as general social apathy.

A Short History of Homelessness in Canada

Homelessness has been politically managed in one way or another for centuries. In feudal times in Western Europe, communities were held responsible for taking care of those who could not work through acts of charity. As populations grew and people became more mobile, poverty was transformed into a political problem requiring unique forms of regulation. The sixteenth century saw a general shift from thinking of the poor as lazy to characterizing them as potentially dangerous (Castel, 2003; Snow & Anderson, 1993). Britain introduced the English Poor Laws to manage those identified as vagrants and beggars through local parishes (Beier, 2004). The crux of the legislation was to control those who did not own land by requiring able-bodied workers to engage in low-wage employment and fill labour shortages. During the latter part of the Industrial Revolution in the early nineteenth century, the Poor Laws were revamped to address migration to urban centres. In an effort to control the onslaught of people moving to the cities, Britain and other Western countries enacted institutionalization techniques that confined the poor to workhouses where they were compelled to perform the most menial and dangerous tasks that other workers refused to do and which were inherited in Canada as houses of industry (Lees, 1998).

The colonization of North America expanded exponentially at this time. As Paradis (2014) explains, homelessness and colonization are intimately linked. British and French settlers brought the colonial concept of "owning" land to Turtle Island,[2] as well as the power to exclude certain people from ownership. In Canada, legislation such as the *Indian Act*, first passed in 1876, prohibited many First Nations people from owning land; for example, First Nations women who married non-status or non-Indigenous men lost their Indian status and right to the land (Vowel, 2016). Indigenous Peoples' oppression during the outset of colonization is mirrored today in the disproportionate number of Indigenous Peoples experiencing homelessness. Thistle's (2017) work on defining Indigenous homelessness as the loss of land, language, culture, and tradition makes evident the connection between homelessness and colonization, criminalization, and cultural genocide (National Inquiry into Missing and Murdered Indigenous Women and Girls [NIMMIWG], 2019; Truth and Reconciliation Commission [TRC] of Canada, 2015).

In the 1950s and '60s, these historical foundations of homelessness in Canada were embedded within the "skid row" and "skid row alcoholic" archetypes, where homelessness was depicted almost exclusively as the experience of older men in dirty and dishevelled clothing who whiled away the day in dingy bars (Bahr, 1970; Olin, 1966). The skid row character fortified the pathologization of poverty and homelessness discussed throughout the book.

The contemporary homelessness crisis in Canada exploded in the 1980s and '90s. The steep rise in homelessness occurred primarily for three reasons. First, the 1990s saw most provinces, most notably Ontario, slash welfarist programs, including health and social services. Canada's most marginalized people had their social safety net pulled out from under them by the privatization of services and widening of the wealth gap, while criminal justice initiatives expanded. Second, in 1993 the federal government disinvested in affordable housing, becoming one of the only G8 countries not to have a national housing strategy (a status that the federal government corrected in 2017 with the introduction of a new National Housing Strategy). The government's withdrawal of new operating agreements to support the capital costs and operating expenses for social housing development resulted in a dramatic decrease in affordable housing options, leaving low-income households to try to make ends meet in the private rental market (Suttor, 2016). Third, economic shifts across the global North led to a decrease in full-time, permanent, well-paying jobs, bringing more people to the brink of poverty. In this new reality, the demographics of the homeless population changed. Young people, women, and families became a more visible part of the homelessness landscape.

Because of the rapid growth in homelessness in such a short period in Canada and across the global North, much of the scholarship at the time grappled with answering questions about who was experiencing homelessness, tracing trajectories in and out of homelessness, and counting, diagnosing, and individualizing the homelessness phenomenon. Given the relatively short, forty-year history of homelessness as a modern topic of research, these early studies set the tone for making sense of the phenomenon, one where individualized and pathologized understandings of homelessness prevail and where critical and social justice oriented research is only beginning to emerge.

Understanding Homelessness: Individualization and Socio-Political Paradigms

The ways in which homelessness is framed dictate social reactions. In Canada, from the influence of England's Poor Laws to the modern reliance on short-term emergency services, the state relies predominantly on an individualized understanding of the pathways to homelessness. To date, interventions have focused largely on managing the crisis rather than preventing or helping people permanently move out of homelessness. Even with the introduction of the Housing First model (discussed below), the emphasis remains on individual factors causing homelessness. This orientation depoliticizes what are inherently socio-political concerns. It also allows homelessness to be aligned seamlessly with deviancy, mental illness, and addiction discourses. Although many scholars and service providers acknowledge structural and systemic impacts on homelessness, dominant modes of intervention continue to privilege individual causes.

Despite the proliferation of individualized understandings of homelessness, there are critical voices in the homelessness sector fighting to bring attention to and address social and structural causes of homelessness. Housing unaffordability, the commodification of housing, widespread under- and unemployment, multi-generational poverty, limited access to social services, deindustrialization, a minimum wage that does not keep up with the cost of living, discrimination based on race/ethnicity and/or disability, historical and contemporary colonization, gender inequality, and reduced benefits (especially pensions) are among the myriad of social, political, and cultural conditions that created the homelessness crisis and allow it to proliferate. Beginning with Snow and Anderson's (1993) seminal ethnography of street life in Austin, Texas, and their subsequent works, critical scholars cautioned against developing a body of research that relies strictly on positivist descriptions of who is homeless:

> We argue that this portrait of the homeless as drunk, stoned, crazy, and sick is partly distorted and flawed. It is distorted in the sense that a makeup mirror distorts the face of its user by highlighting and magnifying only the blemishes or imperfections, and it is flawed in the sense that the picture or image is in part an artifact of the questions asked and the procedures used to pursue those questions. In other words, given researchers' preoccupation with the problems the homeless presumably have, namely, personal disabilities or pathologies, and the procedures used to track this preoccupation, namely, the cross-sectional survey consisting of face-to-face structured

interviews conducted anywhere from 15 to 90 minutes, it is not surprising that the homeless are generally portrayed as being riddled with various "conspicuous dysfunctions." (Snow et al., 1994, pp. 462–463)

In the decades that followed, a handful of scholars took up Snow, Anderson, and Koegel's (1994) call for "a more balanced, contextualized, and adaptive picture of the homeless" (p. 470) by nuancing homelessness and privileging first voices – those with lived experience of homelessness. For example, Allen (2000) writes: "Homelessness does not so much reflect a flawed individual as it does a flawed system" (p. 20). Invaluable critical scholarship is emerging, reorienting the homelessness discourse to prioritize first voices, recognize resiliency and strength, and highlight the structural and social causes of homelessness (Boydell et al., 2000; Feldman, 2004; Kennelly, 2018; Lyon-Callo, 2004; Nichols, 2014; Paradis, 2014; Stuart, 2016). This shift is being led by scholarship from people with lived experience of homelessness, especially in the youth homelessness sector. The research documented in this book is firmly grounded within the bourgeoning scholarship that examines systemic inequity that reinforces the included/excluded binary. This work takes to task the pathologization of homelessness enacted through mental health discourses and practices that seek to legitimize the ongoing exclusion of the homeless population.

Mental Health

Mental health discourses applied in the homelessness sector individualize and pathologize the causes and experiences of homelessness. Assessing the medical model, its relationship with normalization, and the counter-narratives that resist the medicalization of problems in living (that is, the processes that intervene in and reconstitute common challenges people face as medical problems [Szasz, 1974]) allows us to capture how these governing mechanisms work.

The Making of the Medical Model
Contemporary psychiatry came about as a response to the Great Confinement, as defined by Foucault, where specialized institutions incapacitated individuals designated as mentally ill, the unemployed, prisoners, and the poor in degrading conditions. Credit historically goes to physicians William Tuke and Phillippe Pinel, who, in the late eighteenth century, rejected the physical restraints and abuse found in institutions of confinement and introduced

more humane and benevolent techniques to manage people. But as Foucault (1988) argues, power and dominance over marginalized people was transformed, not eliminated, with this change through a shift from physical penalty to moral and social discipline in the asylum, cemented within medicalized knowledges (as well as the continued use of physical restraints [Jacob et al., 2018]). The introduction of "moral treatment" allowed medical professionals to integrate into the field of psychiatry, transforming the asylum into a space of medicalized knowledge. Over time, the medical framework became the primary means for understanding distress and psychiatry became recognized as a branch of medicine (Rogers & Pilgrim, 2014). Psychiatry embedded itself within the medical model by relying on the body as the site for scientific discovery and intervention. In the era that followed, distress became regarded as an illness that derives from a virus, biochemical disorder, or genetic predisposition, all of which are seemingly value-neutral and objective (Tew, 2005).

As psychiatry gained dominance, "psychocentrism" came to permeate everyday life by medicalizing social issues as the failed health of particular individuals (Rimke, 2016). This is not to say that those who subscribe to the medical model do not acknowledge external causes of distress, but they often deem structural, systemic, and environmental factors to be triggers for already existing biochemical conditions. The psy-disciplines are obliged to seek out and prioritize a biological connection to mental distress in order to retain the legitimacy that comes with the medical profession. Doing so requires continuing to look for the causes of mental distress in the body, regardless of whether there is physical evidence to support this strategy (Cockerham, 2003). The search for genetic and neurological links to distress remains a cornerstone of psy-research, with only moderate results. The medical model's dominance within the psy-disciplines does not reside in its fallible relationship with physical health but rather with its ability to minimize social factors as contributing to mental distress (Rogers & Pilgrim, 2014). From this perspective it is no wonder that mental illness treatments are rooted in the medical model, from the heavy reliance on electroconvulsive therapy (ECT) between the 1930s and 1960s[3] to the extensive use of psychotropic medication as the primary means of intervention today.

Psychopharmacology has dominated the medical treatment of distress since the introduction of chlorpromazine in the 1950s, often as the exclusive form of treatment. Since then, there has been an intense increase in the influence of Big Pharma – a term referring to the large pharmaceutical companies who wield tremendous economic and political power convincing doctors and patients alike that the answer to their maladies lies in a patent-protected pill. The overreliance on psychopharmaceuticals misrepresents medication as a cure rather than a tool to manage symptoms, and in some cases generates other, secondary symptoms. Even with the introduction of modern treatment strategies such as psychotropic medication, recovery rates for mental illnesses like schizophrenia have not changed for at least fifty years (Drake & Whitley, 2014). The medical model retains its dominance notwithstanding this failure because, despite public perception, psychiatry does not feign an ability to cure distress but seeks simply to manage those deemed mentally ill. Tew (2005) recognizes this "management" as a technology of power used to govern individuals for a lifetime. Psychiatry's attachment to the medical model has flourished and expanded the discipline, not necessarily because it is a useful paradigm, but because its coupling with powerful medical discourses reinforces dominant conceptions of normality.

The medical model's dominance, emboldened through the extensive use of psychopharmaceuticals, creates the conditions for managing and sometimes punishing poor individuals who do not comply with medication regimes, with the complicity of the criminal justice system. For instance, the criminal justice system can be used as a tool to ensure medication compliance, either as part of a parole or probation order (Redlich et al., 2006) or through a community treatment order (CTO). CTOs are legal provisions that allow individuals who would otherwise be institutionalized in a psychiatric hospital to live in the community under certain conditions, most notably medication compliance. Although CTOs are technically voluntary, requiring someone to choose between a CTO and involuntary hospitalization is coercive in nature, with Fabris (2011) likening CTOs to "chemical incarceration" and a "chemobotomy." Moreover, police can forcibly bring those who fail to comply with a CTO back to the hospital. There is little evidence to support the effectiveness of CTOs; rather, those on CTOs are more likely to be hospitalized involuntarily for longer periods than those without such orders (Klassen, 2016; Rugkåsa, 2016). CTOs are an example of what Moore (2011) calls "benevolent coercion" whereby mandating treatment compliance under the threat of police apprehension is positioned as an act of enabling personal autonomy and choice. CTOs also retain and privilege a pathologized understanding of distress and vulnerability.

The medical model's dominance in Canada is apparent in how it informs organizational rhetoric and policy. For example, provincial and territorial mental health acts provide psychiatric facilities the power to involuntarily hospitalize (or institutionalize) individuals for medical treatment, a practice known as *forming*. Although there are variations throughout the provinces and territories, involuntary hospital admissions generally occur when a physician believes someone has a mental disorder and they are likely to cause serious harm to themselves or another person. While a physician must personally examine the individual and make the application, they can rely on others' reports to reach a decision, such as those of emergency shelter staff. The strictly medicalized definition of mental illness must be disrupted, particularly as it relates to how these discourses are mobilized against those experiencing homelessness. Although it is not my intention to refute any connection between biology and mental distress, I engage with and privilege alternative conceptions of mental distress and account for how individuals make sense of what it means to be diagnosed with a mental illness. This position is especially important when we consider the general resistance to "alternative" therapies, such as peer support offered by the mad movement.

The Mad Movement: Resisting Psy

From Szasz's (1974) problems in living to Rimke's (2016) psychocentrism, resistance to psy's normalization practices has a long history. Using the medical model as leverage, psy-discourses have come to dominate everyday actions and thoughts. The psy-complex proliferates in the landscape of human nature as it pathologizes various aspects of daily life, thereby demanding that all active citizens guard against their potential abnormality through responsibilization strategies.

Key to the psy-disciplines' success are their subtlety and "generosity" (Rose, 1998) in lending terminology, discourses, judgments, and practices to other fields. As diverse groups of experts and para-professionals embrace and implement the techniques of these disciplines, it is easy to lose sight of psy's dominance. Not only psychiatrists and psychologists, but also social workers, teachers, counsellors, nurses, and other professionals and para-professionals have a strong allegiance to psy-discourses, forming a tight network of surveillance and control. The psy-disciplines' insidious and "seductive" nature (Rose, 1988) makes them exceptionally difficult to build a counter-narrative against. Nonetheless, people directly targeted by psy's power, alongside notable scholars, have resisted its dominance and offered alternative paradigms.

The mad movement encompasses several ideologies and advocacy goals related to the rights of individuals involved in the mental health system. Anti-psychiatrists of the 1960s and '70s, led by scholars like Szasz (1989), Cooper (1967), and Laing (1960, 1967), examined mental illness as a social construction and questioned the value-laden judgments inherent in medical diagnoses (Sedgwick, 1982). In parallel, survivors/consumers[4] began to organize more formally to protest the mental health system throughout the 1970s and '80s in North America and Europe (Rogers & Pilgrim, 2014; Tew, 2005). Distinct from the anti-psychiatrists, the mad movement moves beyond solely an intellectual debate and is committed to direct action, including protests against involuntary commitment legislation, ECT, and forced treatment, especially CTOs. The movement now runs community-based mental health services such as outreach programs and crisis intervention services (Diamond, 2013). The mad movement has had to respond to the inadequacy of community resources to support people experiencing distress. They do so by asserting several broad goals, including a quest for self-determination; respecting decision-making capacity and gaining self-esteem among those with distress; privileging the narratives of those who have encountered psychiatry; and focusing on recovery[5] as a holistic response to negotiating symptoms rather than necessarily eliminating them (Cook & Jonikas, 2002; Crossley & Crossley, 2001). With these objectives in mind, the mad movement adopts strategies such as creating strong social networks, participating in social activism, and supporting good physical health, among others, to enable people to exercise self-determination.

Mad movement scholars and activists embody a philosophy of resistance to problematize the constitution of mental illness as strictly pathological and contest the system's normalizing and coercive practices. They do so by questioning who is caught up in the mental health system – disproportionately people living in poverty, women, racialized people, and sexual and gender minorities (Daley & Mulé, 2014; Morrow, 2017; Tam, 2013). They also push against common governance techniques employed by the system, especially the heavy reliance on psychotropic medication, CTOs, professional treatment teams, etc. By problematizing the medical model, the movement opens a theoretical and practical space to challenge the mental health system. For example, psychiatric consumers/survivors have integrated their personal experiences when advocating against the systemic challenges facing the community (Fabris, 2011; Shimrat, 1997) and when undertaking research on more appropriate program design and implementation for those in distress (Church, 2013; Schneider, 2010). Disrupting dominant mental health discourses is vital because there is still minimal support outside the mad movement for individuals who have experienced mental health intervention to achieve autonomy and to scale up alternatives to medicalized forms of treatment; in fact, many people who have not had direct experience with the more invasive aspects of the mental health system are hostile to the idea of such alternatives (Whiting, 2009). Despite national and regional anti-stigma campaigns, fear of those identified as mentally ill is rampant, leading to unnecessary and punitive responses to people in acute distress. For example, in 2014, the federal government amended the provisions in the *Criminal Code* concerning someone found not criminally responsible for their actions, further reducing the rights of the accused, despite evidence that these changes may impede, rather than enhance, public safety (Dej, 2015). Members of the mad movement continue to push to have their voices heard in the mainstream and to influence policy and practice. As the mad movement agenda moves forward, it is essential that people who have experienced homelessness and mental health interventions lead and inform this work.

Uncomfortable Bedfellows: Homelessness and Mental Illness

In the last decade, mad scholarship has bourgeoned (Landry, 2017), but to date there is limited engagement with homelessness in that literature. A small group of scholars are working to bridge that divide, and are worth noting here. Barbara Schneider (2010) and her team used participatory action research to investigate housing challenges for those diagnosed with schizophrenia. Lilith Finkler (2013) conducted research on minimum separation distance bylaws that restrict housing options for psychiatric survivors and perpetuate the exclusion of those identified as "mad." Marina Morrow and her colleagues (2012, 2017) use a social justice lens to unpack the notion of recovery and the intersectionality of feminism and madness. Jijian Voronka partnered with peer researchers to reflect on the intersection of mental illness and homelessness, particularly as these ideas were reflected in the *At Home/Chez Soi* study (see below). Voronka's research injects a much-needed critical orientation into the dialogue on personal experiences, mental health service provision, and homelessness (Nelson et al., 2015; Piat et al., 2014; Voronka, 2017; Voronka et al., 2014). These critical conversations are often outliers within a field dominated by biomedical discourses, something that mad activists and allies are pushing to change.

Psy-dominated constructions of distress reproduce common conceptions of the scope of mental illness among those experiencing homelessness. Estimates are that one third of those experiencing homelessness experience mental illness, although reported rates range from 10 to 70 percent (Holton et al., 2010). The most common diagnosis among those experiencing homelessness is depression, followed by anxiety, bipolar disorder, schizophrenia, and post-traumatic stress disorder (PTSD). Attention is beginning to turn to the role of brain injuries among the homeless population as well (Nikoo et al., 2017; Topolovec-Vranic et al., 2017). *At Home/Chez Soi*, the first study of its kind in the world to evaluate the merits of a Housing First (HF) intervention for those experiencing homelessness with significant mental health challenges, reinforced the implicit affiliation between homelessness and mental illness. HF is both a philosophy and a program model premised on the notion that individuals should receive immediate, no barrier access to housing that includes person-centred wraparound supports. HF contrasts with the "treatment first" model that was used for decades and continues to be used in some programs, which contends that people must meet certain readiness requirements before securing housing, such as becoming sober, treating mental illness, participating in programming, or finding employment, to name a few (Tsemberis & Eisenberg, 2000). There are obvious challenges to meeting these goals while street-entrenched and so *At Home/Chez Soi* tested the efficacy of the HF model for those who are chronically homeless. The study spanned five Canadian cities, and followed 2,000 homeless and precariously housed individuals with identified mental health and/or addiction challenges for two years. Half of the participants received immediate housing and supports while the other half used the usual services and treatments offered in their respective communities. At the study's completion, 62 percent of the HF group had maintained housing compared with 31 percent of the participants who used standard community supports (Goering et al., 2014).

The HF model has altered the Canadian and international homelessness policy landscapes. In Canada, it has led the federal and some provincial governments to reallocate the majority of their funding to HF programs. Although the federal government scaled back the HF requirement in its latest homelessness strategy, Reaching Home, to allow communities greater flexibility in their response to homelessness, HF has arguably become a foundational philosophy and model in Canada. While HF is undoubtedly an important innovation in responding to homelessness, critics are skeptical about its rapid adoption without careful attention to fidelity (Waegemakers Schiff & Rook, 2012). Others argue that HF does not work for everyone and must be adapted to meet the needs of specific populations, for instance women fleeing violence, youth, and Indigenous Peoples (Alaazi et al., 2015; Gaetz, 2014).

Amidst these critiques, however, there is silence on the ways that the HF model reinforces the pathologization of homelessness (for a notable exception, see Katz et al., 2017). There are some important critiques of how Assertive Community Treatment (ACT) and Intensive Case Management (ICM) teams, the common method of coordinating multidisciplinary, community-based treatment for those in housing, fail to adhere to HF's self-determination principle (Matejkowski & Draine, 2008). An alarming example is the integration of police into ACT teams, where treatment takes on an overtly coercive character (Van Veen et al., 2018). Looking broadly at these approaches, there is little reflection on the privileging of the biomedical model of distress and how it impacts the lives of those experiencing homelessness. Most HF programs use some kind of prioritization tool to decide how to allocate limited housing and support resources. Tools such as the Vulnerability Index-Service Prioritization Decision Assistance Tool (VI-SPDAT) use mental health status as one of the key indicators to determine someone's acuity. HF programs only accept those chronically homeless individuals regarded as most severely distressed. That is, by relying so heavily on the HF model to respond to homelessness people must wait until they are chronically homeless and likely facing significant distress and victimization before receiving housing and support. Stephen Gaetz, president of the Canadian Observatory on Homelessness, has made the argument for years that there is a moral and practical obligation to work upstream and provide assistance before people become homeless and that these strategies are as important as supporting people to exit homelessness (Gaetz & Dej, 2017). Moreover, screening tools like the VI-SPDAT frame an individual's vulnerability as a personal flaw to score and rank, rather than a product of the socio-political environment. For example, screening tools do not account for systemic discrimination on a person's housing history and are not culturally sensitive. Instead, the very nature of homelessness and common adaptive responses to homelessness (inappropriate dress/appearance, depression, agitation, unresponsiveness, etc.) are pathologized (Snow et al., 1986; Snow & Anderson, 1993). This mode of governance is quite nefarious. Systems and a social climate that produce distress go on to judge and rank those who react to those conditions as mentally disordered.

A note about addiction is warranted here. Anywhere from 50 to 82 percent of the homeless population identify as struggling with substance use (Milaney et al., 2018). Contemporary mental illness and addiction discourses and practices are overlapping, especially among the poor where access to services and treatment is limited. Participants in my research project spoke about the two interchangeably and as a result, so do I in many instances throughout this book. Still, it is worth noting the varied history of the two categorizations, particularly the state's early response to substance use which relied largely on the criminal justice system rather than a medicalized framework. The criminalization of opium at the beginning of the twentieth century as a mode of governing Chinese immigrants in Canada relied on racialized discourses purporting that opium users were "weak willed" and had a "low moral constitution" (Conrad & Schneider, 1992; Valverde, 1998). While its inclusion in the *Diagnostic and Statistical Manual of Mental Disorders* (*DSM-V*) definitively situates addiction as a biomedical problem, its moralistic origins have not disappeared. We only have to look at the ongoing "war on drugs," despite its abysmal failure in eradicating illicit substance use, and the legal, political, and social barriers to developing safe consumption sites and overdose prevention sites in communities across the country, to make claims of the ongoing moral repudiation of addiction in a way that is distinct from responses to mental illness.

Despite possible ideological differences, responses to mental illness and addiction share many similarities. They both exist tangentially to the traditional disease framework because they are assessed primarily through self-reporting and "abnormal" social behaviour rather than through physical observation or measurement (i.e., blood test, body scan, etc.). In this way, mental illness and addiction are regarded as somewhat suspect and less legitimate than other physical ailments. Another factor binding addiction and mental illness together is their characterization as the breaking of social norms. Their relationship with normalization and self-regulation leads those who are identified as mentally ill or as addicts to be governed through a variety of institutions, including in the homelessness industrial complex and the criminal justice system. Since the late 1980s, biomedical research has increasingly come to terms with mental illness and addiction as sometimes existing as concurrent disorders or as a dual diagnosis, recognizing the interplay between the two. Whereas, in the past, practitioners would only treat substance abuse once mental health was effectively managed (or vice versa), dual diagnosis allows mental illness and addiction to be addressed simultaneously. However, while medical standards have changed, service delivery, especially among the poor, has not kept pace (Kuehn, 2010; Priester et al., 2016). While few people who are homeless and identify as suffering from both mental illness and addiction receive concurrent disorder treatment, the disorders are regarded as part and parcel of one another among many frontline workers, counsellors, and individuals in distress.

Criminalizing the Vulnerable

Mental illness and substance use share another, dubious connection – they are both criminalized as a means of social control. The criminal justice system is a major cause of, and contributor to, the social exclusion of already marginalized people. Punitive tactics exist beyond the prison walls to surveil and manage those deemed unable or unwilling to align with dominant social norms. If we focus our attention on the ever-widening carceral net (Cohen, 1985), the unique histories of criminalization among marginalized groups come to form a troubling, prevailing pattern of criminal justice knowledges, discourses, and practices that incapacitate, separate, and harm those who are deemed Others.

Criminalizing Distress

The forces linking mental illness and the criminal justice system are not new. In 1939, Lionel Penrose equated the relationship between the mental health and criminal justice systems with the "balloon effect" – when you push one part of the balloon in, the other part will bulge out (Lamb et al., 2004). While the incarceration of people experiencing distress has existed in one form or another for centuries, the deinstitutionalization of psychiatric hospitals between the 1960s and 1990s throughout the global North acted as unique historical and cultural moments, the effects of which are still felt today.

Deinstitutionalization was the process of transferring mental health treatment from psychiatric hospitals where people were held for years, or indeed their lifetime, to the community. Community alternatives were considered more humane and cost-effective than hospitals and so over 27,000 psychiatric beds were lost across Canada (Sealy & Whitehead, 2004).[6] However, community alternatives were not adequately funded and resourced, creating a chasm in mental health treatment. The common understanding in the scholarly literature on the subject is that this lack of care thrust police into a quasi–social worker role to respond to and manage those deemed abnormal, resulting in the criminal justice system acting as an "institution of last resort" or the "dumping ground" for those in distress (Etter et al., 2008). While it is undeniable that deinstitutionalization left people in distress with a dearth of support and care, Ben-Moshe (2017) cautions against uncritically adopting this historical narrative. She astutely notes that pointing to deinstitutionalization as the primary cause of the swelling population of those managed by the criminal justice system retains the focus on individualized faults and obscures the socio-structural shifts that also occurred at the time, namely the gutting of the welfare state, increased poverty and marginalization, and the rise of neoliberal domination. Still, the reality remains that people experiencing distress came to have extremely limited access to care, leaving them vulnerable to the intervention of the criminal justice system.

Police have become increasingly responsible for managing those perceived to be in distress. Indeed, people in distress are criminalized in such a way that those who have not committed a crime (for example when people act erratically in public) or who commit minor infractions (such as trespassing, traffic violations, disorderly conduct, etc.) can end up ensnarled within the criminal justice system. While collaborations between psy-professionals and police officers through police-mental health units have shown some success in diverting people from jail,[7] negative interactions between police and those in distress remain common. We only have to look at the death of Sammy Yatim, the young man shot and killed by Officer James Forcillo on a Toronto streetcar in 2013, or Abdirahman Abdi who was killed by Ottawa Constable Daniel Montsion in 2016,[8] to recognize how ill-equipped and inappropriate it is for police to act as first responders in situations where someone is experiencing acute distress, and thus how inappropriate it is for them to do so. Crucially, the intersection of distress and racialization in both of these examples is exemplary of the anti-Black and anti-Brown racism prevalent in police forces that was the catalyst for the Black Lives Matter movement (Rickford, 2015). Not only are people of colour who experience distress significantly more likely to have involvement with the criminal justice system than white people in distress (Omonira, 2014; White, 2015), but the aggressive policing tactics regularly used on communities of colour negatively impact the mental health of people in those communities, particularly Black men (McLeod et al., 2019). This means that the racially motivated policing practices that many people of colour experience may in part be the cause of the very distress that leaves them vulnerable to police brutality.

Unsurprisingly, people identified as mentally ill pervade the correctional system. Ivan Zinger (2012), Correctional Investigator of Canada, argues that "addressing the criminalization and warehousing in penitentiaries of those who suffer from mental illness is not simply a public health issue, it's a human rights issue" (p. 25). Around 70 percent of men and almost 80 percent of women serving time in federal custody meet the criteria for at least one mental disorder, including substance use disorders (Beaudette et al., 2015; Derkzen et al., 2017). Provincial numbers are harder to come by, but we can deduce that rates are just as high, if not higher than federal numbers, given that provincial detention centres hold the most marginal and least violent prisoners on remand or with short custody sentences. While these numbers clearly demonstrate the inappropriate use of the criminal justice system to manage those in distress, we must think critically about how mental disorders are defined and assessed within such oppressive and harmful institutions. We must also consider the role the criminal justice system and similar systems play in creating and perpetuating the dehumanizing conditions that would cause anyone in those circumstances to experience distress.

Mental health treatment is sorely lacking in federal prisons and even more so in provincial and territorial jails. The tough-on-crime agenda, a cornerstone of Prime Minister Harper's platform from 2006 to 2015, prioritized punishment and security, further diminishing correctional facilities' ability to deliver already limited mental health resources while creating structural conditions for distress, such as lengthier sentences, overcrowding, and a heavy reliance on segregation. Using prisoners as political pawns has had very real consequences. Ashley Smith, Edward Snowshoe, Justin St. Amour, Cleve Geddes, Yousef Hussein, Terry Baker, Guy Langlois, Camille Strickland-Murphy, Christopher Roy, and so many others who were held in segregation for months, and in some cases years, subsequently died by suicide. According to the Mandela rules, segregation lasting longer than fifteen days amounts to torture. In the case of Ashley Smith, who spent over one thousand days in segregation in four years, her death by asphyxiation was ruled a homicide because of Correctional Service of Canada's negligence in ensuring her safety and care.

Of the mental health resources that are available in correctional facilities, critical feminist criminologists warn that they can be more harmful than beneficial. The mental health needs of women prisoners in particular transform into security risks, placing them in higher security institutions that are detrimental to their mental health and well-being (Hannah-Moffat, 2016). These practices are racialized as well, given that Indigenous women make up 42 percent, and Black women make up 9 percent, of the federal female prison population (Savage, 2019; Zinger, 2020). Therapeutic interventions are applied coercively and inappropriately, where correctional officers take on the therapist role and where women are unsafe to disclose their distress for fear of institutional repercussions, such as the disclosure negatively affecting their chance for parole. The "therapunitive rhetoric," a term coined by Carlen and Tombs (2006), presents the prison as a place for correcting the causes of crimes and facilitating rehabilitation, while downplaying the role of the prison as an essentially coercive and exclusionary carceral space. Furthermore, the kinds of therapeutic interventions available to prisoners are highly disciplinary in nature, emphasizing individual fault, poor self-regulation, and cognitive distortion, thus concealing the socio-structural contributors of criminalization and distress. Pathologizing prisoners works because it acts as a relatively easy fix for large, complex social problems and because it objectifies, neutralizes, and legitimizes structural disadvantage and discrimination (Kendall, 2000; Kilty, 2012; Maidment, 2006; Pollack, 2005, 2006, 2009). These themes are replicated in the homeless population.

Criminalizing Homelessness
Homelessness acts as a vulnerability point for those experiencing distress to be caught up in the criminal justice system. Individuals experiencing homelessness are more likely to identify as suffering with distress while incarcerated and are between seven and eleven times more likely to be incarcerated than housed individuals (Greenberg & Rosenhck, 2008). The link between incarceration and homelessness is bi-directional: involvement with the criminal justice system contributes to homelessness and street involvement leaves people vulnerable to criminalization.

Those who have interacted with the criminal justice system, especially those who have experienced incarceration, are at risk of homelessness. One study revealed that those who were incarcerated in the past year were 25 percent more likely to be homeless than marginalized people who had not been in custody (To et al., 2016). A Toronto study showed that in one year more than eight hundred shelter admissions came from individuals discharged from a correctional facility and their shelter stays tend to be longer than those of other shelter residents (Novac et al., 2009). Similar research found that one in five prisoners in southern Ontario provincial correctional facilities were homeless on entry into custody and, of those, 85 percent expected to be homeless on release. In total, almost 45 percent of individuals released from custody had a plan to be homeless or precariously housed (e.g., couch-surfing) on release from jail (John Howard Society of Toronto, 2010). Ottawa's point-in-time count revealed that 60 percent of prisoners at the Ottawa-Carleton Detention Centre (OCDC) are chronically homeless (City of Ottawa, 2018a). There are several reasons for the high rate of homelessness following incarceration: housing loss upon incarceration, trouble maintaining employment while incarcerated and finding new employment once released, disconnection from support networks, and housing discrimination based on criminal record status, to name a few. Where discharge planning from correctional facilities exists at all it is woefully inadequate, especially in provincial and territorial jails. Indigenous prisoners are less likely to receive any kind of discharge planning than non-Indigenous prisoners (Gaetz & O'Grady, 2009). Around 60 percent of prisoners across the provinces are on remand, meaning that they are awaiting trial and are legally innocent, but they are rarely eligible for discharge planning (the Winnipeg Remand Centre being an exception). Given the inadequacy in terms of time, resources, and support devoted to discharge planning, even those who do meet with a discharge planner may still be discharged into homelessness.

Not only are those leaving correctional facilities at risk of becoming homeless or returning to homelessness, but the very nature of being street involved makes people a target for criminalization. Numerous studies show that individuals living in poverty do not commit more crime than wealthy people but are unfairly targeted by law enforcement. People experiencing homelessness are much more likely than housed people to be fined for "disturbing" or "nuisance" behaviour such as public intoxication, loitering, spitting, or urinating in public (Allen, 2000; Bernier et al., 2011; Mosher, 2002; Sylvestre, 2010b). While many people experiencing homelessness have been arrested at least once in their life and incarcerated at some point, their sentences are often short, lasting six months or less (Novac et al., 2009), suggesting that marginalized people are often incarcerated for minor offences. Additionally, research shows that homeless Black and Indigenous youth are subject to greater surveillance and ticketing for minor offences, such as loitering, than are white homeless youth (O'Grady et al., 2011).

Criminal justice policies and actors target the homeless population specifically. Aptly dubbed "anti-homelessness" legislation, Ontario's (1999) and British Columbia's (2004) *Safe Streets Acts* (*SSA*) penalize and criminalize panhandling. The legislation came about in Ontario as a response to public complaints about aggressive panhandling and "squeegee kids" (Hermer & Mosher, 2002). Mirroring Stanley Cohen's "folk devils" of 1970s England, young people on Toronto's street corners, clad in ripped jeans, leather vests, and bright-coloured, spiky mohawks, were claimed to be intimidating to commuters as they cleaned car windshields at busy intersections. The Ontario *SSA* was introduced after a few incidents where youth became aggressive, making it a violation to squeegee or "solicit a captive audience" (panhandle near a public space such as a bus stop or bank machine). The average fine for violating the *SSA* is $60 but can reach as high as $1,000. Despite surviving a constitutional challenge (Esmonde, 2002), the *SSA* is objectively a failure.

In the ten years followings its enactment, the rate of ticketing for panhandling increased 2,147 percent in Toronto alone. Around 80 percent of tickets issued were for non-aggressive panhandling, providing further evidence that the latent purpose of the legislation is to criminalize homelessness, and is not a matter of public safety. Over eleven years in Toronto, *SSA* tickets were issued for a total of over $4 million at a cost of almost $1 million in police time for the Toronto Police Service. Only $8,086 in fines were collected during this time period, demonstrating that the *SSA* is not economical or effective at deterring panhandling (O'Grady et al., 2011). Garland (2001) reminds us to look at the veiled objectives that sustain the criminal justice system if it consistently fails to meet its stated goals. In this case, the *SSA* is a tool used to manage and exclude those experiencing homelessness and maintain the capitalist agenda by responding to complaints from business owners to force people to move along and out of view.

Despite its failure, municipalities have followed suit, developing their own bylaws and ordinances to effectively criminalize homelessness. Several small communities across British Columbia have recently created their own bylaws against panhandling, with the City of Penticton spending over $26,000 in legal fees to prosecute a man experiencing homelessness who did not pay $880 in fines (Strachan, 2018). In Montreal, a neighbourhood police system sought to crack down on incivilities such as panhandling, squeegeeing, and sleeping in public by increasing their ticketing practices by 500 percent over the span of ten years (Bernier et al., 2011; Sylvestre, 2010a). There is something perverse about fining people who are so poor they are asking for money on the street. The zealous use of law enforcement on the homeless is a response to housed individuals feeling uncomfortable with the mere presence of homeless individuals. Sylvestre's (2010a, 2010b) study of policing among Montreal's homeless found that the priority is protecting public and semi-public space as sites of capitalist consumption over the well-being of marginalized people. Police are expected to take action to eliminate disorder and incivility. Those experiencing homelessness are regarded as always-already risky and are thus taken up by the criminal justice system at an alarming rate.

Not only are members of the homeless population more likely to be ticketed and arrested for minor infractions than housed people, but they are also significantly more likely to be detained because they cannot make bail. Those identified as homeless and/or mentally ill are more likely to end up on remand because they are denied bail, do not make their court appearance, or breach their bail conditions, many of which are contradictory or seemingly impossible to keep track of (Baldry et al., 2012; Bernier et al., 2011; Myers, 2016; Sylvestre et al., 2017). They are also more likely to plead guilty to an offence than those with a fixed address (Novac et al., 2009). It is clear that the criminal justice system is used to manage and exclude those experiencing homelessness and that, by complicating normative understandings of punishment and carceral spaces, the homelessness sector is reframed as a site of social control and an extension of the prison industrial complex.

Conclusion

Homelessness, mental illness, and criminalization form a triad of exclusion, social control, and Othering. While not mutually exclusive, these phenomena have all led to a contemporary entanglement where marginalized people are regarded as in need of surveillance, management, and in some cases, punishment. The capitalist regime creates and subsequently condemns poverty, difference, and distress. Society has responded to this self-made crisis by further individualizing and pathologizing marginalized people, thus creating and sustaining the homelessness epidemic we have today.

This exclusionary and punitive response to homelessness in Canada was not inevitable. The mental health system privileges dominant psy-knowledges that emphasize individual pathology and weakness, thereby silencing the social, cultural, and economic conditions that lead to distress. Critical mad scholars have worked for decades to reimagine the response to distress, but the medical model and Big Pharma's discursive and economic power make resistance challenging. Those experiencing homelessness, whether it be due to distress, addiction, or poverty, are at significant risk of criminalization. Homelessness is criminalized in the name of public safety and protecting businesses, with little evidence that this is necessary or effective. Criminalization further marginalizes already vulnerable populations by positioning them as both risky and at risk. Those experiencing homelessness are at higher risk of being incarcerated than housed individuals, and in turn, people leaving correctional facilities are highly vulnerable to homelessness. The prison industrial complex and homelessness industrial complex carry on this largely unspoken relationship that allows for marginalized people to be continually watched, managed, and excluded.

3

Managing in Place: The Shelter as Neoliberal Total Institution

> *"We may say that the prisons are ghettos with walls, while ghettos are prisons without walls."*
>
> – Community: Seeking Safety in an Insecure World

The homelessness sector, and specifically emergency shelters, are sites of paradox. Shelters are chaotic but boring; used for self-protection, but infamously insecure; spaces completely devoid of privacy but also filled with abject loneliness; and places to access resources and care, but in an environment that breeds physical and mental distress. The purpose of this chapter is to explore what the homelessness industrial complex looks like in practice with an emphasis on emergency shelters, given their place of prominence as described by research participants. As noted in Chapter 1, unpacking the homelessness industrial complex is fraught with moral, intellectual, and practical tensions. Having spent over a decade in and around shelters, I have a deep respect for much of the work people in these spaces do, and as I note below, so too do many recipients of the services they offer. Understanding shelters within the framework of the homelessness industrial complex, however, alerts us to the structural, ideological, political, and bureaucratic boundaries of this work that are rendered invisible in day-to-day interactions and practices between shelter residents and service providers, and that severely limits opportunities to understand homelessness as a social problem and solve homelessness by addressing structural inequity. Of particular importance in this chapter is the way the notion of personal autonomy is mobilized to downplay the constraints placed on people's choices (to stay in the shelter or not, for example) and to stifle discussions about broader systematic causes of homelessness that would require us as a society to make changes, rather than placing the burden for change on those who are homeless.

The role of the emergency shelter has changed dramatically over the last thirty years. The homelessness industrial complex's growth and transformation broadened the scope of many shelters beyond simply "three hots and a cot" (three meals and a place to sleep) into a hub of social supports and resources: food pantries; clothing banks; employment and life-skills development; physical and mental health care, etc. The shelter is an essential component for the survival of those who are homeless and vulnerably housed; however, like so many other homeless-serving organizations, shelters have policies, funding structures, and practices that are designed (intentionally or not) to manage and maintain rather than end homelessness. The homelessness crisis that grew in the 1990s from federal and provincial cuts to the welfare state left charitable and non-profit organizations to fill the gap and provide services that would otherwise disappear (Munshi & Willse, 2007). The modern shelter was compelled to adapt and did so within a social, economic, and political context that was rooting itself in a neoliberal ethos. Neoliberalism epitomizes governmentality's focus on "governing at a distance," where formal state intervention is supplanted as much as possible by arm's-length institutional directives, social pressure, and individual self-governing. Governance under a neoliberal framework means shaping how non-political entities engage with targeted populations and deliver services in lieu of direct state involvement (Miller & Rose, 2008; Rose, 1999). As the state distanced itself from the welfarist social safety net (i.e., social assistance, universal health care, publicly funded child care, etc.) people were expected to take on greater responsibility for managing any number of risks related to employment, finances, health, and well-being. The irony of the neoliberal logic is that it privileges the capitalist free-market, entrepreneurial spirit, and achieving social cohesion through individualized projects of the self, while at the same time encouraging, and indeed depending on, non-state actors such as charities, non-profit organizations, and private enterprises to take on the needs of those who "refuse the project of individual freedom" (Rose, 1999, p. 135).

Part of this neoliberal shift was to distribute carceral power beyond state-run sites such as prisons to community settings where non-state actors could surveil and govern particular people. Transcarceration (Lowman et al., 1987) describes the system of cross-institutional arrangements used to control those who cannot or will not self-govern, such as between the jail, prison, hospital, and, I argue, the homeless shelter. The homelessness industrial complex makes up part of the transcarceral process because, although few emergency shelters have a direct partnership with the criminal justice system, they are crucial in the social control of those at risk of entering the criminal justice system and act as a holding place for individuals who cycle in and out of correctional systems. By situating the shelter within this expansive mechanism of control we become attuned to two otherwise opaque ideological apparatuses: the primacy of the shelter as a site of security and control, and the discursive gymnastics used to position residents as autonomous consumers of shelter services, with little regard to the constraints and limits on their choices.

In this chapter, I consider the role of emergency shelters as a neoliberal disciplinary space. Situating the shelter as a site of social control allows us to bear witness to how social exclusion manifests discursively in policy and practice as well as through interpersonal interactions within these spaces. To get at the complexity through which shelters act as sites of intense governance I draw on Goffman's notion of total institutions to explore the structural, practical, and spatial arrangements that seek to create docile subjects (Foucault, 1977; Goffman, 1961). I argue that shelters act as a new kind of *neoliberal total institution* by positioning shelter life as a freely chosen enterprise while maintaining much of the deprivation, discipline, and control of traditional total institutions, such as the prison and psychiatric hospital. The paradox of the shelter as a neoliberal total institution rests in the implication that people's so-called choice to stay there is framed either as a positive step toward empowerment or as resignation to the hopelessness and permanence of their excluded status.

To make the argument that emergency shelters are neoliberal total institutions is not only an exercise in theoretical debate, although there is intellectual merit to adapting Goffman's work to the twenty-first century. It also underscores how people who are homeless are managed through their freedom and how they negotiate these techniques of control. Just as the mad movement fought for the liberation of people confined indefinitely in hospitals and as prison abolitionists have argued for decades against the mass incarceration of largely marginalized people, positioning emergency shelters as a form of total institutionalization provides the groundwork for reorienting our response to homelessness within a social justice and human rights framework. In the last five years, some shelters have begun to provide Housing First programs and, even more recently, build in homelessness prevention programs (Gaetz & Dej, 2017). The Canadian Alliance to End Homelessness recently launched the Canadian Shelter Transformation Network, which serves to support shelters across Canada as they reorient their work toward ending homelessness. As outlined in James Hughes's (2018) *Beyond Shelters,* there are examples of shelters across Canada, such as The Old Brewery Mission in Montreal, that have completely reoriented their mandate and practices to drive toward ending homelessness. These innovative practices show enormous promise but to date make up only a fraction of the investment and resources allocated to addressing homelessness. For now, we continue to rely heavily on shelters to manage the homelessness crisis. Because shelters are situated within the neoliberal ideology, the institutionalization practices that are obvious in prisons and hospitals are muted in emergency shelters through logics of autonomy and choice. If we recognize that neoliberal governing rationales download surveillance and governance responsibilities onto non-state actors and if we understand that shelters, as they are currently designed, inevitably fall into that role, then we can build an argument that institutionalization is not an ethical, economically sensible, or practical response when someone becomes homeless. Shifting to an approach that seeks to prevent and end homelessness has the potential to stop the perpetuation of social exclusion couched in the homelessness status.

To qualify emergency shelters as neoliberal total institutions I compare them with three key characteristics of total institutions and make note of the shelter's uniquely neoliberal qualities. First, the spatial arrangements of the shelter reinforce the exclusion of those living on the margins. Second, shelters exert minute and totalizing control over the lives of their residents. Finally, the demarcation of power between staff and residents creates a tense and insecure environment but also acts as one of the few sources of care and attention available to people experiencing homelessness in what can otherwise be a lonely and isolating atmosphere.

Framing the Issue: Theorizing the Shelter as a Neoliberal Total Institution

Goffman (1961) defines total institutions as: "A place of residence and work where a large number of like-situated individuals, cut off from the wider society for an appreciable period of time, together lead an enclosed, formally administered round of life" (p. xiii). Goffman's *Asylums* (1961) describes the characteristics of total institutions, namely the prison, the psychiatric hospital, military bases, and religious orders, and finds similarities in the ways they act as physical and social barriers to the social world. Individuals sleep, eat, engage in leisure activities, and work (arguably working on the self) in the same space and under the gaze of the same authority. Individuals go about these often tightly scheduled and highly routinized activities with the same people every day doing the same thing. Finally, these activities and routines serve the mandate of the particular institution. In the prison, for example, prisoners are spatially limited to their cell, common room, or other quartered off areas of the prison. They are constantly surrounded by others who were likewise accused or found guilty of violating the law and interact with this group in every aspect of their life: they share meals together, work together, and sleep in close proximity.[1] The mandate of the prison is primarily to be a security-driven institution of confinement. While the totalizing quality of a shelter is less obvious, as I explore in the next section, research participants were quick to note the similarities between shelters and prisons. Goffman (1961) articulates that spaces such as the prison, psychiatric hospital, and military base act as ideal types, providing the opportunity to expand beyond his study and explore the modern manifestation of the total institution.

While traditional total institutions continue to be used as a mode of governance and punishment, social theorists invite us to think more broadly about the ways community-based institutions are independent of, but related to, the disciplinary tactics used by the criminal justice system. Cohen (1979) refers to this phenomenon as the "punitive city" whereby systems of control are dispersed into the community. Similarly, Beckett and Murakawa's (2012) "shadow carceral state" describes the policies, laws, and institutions that are not part of the criminal justice system per se, but have the power to cause harm and deprivation that closely resemble criminal sanctions. This "submerged" form of punishment opens up multiple sites for analysis beyond those officially deemed carceral by the state. The social assistance office, community-based services, and homeless shelters engage in surveillance and management to form a kind of "social panopticism" (Wacquant, 2009) that expands the penal system beyond the prison walls. By considering different spaces as sites of discipline we can situate the emergency shelter as part of the "net widening" (Cohen, 1979, 1985) designed to monitor and manage risky individuals.

Despite the fact that the homeless shelter is a (usually) non-mandated,[2] community-based, and relatively accessible space, scholars have followed Goffman to argue that the shelter's very purpose is to maintain security, through institutionalizing and controlling the poor (DeVerteuil et al., 2009). Seeing homeless shelters as a form of transcarceration, Stark argues that they mirror the institutionalization felt by those coming from the prison and/or the psychiatric hospital: "Goffman's (1961) thesis [is] that the chief aim of institutional culture, in this case the homeless shelter, is to bring about control of its clients, control that must be maintained in spite of the client's welfare" (Stark, 1994, p. 555). Ranasinghe (2017) concurs, finding that the emergency shelter acts as a space of security first and a place of welfare and assistance second. The addition of treatment programs, mental and physical health care, and other services within the shelter space during the rise of neoliberalism indoctrinates individuals into the shelter regime and situates residents as consumers,[3] choosing which (if any) services they wish to partake (DeVerteuil et al., 2009; Gounis, 1992; Lyon-Callo, 2004). The shelter monitors residents' movements, eliminates any sense of privacy, and creates regimented schedules, much like other total institutions. While emergency shelters do fit many of the parameters of a total institution, the technologies of governance are decidedly different from Goffman's descriptions of institutions in the 1960s. Shelters represent a new form of total institution, one that emphasizes individual autonomy irrespective of the social context that limits a marginalized person's alternatives to shelter and service dependency.

Locating Discipline in a Post-Disciplinary System

Some scholars (Marcus, 2003; Ranasinghe, 2013) challenge the notion that the shelter is a total institution because it is part of a larger network of surveillance and risk management rather than adhering strictly to the panoptic design of the prison and hospital (Foucault, 1977). But this difference does not disqualify shelters from being total institutions; rather, it highlights the evolution of institutionalization as a governing strategy in the neoliberal age. While Feldman (2004) sees this evolution in terms of a move toward a "post-disciplinary" society, I see it rather as a move toward more subtle and hidden strategies and technologies of disciplinary power. Disciplinary techniques within traditional total institutions are hyper-individualized, focusing on the minute actions and thoughts of those it seeks to normalize, while people experiencing homelessness, Feldman argues, are largely warehoused in shelters and not categorized, segmented, and worked on in any systematic way. Post-disciplinary techniques target the physical environment, engage in risk management, and do not seek to manipulate individual subjectivities. In contrast to Feldman, rather than assume that we live in a post-disciplinary (and post-colonial, -feminist, -racial) world, I argue that it is imperative that we uncover the obfuscation of disciplinary strategies and technologies of power in the late-modern era. Johnsen et al. (2018) developed a typology of social control techniques deployed among people experiencing homelessness, including force, coercion, and bargaining. The authors point out that these practices do not constitute a continuum from severe to "softer" forms of control but point to the range of practices, each with their own complexities and challenges, used to mould behaviour. Strategies that emphasize responsibilization and choice-making in the neoliberal total institution are in keeping with the "influence" type of control, where professionals and para-professionals use persuasion to encourage behaviour modification. These social control strategies are not less serious than coercive tactics commonly used in traditional total institutions.[4] Rather, they are a form of social control that encourages people experiencing homelessness to engage in self-discipline and to manage themselves by seeking out professionals who will foster normalization.

Despite the individualization and responsibilization of people who are homeless in the neoliberal era, Foucauldian scholars remind us that power dynamics are constantly in flux (Foucault, 1980a; Gordon, 1991; Rose, 1999) and shelters do deploy some traditional disciplinary strategies. The shelters in this study incorporate disciplinary measures into their spatial and organizational layout. The front desks at both shelters house a series of screens from which staff can monitor every corner of the shelter. At Crossroads, staff often zoom in on individuals outside the main gates when they suspect a drug deal is occurring. Haven is designed with a series of locked doors so that residents' movements are restricted by staff members who must give permission for them to move from room to room or to a set of hallways (see also Ranasinghe, 2017). Staff constantly observe individuals in and around the shelter and document problematic behaviour in residents' files. As one shelter manager noted with reference to signs of mental distress specifically: "We have a database that we see and front desk will identify that somebody's unusual or their behaviour's changed, and then the whole place is aware of that and then people can observe it, right? And you can see what's happening" (Anthony). This kind of surveillance is designed to maintain the security of hundreds of people at a time who need the shelters' services; both

Haven and Crossroads are at capacity almost every night, and often over capacity in the winter months. The creation of the homelessness crisis and the subsequent response of warehousing people in emergency shelters compels frontline staff to develop techniques for managing these problematic circumstances and leads them to occupy incredibly complex positions as security officers, crisis intervention specialists, and mental health providers. This leaves people experiencing homelessness to contend with the insecurity and distress that comes from institutionalization and hyper-surveillance. Someone behaving differently in their own home would go unnoticed or at least undocumented, but in the shelter space a change in behaviour is identified as a potential security concern.

One of the techniques of normalization that is concomitant with disciplinary institutions is the case file (Foucault, 1977). It is common for those who are most excluded from society to have the largest and most detailed files. The case files of those who use emergency shelters act as a mode of "digital rule" – a modern form of "at-a-distance monitoring" (Jones, 2000, p. 11) that is accessible to a variety of professionals, para-professionals, and staff through electronic devices, and that provides a new body of information and evidence that can be used in decision making. In the emergency shelter, individuals are observed and documented by a number of para-professionals who work in the shelters, including frontline staff, case managers, and those involved in treatment and counselling, blurring the line between security and social welfare. Focus group participants described how staff are able to use this database to "track" individuals with "perceived mental health issues":

> Mental health does come up [during intake meetings] and sometimes an individual will identify as having mental health issues whether it's a diagnosis or they're feeling depressed or anxious, or I may perceive that they have mental health issues and we're actually starting to track that. If somebody identifies as having that I will write in my database that whatever their diagnosis is or if I perceive it, then I will mark that they have perceived mental health issues. So, usually if there are some pretty obvious signs of mental illness. (Candace, intake worker)

There are consequences to this kind of observation and documentation. Haven and Crossroads each hold weekly mental health meetings where shelter staff and para-professionals from outreach organizations discuss individuals whom they identify as suffering with mental illness. There are several potential outcomes from these meetings. Most often, staff will continue to monitor individuals, especially regarding their safety and the security of the shelter. Case managers may also connect individuals with resources within or outside the shelter, for instance sending them to have their acuteness assessed to determine their eligibility for Housing First programs or access to a Canadian Mental Health Association (CMHA) worker, or referring them to the mental health nurses or psychiatrists who visit the shelter. Alternatively, shelters can "form" someone and detain them involuntarily in a psychiatric hospital, demonstrating the continued presence of traditional total institutions for those who cannot or will not engage in self-discipline. Kathy, a mental health nurse who routinely visits Ottawa's shelters, described the reluctance on the part of medical staff working with people experiencing homelessness to form someone:

> We don't form people very often. The reality is, our clients go to the hospital and they often get sent right back. And we like to keep people's rights in place for as long as we can. So we don't form often because the hospital doesn't respond, we lose our therapeutic rapport, and we're right back at zero with that person so it doesn't really make a lot of sense.

Focus group members echoed the notion that the mental health system does not respond to the needs of the homeless population; this is explored further in Chapter 6. Kathy's response makes clear how rarely professionals who work in the homelessness sector form someone, but at the same time she reinforces the disciplinary power of those working in the shelter. By stating that "we like to keep people's rights in place for as long as we can," Kathy insinuates that professionals and para-professionals are the gatekeepers of homeless individuals' rights. With the surveillance mechanisms available at shelters, they have substantial power to retract these rights when they deem this to be necessary, translating their role as health care workers into one where they act as quasi-legal actors (Moore, 2007b). Herein lies the tension between freedom and disciplinary technologies; individuals have the right to be free so long as they perform their freedom according to the norm. Stuart's (2016) ethnography of policing residents of Skid Row in Los Angeles provides an example of the integration between discipline and freedom, finding that police use the threat of tickets or arrest to encourage people to sign up for rehabilitative programming. Those identified as suffering with mental illness are often thought to be less capable of using their freedom "properly" and are subject to disciplinary strategies in the form of observation or, at the most coercive end of the spectrum, involuntary incapacitation.

The notion that shelters are post-disciplinary is problematic not only because it ignores the disciplinary tactics they continue to use, but also because it assumes that shelters do not categorize people. Shelter staff do categorize some of the residents, often through the types of programming they participate in, thus delineating how responsible – and thus how redeemable – they are. People's mental health and addiction statuses, as well as their general behaviour, can put them on the staff's radar, either positively or negatively depending on their obedience, perceived dangerousness, or motivation to work on their projects of the self. However, in an institution housing hundreds of people a day, many of whom are transient, people are often anonymous. Some, like Seamus, prefer this status:

> I was very standoffish and I didn't really talk to really anyone for a long time and I still swore after three months here the staff didn't even know who I am or after that, you know, 'cause every time, the checking in thing, and a lot of guys it's just, yep, yeah Seamus, good. Gotcha, or Steve or Dave, whatever. But it was like, you got a bed here? [whispers] yeah, I've been here three months. But that's ok, I'm fine with that. I was happy that way. Actually, one of the guys I do spend time with here, he's like, "I don't know how you do it. You're like Teflon, you can do whatever you want." I'm like, "what are you talking about?" "No one knows you." I'm the guy with the hat who reads.

Seamus, a 42-year-old white man who had recently become homeless at the time of the interview, relished his anonymity as it afforded him a semblance of privacy in an otherwise public space. The fact that staff did not know his name is characteristic of post-disciplinary warehousing, but is likewise a mortification strategy used by other total institutions, often unintentionally, that breaks down people's former selves and introduces a new, institutionalized identity. As Goffman notes, total institutions often limit people's tangible connection to the outside world: "Perhaps the most significant of these possessions is not physical at all, one's full name; whatever one is thereafter called, loss of one's name can be a great curtailment of the self" (Goffman, 1961, p. 18). For three months, Seamus checked in to Crossroads for his meals three times a day and secured his bed every evening using his shelter number rather than his name. In this way, he was not unknown to staff, but his identity was entirely shaped through, to borrow from Goffman (1961),[5] his *moral career of the homeless person* rather than his personal identity outside of the shelter. Of course, Seamus's friend is wrong; Seamus cannot "do whatever [he] want[s]." If staff take notice of Seamus, either because he becomes a security risk or because he begins using the services offered by the shelter, for example attending outpatient addiction treatment or requesting education or employment services, he will be observed, categorized, and subject to normalization processes in keeping with typical total institutions.

As neoliberal total institutions, emergency shelters are more likely to rely on strategies that encourage self-discipline, such as offering workshops on money management and career counselling, but traditional disciplinary strategies that rely on observation and surveillance exist as well. In this way, the shelter retains its similarity with other total institutions that use analogous, although often more sophisticated and coercive, disciplinary techniques. Shelters act at a distance from these more formalized systems, such as the criminal justice system, and use neoliberal governance techniques to position the homeless person as a voluntary disciplinary subject. In the next sections I explore three key characteristics of total institutions in order to situate the shelter as their neoliberal counterpart: spatial restriction; minute control over daily activities; and the power differential between the watchers and the watched.

The "Freedom" to Leave and the Need to Stay: Managing Shelter Space

Emergency shelters are distinguished from traditional total institutions for two reasons. First, their permeability and connection to the wider social world is thought to negate their totalizing effects. Second, the voluntariness of residents' admission to the shelter and their freedom to leave at any time leads some scholars to suggest that the shelter is a "near" but incomplete total institution (Marcus, 2003; Ranasinghe, 2013). I argue instead that these qualities do not disqualify shelters from being total institutions; rather they illustrate the transformation of the total institution in light of neoliberal governing logics that emphasize self-governance and personal responsibility.

The Permeable Institution
Although Goffman (1961) describes total institutions as having "variation" and "degrees" (p. 119) of permeability, total institutions tend to bring to mind the high brick walls of the psychiatric hospital, the barbed wire fence of the prison, and the inaccessibility of these spaces to the public. In

contrast, most homeless shelters, including those in this study, are located in downtown cores, and residents, staff, volunteers, and visitors move in and out of these spaces throughout the day. As Gounis (1992) describes, "shelters remain relatively open institutions, a hybrid between a degraded type of public housing and a new form of institutionalization" (pp. 687–688). Most shelters require residents to leave their quarters during the day, although some shelters permit people to stay in common areas, such as the lounge, TV room, and dining hall, during mealtimes. Shelter policies encourage people to leave during the day, such as Crossroads' policy not to turn on the TV until the six o'clock evening news.

Not only do shelters encourage people to leave during the day, but this encouragement is often welcomed by residents; a common narrative found among research participants was their desire to escape the shelter whenever possible:

> KARLA: I stay out of here and go to drop-ins during the day or am looking for apartments or looking for programs to get into, to get away from here.
>
> JOSEPH: Well during the day I'm not here. After I eat my breakfast I go for a walk somewhere and I read a book and then I go to the [employment] centre and go job hunting. To me it's a base so I try to go there for lunch and come back to the job centre and then I go back at 4:00, I eat, I walk away and when I finish eating I go to my dorm and I'm by myself. Some nice people chat with me but I don't hang around.
>
> GERRY: Well I try to stay away from Crossroads as much as possible, come back for lunch and dinner. It's boring. It's not good to be bored and so I usually do a lot of walking.

The shelter is the site of ennui, drug pushers, and heightened vulnerability to victimization. Joseph, a 49-year-old biracial man who had been on and off the streets for four years, uses the shelter as a "base" to eat meals and sleep but otherwise finds the space unconducive to his project of the self, namely securing employment and rebuilding relationships with his family. In this way, interviewees suggest that laziness and dependency are by-products of the shelter environment. Karla, Joseph, and Gerry see it as their responsibility to avoid these pitfalls by leaving the space whenever possible.

For some scholars, the freedom residents have to leave the building and interact with whomever they wish minimizes the shelter's totalizing quality. Most importantly, those experiencing homelessness are able to maintain familial ties that are essential to one's identity (Gounis, 1992; DeOllos,

1997). However, while shelters do not physically prohibit individuals from spending time with family and friends, being homeless creates significant impediments to performing the roles of partner, parent, or friend (Stark, 1994). Although isolation is not a goal of the homeless shelter, the very nature of the homeless identity as an excluded group and their rejection from the social world have isolating effects. Moreover, some people's homelessness directly relates to family breakdown, especially among women and youth (Karabanow, 2006; Mayock et al., 2016). The neoliberal total institution exists within a social and cultural context where the institution itself does not need to erect barriers between residents and the community; the exclusion of the homeless population from mainstream society, including their kin network, reinforces their confinement within spaces relegated for others, such as emergency shelters. Shelter residents may be free to see their family and friends, but often they do not, given their emotional and felt exclusion.

Mary's story illustrates the complexity of maintaining her role as a partner while homeless: "I was on the street for a while with my boyfriend sleeping outside in the wintertime, for nine months. We were together, that was the main thing. We wanted to be together. It was ok. We were never cold. Under the bridge we made a home there." Mary, a 55-year-old Inuk woman, spent months living outdoors so that she could be with her boyfriend. Like most shelters, Ottawa's are gender segregated so the only way she could live with her boyfriend was if they slept on the street. Eventually Mary entered an intensive substance abuse treatment program run by a shelter and she now lives separately from her boyfriend. She struggles to balance her role as a partner with her physical well-being: "I'm getting older so I cannot be out, I wish to be but I can't. I tried when I first came back last August, can't do it anymore. It's not like before. 'Cause I had no problem sleeping outdoors with my boyfriend at that time. But now I can't do it." Mary stated that she and her boyfriend try to have the odd date night, consisting of dinner at Wendy's and a "cuddle in the bushes," but that her move to the treatment program in the shelter greatly diminished her ability to spend quality time with him. Deep, meaningful, and supportive relationships with others and connections to community are rarely designed into programs and services for people experiencing homelessness.

Mary's predicament illustrates how homelessness, distress, and personal and institutional identity coalesce. The reality of shelters as permeable spaces where people are free to come and go as they please and to interact with whomever they choose is complex. Residents who are not engaged in programming (and thus are assumed to not be working on the project of the self in appropriate and normalized ways) are discouraged from spending the day in the shelter, and are not welcome in other public sites, such as parks, shopping malls, or on sidewalks (Beckett & Herbert, 2010; Mosher, 2002). While they are free to come and go from the shelter, many of the research participants spoke of finding refuge in other services geared to the homeless, such as drop-in programs, public health clinics, and friendship centres. Others use public spaces more tolerant of people presenting as homeless, such as the public library, to pass the day. Still, participants' most common response when I asked them how they spend their days was that they simply walk. They are not welcome to stop in any one place for too long and cannot always pay for the privilege of using spaces like coffee shops and restaurants. Sometimes, even when they can pay, they are still told to leave. They walk in and among, but separate from, the included world. The experience of homelessness, as embodied in the shelter, is not very permeable at all. There are no high brick walls or barbed wire fences separating "us" from "them" but there are practical, symbolic, and ideological distinctions between the homeless and the housed that redefine total institutions in the neoliberal era and draw attention to the ways in which the homelessness industrial complex sustains exclusion by relying on techniques of institutionalization.

The Voluntary Inmate

Freedom – the ability to determine for one's self a course of action – is the bedrock of neoliberal society and the institutions that make it up. For some scholars (Ranasinghe, 2013; Marcus, 2003), the possibility that people experiencing homelessness can enter and leave the shelter voluntarily, unlike the prison or psychiatric hospital, distinguishes these places from total institutions. The logic goes that because people can find a bed in another shelter, couch-surf, or sleep on the street, emergency shelters do not qualify as total institutions.

The nature of "choice" with reference to staying in a shelter is worth scrutinizing. First, the voluntariness of entry is questionable. When discussing total institutions, Goffman (1961) refers to degrees of voluntariness that change the dynamics of the institution itself. While people are not coerced into residing in a shelter, the lack of affordable housing, anti-homelessness legislation that represses and criminalizes how people who are homeless use public space, and environmental designs such as arm rests in the middle of park benches and sculptures in doorways to prohibit people from lying down, creates a reliance on emergency shelters. For those research participants who had spent time on the street, the cold Canadian winters strongly influenced their decision to enter a shelter, despite fear of victimization:

> GREG: I was scared. I didn't know what was there.
> ERIN: So how did you make the decision to go in and what was that like?
> GREG: Um, it was fucking cold. All I had was a sleeping bag and a couple of pieces of cardboard just to block the wind. That's not much of a shelter, so I came in ... December 15 I got in. So, I remember the day [laughs]. Fuck it was cold. Hands all red and everything. And I walk up the stairs. I'm like excuse me is there any beds available? She was like, it was five something in the morning. She's like "no. You can put your head down on the table and come at seven o'clock."

For Greg, the danger associated with homeless shelters convinced him that sleeping on the streets was a safer alternative, but the winter temperatures left him with no choice but to seek refuge from the cold. Greg told me that he had heard "crazy things" about the violence in shelters, but that by the time spring arrived he was comfortable there.

Conversely, others entered the shelter because they experienced victimization on the street. Al recounted being urinated on while he slept on the sidewalk. Mac, a 57-year-old white man, described why he entered the shelter system:

> I slept under the bridge over here for a year before moving into the boarded up building. One night there was three Inuits[6] who were out having fun and I was in my sleeping bag, it was wintertime and they started kicking me and they broke my sternum in three places.

Mac later found himself in a poorly maintained rooming house, which later caught fire. He managed to escape but one of his close friends died. For Mac, his move to the shelter was not so much an active choice as it was a last resort to save his life. Goffman (1961, p. 118) would describe Greg's, Al's, and Mac's entries into emergency shelters as semi-voluntary. In keeping with neoliberal logic that emphasizes personal risk management and the individualization of social problems, entry into a homeless shelter is characterized as voluntary but the choices people make are constrained by their marginalization and lack of resources from a dismantled welfare state.

More than the voluntariness of entry, it is the freedom to leave the shelter at any time that scholars argue distinguishes emergency shelters from total institutions (Marcus, 2003; Ranasinghe, 2013). Because some residents spend nights away from the shelter by couch-surfing, squatting, renting a motel room, or sleeping outside, and because people stay in shelters for a short period of time,[7] Marcus (2003) argues that shelters do not institutionalize residents. Responding to these claims puts the question of "freedom" under the microscope, when the choice to leave a shelter is constrained by challenges that make it difficult to meet basic needs such as accessing food and clothing and finding a warm and safe place to sleep. While shelter residents are not physically confined to the shelter against their will, their freedom to leave is constrained by their marginalization (DeWard & Moe, 2010). According to the Social Housing Registry of Ottawa (the Registry), there is a five-year wait-list for social housing. In other Ontario communities, the wait time can be more than eight years (Ontario Non-Profit Housing Association, 2016). J. J., a 50-year-old white man who identifies as suffering from obsessive-compulsive disorder (OCD), claims he chose to enter the shelter system because of the wait-list:

> Eighteen months and I did my time so I could subsidize and get my health. Three to five years for subsidized housing, but if you're homeless at the shelter you're a priority for anybody who's on the registry, which is for subsidized housing. [Social housing provider] can subsidize you, or co-ops, or everything, or [supportive housing], whoever it is that house people, their priority are people that are homeless.

The Registry (2014) specifies that individuals who live on the street or in an emergency shelter can receive "homeless status" and be assigned as a priority case, as can people fleeing violence or who have a life-threatening illness. J. J. spoke at length about his struggles with addiction and mental illness and how this distress caused him to become homeless, but he characterized his transition to the shelter as a strategic manoeuvre. J. J.'s remarks are useful because they pinpoint the tension in the notion of "choice" when people enter or leave the shelter. The ability for J. J. and others in his situation to leave the shelter depends on an overburdened social housing system that does not have nearly enough supply to meet the demand. It is the external pressure to enter and stay in the institution that distinguishes the shelter as a neoliberal total institution. Other semi-voluntary institutions described by Goffman (1961), such as religious orders and the military, use mortification processes to convince subjects to stay. While shelters use some of these strategies, the neoliberal total institution relies heavily on external factors to influence people's experiences of voluntariness. The neoliberal total institution does not coercively isolate its residents in the same way as traditional total institutions do, but the surrounding socio-cultural and political landscape compels marginalized populations to enter the shelter of their own volition.

We must also think critically about the assumption that the freedom to leave the shelter is tantamount to escaping homelessness. Often, people leave shelters to temporarily stay with a friend or live in unsafe and unhygienic rooming houses (Gaetz et al., 2016). True to Cohen's description of the punitive city, there is a wider network of social control at play:

> We are seeing, then, not just the proliferation of agencies and services, finely calibrated in terms of degree of coerciveness or intrusion or unpleasantness. The uncertainties are more profound than this: voluntary or coercive, formal or informal, locked up or free, guilty or innocent. (Cohen, 1979, p. 346)

Even among those who do exit the shelter, many struggle to maintain permanent, safe, and appropriate housing, some cycle in and out of homelessness, and others continue to identify as homeless given their material and felt exclusion (Chamberlain & Johnson, 2018; Kidd et al., 2016).

The institutionalization of homelessness extends beyond the reach of the shelter. Research participants considered alternatives to staying in an emergency shelter to be more precarious and dangerous. Gaston is a 59-year-old white man who cycles between subsidized housing and emergency shelters. He described his social housing unit this way: "Lots of crack head[s] there. Lots of coke … Lots of [makes banging noises] two or three o'clock in the morning. That kind of building. So it's not easy to live there." Gaston found his current home unsafe and not conducive to maintaining his sobriety but resigned himself to this living situation because in his experience other subsidized housing complexes share similar traits. For Gaston, there is no alternative to precarious living.

Mac shared his story of living in a rooming house:

> Like where I live now, it's just swamped with drugs. There's people banging on my door all night long with drugs. They put it on the tenants. It's my fault. They have security there but if I was to complain, it's my fault. You

know? I've been beaten with bats, pipes, you name it, so they can deal out of my place. But it's all my fault. It's the same with the police if I call them. Well you opened your door, but they bang away at it. It's hard to stay clean in those buildings. I'm trying to get out. I've been on a high priority waiting list for two years and my life has been threatened, and, I've been on this waiting list for two years. Yeah, I'm at the top of the list, but there's no such thing as priority or caring about me.

Mac is describing home takeovers – when a legitimate tenant or homeowner is threatened physically, financially, or psychologically when people will not leave their home (Butera, 2013). Precariously housed individuals are at great risk of victimization and, as Mac recounts, negative relationships with police often limit options for a resolution to the takeover. Anecdotally, people who are homeless have told me of friends who had a social housing unit but stayed in the shelter because they were not safe in their homes, which were taken over by drug dealers. Mac's narrative also questions the usefulness of the priority wait-list described by J. J. Mac uses shelter services and feels insecure in his home but does not meet the Registry's definition of homeless and will therefore have to wait years to access housing.

Given the above discussion, the permeability and voluntariness of the shelter does not disqualify it from consideration as a total institution; instead, these features account for how institutionalization takes shape in the neoliberal era. Although many participants spent as little time in the shelter as possible, the space acts as an anchor through which they access living essentials and, in some cases, escape the vulnerability and danger of living on the streets or in unsafe housing. The lack of safe and viable alternatives to the shelter acts as a significant constraint for those experiencing homelessness to exercise their freedom to leave. Outside pressures reinforce the neoliberal total institution, namely the lack of safe alternatives to shelter living and the possibility of facing death on the streets during winter. Moreover, leaving the shelter does not always mean escaping homelessness because housing arrangements are situated within a group of loosely connected institutions that target risky populations in different venues. Rather than rejecting the idea of the shelter as a total institution, it is useful instead to consider the institutionalization of poverty and hopelessness found in emergency shelters as a manifestation of the total institution in the neoliberal context. The shelter maintains its totalizing quality by acting as a site of control that residents often describe as similar to the prison system.

Controlling Time and Space in Emergency Shelters

One of the key characteristics of the total institution is its highly regimented schedule and routine, with people's "essential needs" planned by the institution (Goffman, 1961). The timetable is a disciplinary tool meant to control activity and create docile bodies, whereby discipline becomes "a political anatomy of detail" (Foucault, 1977, p. 139). Marginalized people's bodies act as sites of governance where professionals and para-professionals across social service sectors seek to normalize and regulate the movements, actions, and behaviours of those living on the margins, giving little attention to how social systems create and perpetuate inequity (Lyon-Callo, 2004). Time is highly scrutinized and regulated in spaces like the asylum, hospital, and prison, even when much of that time is unstimulating and monotonous (Castel, 1988; Foucault, 1976, 1977, 1988). Residents' schedules are not as strictly fixed in a neoliberal total institution but the regimented and rules-driven nature of services geared toward those experiencing homelessness ensures they act as external constraints on residents' routines, in turn reinforcing the regulative power of the shelter. Most residents rely on the shelter to meet their basic needs, and in order to manage so many people in a single space, shelters control when residents eat, sleep, watch TV, have a coffee, take a shower, do laundry, and access their bedroom. Indeed, while the daytime is not tightly controlled, the fact that almost every other activity is scheduled limits residents' freedom to plan their days. For example, Chico, a 50-year-old white man who has spent years in shelters across Canada, described the difficulty he experienced working around shelters' schedules:

> I mean, coming and going, you have to report, have to check in, I mean sometimes I'm over in Gatineau [an adjacent city] and I'm like Jesus I gotta go book in. I don't really want to go for supper but I have to come and book in because ... but that's a good thing because it keeps you in check.

Chico went on to say that although he aspires to live independently, he realizes there would be no incentive to stop drinking for the evening to ensure he gets back in time to secure a bed. The tight schedule serves as a form of accountability by limiting how far he can be from the shelter and for how long, thereby acting as a method of personal and social control. In this way, the neoliberal total institution uses residents' autonomy to encourage, but not coerce, them to self-regulate by imposing administrative requirements throughout the day that restrict their freedom if they choose to stay in the shelter.

The daytime is more closely scheduled for those who participate in the programs offered by the shelters, such as outpatient addiction treatment and case management. Group therapy, individual meetings, employment training, and homework such as journal writing require residents to regulate their days through the schedules set by social agents. Many participants spoke positively about having their days managed, such as Mick, a 53-year-old white man who was actively seeking support for his substance abuse and mental health problems:

> And so all these programs I'm involved with and have busy days so I'll start out with the [outpatient addiction treatment] program. Then I'll go to a meeting at noon, either, like NA or AA [Narcotics Anonymous or Alcoholics Anonymous]. And then in the afternoon I'll go for a workout, I'll go to the gym or something. So I'll grab a nap if I'm tired, and in the evening I'll have some, something like the Men's Project[8] or I'll have a workshop at [a counselling service]. Or I have a sponsor now in AA and on Tuesday nights we go to [a building] that's behind the ROH[9] and from 6:00 to 7:00 there's a men's meeting.

Mick moved into subsidized housing with a friend a few weeks before the interview, garnering more freedom to manage his day and allow for a nap, but continued to rely heavily on the shelter for its meals and services. He was involved in several mental health and addiction programs that create a highly regimented schedule. This kind of schedule is not mandatory, but it is strongly encouraged by psy-experts situated within the neoliberal total institution and is helpful to achieving and maintaining the redeemable status. The more individuals take on the project of the self by deferring to professionals and para-professionals, the more active the disciplinary measures imposed on them become because they are characterized as worthy of the time and money required to regulate them. Mick goes on to describe the value in such a structured day:

> I've realized I'm not good yet with idle time. I still don't know how to relax properly, so that anxiety's still active. I don't know how to enjoy myself properly, so I can't have fun doing things too easily so that's still depression that keeps going, that's in there somewhere. If I stay busy with productive, positive, recovery related, self-healing related activities then I will avoid idle time.

Mick identifies as struggling with post-traumatic stress disorder (PTSD), OCD, social phobia, and attention deficit disorder (ADD), as well as addictions to crack and alcohol. Because of this distress, Mick is not confident that he can make what he envisions are healthy and smart decisions. He connects his mental well-being with a highly structured routine. In order for him to engage in "productive" and "positive" (read "normalized") activities, Mick relies on the disciplinary techniques offered by the homelessness sector. The presumption by staff and those experiencing homelessness alike that people living in a shelter "lack judgment" and are incapable of governing their own lives is consistent with the idea of the shelter as a total institution (DeWard & Moe, 2010). In the neoliberal total institution, residents are expected to come to terms with their faults on their own and then to seek support to manage their time. This is not to disparage Mick's hard work or the benefits he acquires from his schedule and the mental health and addiction programs he attends; however, it does point to the narrow, medicalized conceptualization of engaging in self-improvement and its limit to strictly individualized mechanisms of change.

"It's True Hell": The Emergency Shelter as a Prison

Some research participants, such as Mick, framed shelters positively. Vince, a 36-year-old white man, described how the shelter "helped save my life," in particular citing the health care and addiction services offered through the shelters. Others characterized the shelter system in unequivocally negative terms. Both Katie and Karla, who stayed in the same shelter, claimed it is "pure hell," describing being surrounded by drug pushers, people screaming throughout the night, dirty needles in the bathroom, and physical violence. Milan referred to the shelter as "toxic"; Shadow called it "the jungle"; and Lenny claimed the shelter was "ground zero" for the chaos of living in close quarters with people struggling with addiction and facing debilitating distress. Sheela, a 48-year-old First Nations woman who underwent significant trauma in her childhood and spent considerable time in foster care, paints the shelter in similar terms but gains a sense of comfort from the commotion:

> And every day I gotta go back there and deal with that shit again. "So-and-so did this or the staff did that." But then in a way, because I grew up in a place that wasn't always settled, that there was always commotion going on, it kind of felt like home also, in a way. So the banging of the doors kind of felt in a way comforting. But then again, it shouldn't be like that. It shouldn't feel comforting [laughs]. You know what I mean? 'Cause you get used to it.

Sheela connects the shelter's chaotic environment with the instability of her childhood, one that is rooted in intergenerational trauma stemming from settler-colonialism (Christensen, 2016). Although Sheela is unhappy in the shelter, it offers a certain level of comfort in its familiarity, even when the familiar is negative. Gounis (1992) notes that shelters provide the material conditions of a home but without the same symbolic significance. The representation of home as a place of reprieve, safety, and relaxation did not exist for Sheela in her childhood and so her conception of home lies in the conditions of material necessity, such as food, shelter, and clothing.

For many of those who had spent time in jail and/or prison the shelter is a reminder, or continuation, of their confinement. Lenny, a 57-year-old white man who was incarcerated for many years, compared the shelter to his time in prison: "It's very similar. Oh sure you're told when to eat, when to lie down, when to go to bed. You're not asked what you want, you're told what to do, or what you need." Lenny pinpoints his lack of personal autonomy as the common denominator between the prison and the shelter. He highlights the paradox of the shelter, where the organizational mandate is to foster independence among residents, but the nature of the institution requires obedience and conformity. This same critique is made by critical criminologists who question whether prisoners can be empowered and gain self-esteem in a place completely devoid of freedom and in the absence of the most basic independent decision making (Kilty, 2012; Maidment, 2006; Pollack, 2006). The shelter, as a neoliberal total institution, differs from the prison in that it positions its residents as choosing to stay and thus as choosing to adopt its rules; however, like in their traditional counterparts the strict regulation of time and space often has a demoralizing or infantilizing effect. Those who come to rely on the shelter to meet their needs are problematized as dependent.

Getting Too Comfortable
In their groundbreaking research on the deinstitutionalization of psychiatric hospitals and its impact on communities, Dear and Wolch (1987) described "service dependent ghettos," the geographic concentration of those accessing public assistance and resources. As the spread of urban renewal projects and gentrification dismantles these spaces, urban geographers and sociologists are now inclined to describe groups rather than spaces. The focus is now on "service dependent populations" (Ruddick, 1996), which individualizes and problematizes service users. Dependency carries the connotation of being a "dirty word" (Bauman, 1988, p. 80). Dependency undermines

the neoliberal principles of self-actualization, entrepreneurship, and responsibilization and individualizes structural inequities, especially those based on race, class, and gender. Given their institutionalization, those experiencing homelessness are deemed particularly susceptible to dependency. However, this logic fails to consider that, rather than antithetical to neoliberalism, interdependence is a necessary component of a globalized and industrialized world (Reindal, 1999; Ruddick, 1996). In our hyperspecialized social order we are all dependent on each other. I do not know how my car's radiator works so I depend on a mechanic. I do not have the land, nor the green thumb, to grow my own food so I depend on farmers for my food. The very nature of modern industrialized society is mutual dependence, yet when marginalized people come to depend on particular spaces or professions it is characterized as a personal failing requiring targeted policy responses, while ignoring how dependency is built into the shelter system through its social control mechanisms.

Some interview participants saw a connection between the highly controlled atmosphere of the shelter and the passivity of many of its residents. Milan, a 38-year-old white man, considers his transition to the shelter as contributing to his alcoholism and bipolar symptoms:

> One year led to the other, to the other, working in the restaurant, in construction, having a beer, just being like in a fog for many years and eventually I ended up in the street and that was even worse because the street, they pay your shelter, they pay your food, all I have to do is drink now. I know the shelters have a purpose, but I feel it's a big enabler for a lot of people. Without the shelters I don't think I would have stayed in the street more than a couple of months, 'cause it's cold in the winter outside. I slept two winters outside and I know how cold it is.

Milan is highly critical of other men in the shelter who he thinks are wasting their time and lack sufficient motivation to exit the shelter system. Milan regards efforts to make the shelter more hospitable as contributing to the laziness of its residents. He claims that he resists becoming dependent on the shelter by participating in the outpatient treatment programming offered by Crossroads, seeing a psychiatrist, and applying to university; however, Milan's mental health care, addiction treatment, support network, and social assistance all come from the homeless-serving sector. This suggests that he is fully entrenched in the shelterization process but because a neoliberal total institution provides voluntary assistance to the project of the self, Milan characterizes his reliance on the shelter as a choice. Funding shelters in lieu of creating affordable housing endorses the "discourse of personal inadequacy and deficiency as the cause of homelessness" (Foop, 2002, p. 63). Whereas Milan believes he uses shelter resources to avoid becoming passive and dependent, having been homeless for nine years appears to have deepened his dependency on the system rather than thwarted it.

Milan and others are in a Catch-22 whereby if they do not vie for redeemability by adopting the obedient shelter resident role they lose access to the services and supports they need for basic survival, but if they accept this role they are likely to become dependent on that system and stay homeless longer (Stark, 1994). Milan's narrative demonstrates the pitfall of the redeemable status – while he gains access to resources and privileges, such as scarce one-on-one therapy, he remains mired in homelessness and thus excluded from the mainstream social body.

The research participants who spoke about "getting comfortable" had a decidedly negative attitude toward dependency. Many characterized getting comfortable as being detached from their lives and lacking the motivation for self-regulation. Otto, a 43-year-old white man who experienced homelessness for six years, described the moment when he realized he was shelterized:

> I was kicking my heels, I was getting comfortable living in a six-man dorm with a bunch of snorers and smelly feet and people coming in all cracked up in the middle of the night, you know, it was normal life for me. Waking up on Christmas day to find somehow the front desk staff had managed to sneak, I'm going to say like stocking kind of thing. We got a little pack of cigarettes, Native cigarettes that they'd obviously confiscated from some poor fucker and decided to hand them to us. It's really nice, but to have Christmas be dissolved down to whatever you can take from a bunch of strangers and stuff like that, it kind of makes you think hmm … my life's really changed and not just the physical aspects, the mental aspects. Fifteen, twenty years ago I would have thought my God, what a pathetic Christmas that is, like that's so horrible and most people today would think, my God that's sad. That somebody would wake up and look forward to that little stocking that they get from the homeless shelter. But it's all a matter of perspective. So that's when I decided I gotta get out of here, one way or another I'm not dying in a shelter. I gotta get out and if I fail at least I would fail sort of living on my own.

This excerpt from Otto's story illustrates his felt exclusion from the mainstream social body. Comparing the depressing state of Christmas morning in a shelter and gifts coming from "whatever you can take from a bunch of strangers" to previous holidays spent with his wife and daughter illustrates his felt descent into the excluded world. Norms are sites of comparison; Otto qualifies his life in the shelter as "normal life for me" but one that is inherently abnormal and thus deviant to the wider social body. He sees his abnormality as coming from his contentment with being a passive recipient of services rather than actively managing his own life. In this way, Otto embodies Milan's critique that the comfort of the shelter encourages complacency. A more nuanced reading of Otto's narrative, however, reveals both individual and social factors contributing to his continued homelessness. He described a series of attempts at stabilizing his life by attending college and finding employment that were complicated by failed relationships, limited opportunities due to his criminal record, unrecognized credentials, substance use, and distress (he is diagnosed with attention deficit hyperactivity disorder (ADHD), as well as bipolar disorder, and unspecified "social disorders"). Certainly, Otto's moral career of the homeless person is not simply one of laziness and passivity. After multiple recovery programs, job interviews, and attempts at independent living, Otto conceded that his normal is different from the mainstream standards and is more in keeping with those who are institutionalized.

The Bubble Boys: Staff as Producers of the Total Institution

In *Asylums*, Goffman (1961) writes at length about the demarcation of power between staff and inmates. He refers to the two groups as exhibiting "different social and cultural worlds" (p. 9), characterized by a large, subjugated, and managed group and a small, powerful faction of professionals and para-professionals. Given the power imbalance, inmates and staff often have a strained relationship where "staff often see inmates as bitter, secretive, and untrustworthy, while inmates often see staff as condescending, highhanded and mean" (Goffman, 1961, p. 7). Like traditional total institutions, there is often a strain in the shelters between staff and those experiencing homelessness, with research participants comparing shelter staff with correctional officers and mental health workers. The ways staff exert power, even with compassionate intentions (Moore, 2011), reinforce the perception of the homeless population as incompetent and in need of management. As such, the role staff play in prioritizing the security of the shelter (Ranasinghe, 2017) harkens back to a more disciplinary conceptualization of total institutions, albeit within a neoliberal discourse that assumes residents' voluntary acceptance of the regime.

Conflicts between shelter residents and staff are common, with countless stories of how staff members use their power to dominate people experiencing homelessness. However, an analysis of power relations in the shelter would not be complete without making sense of the substantial number of positive comments interviewees made regarding shelter workers. Greg advised that as long as you respect staff, they would respect you. Jon, who also stayed at Crossroads, claimed that case managers and counsellors "bend over backwards" to help those in need. Most (but not all) of the research participants mentioned at least one staff member they felt they could open up to. People who have exited homelessness and gone on to achieve the redeemed status often ascribe their success to a staff member or a small group of champions who played a special role in their lives. For Katie, who frequently moves between supportive housing, shelters, and jail, the importance of staff to her mental well-being was clear:

> Meds don't work. It's Charlene. Charlene's the one I talk to the most. Because she'll know if I show up and I'm in a pissed off mood. [A resident] actually said something to me and it was Charlene that was working. She said something really bad about my kids. So she goes running to her room. I turn around and I said to Charlene, "you heard that right?" She's like "yeah." She opened the door to her [office] and let me in there.

Katie, a 32-year-old mother of five who has been homeless for more than sixteen years, identifies as struggling with anxiety. Although she does not have custody of her children, she maintains a relationship with them and strongly relates to her role as their mother. Stressful situations such as the one described above often cause Katie to have panic attacks or angry outbursts. She does not find that Seroquel[10] helps her cope in times like this and relies heavily on staff members, with whom she has built relationships over many years, who know her triggers and de-escalation strategies. Katie recognizes that she is dependent on staff as an integral component of her mental health care.

At the conclusion of each interview, I asked participants if there was anything further that they would like to discuss. Matilda used this opportunity to speak positively about the shelter staff. She added: "Yes, I'd like to put in and mention to the staff, because they have their hands full and they do a lot, and they try and do a good job, and they're good and it must be difficult at times, and they get frustrated too sometimes but they're really good." Matilda relayed to me that she sometimes has a tense relationship with staff, which she attributed to their stressful work environment and compassion fatigue (Fahy, 2007). Although Matilda expressed genuine gratitude for the work frontline staff do, she is hesitant to approach staff when in trouble because "they get bugged so much." Instead, she volunteers her time folding laundry and cleaning Haven's kitchen to maintain a favourable relationship with staff. In this way, power takes on a productive rather than repressive form (Foucault, 1980a). Performing the redeemable role paid off for Matilda, as staff chose her to receive a coveted spot in another shelter with a reputation for less violence and drug use. As explored below, a shelter resident's relationship with frontline staff and para-professionals, such as case managers, can have a profound effect on their quality of life.

"We're Not the Enemy": Frontline Staff as Police

In noting the similarities between traditional and neoliberal total institutions, some research participants compared frontline staff to police and correctional officers when describing their overt displays of power. Residents commonly refer to the front desk as "the bubble," a term borrowed from prison to describe the glass office where correctional officers are stationed. In turn, front desk staff at the shelter are referred to as "bubble boys" (regardless of their gender). The bubble acts as a symbolic display of power, where frontline staff wear a "badge of privilege" (Bauman, 2004, p. 104) that comes from accessing spaces that are off-limits to residents and enforcing rules that only residents must uphold. Daniel finds the title "frontline," which is embroidered onto the uniforms at Crossroads, to be a display of power:

> You know, they call themselves frontline like we're the enemy? We're not the enemy, you're not against us, you're not punishing us, we're not in the penal system, we're in a supportive environment. Not frontline, no, no, no, no. Helper. Support worker. Service delivery agent, or something. Not frontline.

It is interesting to note that Daniel was among those research participants who described the shelter as "halfway between the ROH and Innes Road." The Royal Ottawa Hospital (ROH) is the city's mental health care centre. Innes Road refers to the street where the Ottawa-Carleton Detention Centre (OCDC) is located. Daniel's description of shelter staff's authoritative presence is consistent with traditional total institutions. He highlights the paradoxical nature of staff roles that requires them to be compassionate and tolerant while upholding strict rules. Goffman (1961) notes this juxtaposition as well, describing staff's dual role in total institutions as using coercive tactics to ensure obedience among inmates while also acting with humanity and rationality. This ambiguity derives from a widening carceral net that downloads responsibility for surveillance and management from the state onto charities and service providers through formal and informal channels and that requires staff to accept or challenge this arrangement in various instances (Tomczak & Thompson, 2019). Daniel, a 47-year-old white man who has experienced homelessness for a decade, describes the tension arising from staff using predominantly disciplinary tactics, such as sanctions for rule violations and engaging in surveillance, within a neoliberal total institution. The residents of the shelter get caught up in the confusion and inconsistency of witnessing staff trying to balance security and care.

Arbitrary Rule Enforcement and the Division of Redeemability
Shelter staff have divergent perspectives on how they carry out their role, leading to inconsistent rule application and enforcement. This incoherency likely stems from the impossible position shelters have been placed in, both as purveyors of charity and as agents of social control. For example, in his research on shelters, Ranasinghe (2014) describes one staff member who subscribed to the "tough love" approach, strictly enforcing the rules while another who had personal experience with homelessness took a more nurturing approach and was much more flexible with the rules. This inconsistency creates frustration among shelter residents, where rules are applied differently depending on which staff are working at any given time. A staff member's approach has a significant impact on shelter residents' lives given that so much of their day is governed by shelter rules. Seamus was obviously annoyed when he stated:

> They need to be less cop-like and more social worker type. Or find a nice blend. And I know that there's rules and there has to be rules. Not black and white though. I've never been black and white rule guy. And they do that but they do it really poorly because they do it black and white for one day and then grey the next and then black, white, and grey in the same day.

Seamus understands that shelters employ rules as a means to maintain the security and functioning of the institution, but he finds that staff implement rules arbitrarily, creating a challenge for residents who have to change their behaviour on any given day. While Ranasinghe (2014) argues that this discrepancy results from ideological differences between staff, we might also look at discretion in terms of the redeemability of the resident, and whether they are afforded the privilege of bending the rules.

Wanda is a quiet and meek 61-year-old white woman who had lived at Haven for ten months at the time of the interview. She suffered with a host of physical illnesses, including chronic foot pain, suspected osteoporosis, as well as being in remission for cancer. Wanda tried to avoid trouble in the shelter but was assaulted by other residents and hospitalized six months prior to the interview. She was understandably very nervous to come back to the shelter once released from hospital, but after a brief stay in a motel she ran out of money and had no choice but to return. On re-entering she found that the frontline staff provided her with extra assistance:

> They let me, I know it's not much to ask for, that I ask for a piece of toast this morning and a little bit of tea because I'm not eating and usually the hours they'd say no. And they did say yes. I know it's not asking a lot but they let me have a cup of tea for my throat and a piece of toast. They have certain hours so they could have said no, but maybe they ... I asked [a staff member] personally, I said, "if you say no it's ok."

Wanda is aware that for housed people having a cup of tea and a piece of toast at one's leisure is of no concern. At the shelter, however, where staff strictly control mealtimes and room access, Wanda's request for food outside the schedule is a request rarely granted. Goffman (1961) contends that requesting permission for minor activities is one of the primary methods of mortification in a total institution. Wanda acknowledges the power differential between her and the staff, but she also qualifies her request for "special treatment" by stating, "if you say no it's ok." In this way, Wanda acknowledges her subjugated position and confers on staff her willingness to abide by the rules even if they do not meet her needs. On her return to the shelter, staff members were cognizant of Wanda's vulnerability and took an increased interest in her care, finding her specialists and helping her navigate the health system. Staff characterized Wanda as redeemable given her willingness to submit to the disciplinary regime of the shelter and as such, granted her seemingly small but significant request for tea and toast.

Louise also stayed at Haven at the same time as Wanda but had a decidedly different experience with staff. Louise is a 48-year-old white woman from the United States who came to Canada seven months before the interview after extradition following a prison term.[11] Haven had barred Louise a few months previously for fighting but she returned after being evicted from a rooming house for drug and alcohol use. Since her return, she had been in a number of other fights but was rarely the instigator; she claimed women assaulted her while she was passed out from smoking crack. Louise was diagnosed with bipolar disorder and depression and found that her Seroquel and Prozac prescriptions were not as effective as alcohol in relieving anxiety. Louise made several requests to stay in her room during the day due to her physical and mental distress but staff were unwilling to bend the rules for her:

> You go get an x-ray on your lungs because I had pneumonia here. Three months I was stuck in bed, three months this winter. Nobody even knew I was alive. And then all of a sudden one day I get a, ok, so no more bedtime. I said, who are you? How do you know how I feel? Because pneumonia is like mono, you're just exhausted.

Louise also recounted asking for bedrest on account of her distress:

> I don't think people recognize, like, when I say I want to stay in my bed and it's because I'm depressed and I don't want to do anything, I don't want to go out, I don't want to see anybody. It's almost like a panic feeling, a paranoia, and you know, they're "get up! You've got no bed rest." And I said "I'm depressed." Uh, "you'll feel better when you get up." It's like, are you a doctor?

Louise describes the shelter staff as unsympathetic and judgmental. She was afforded permission to access the bedroom area when she was acutely ill with pneumonia, but this exception was only temporary. Louise believes she is entitled to stay in bed when she wants and does not appreciate having to make a request to do so. Unlike Wanda, Louise does not defer to the staff's power and is instead confrontational, demanding "who are you?" and "are you a doctor?" Because Louise is resistant to shelter policies and the staff who enforce these rules she is not positioned as redeemable and thus not afforded the benefits that come with playing by the rules. As Chico stated: "You've gotta get along with staff, man. These are the guys that are running the place." Louise confronts these power relations through acts of resistance. But by not playing the part of the docile subject working to "get along" with staff, she is not privy to relaxed rule enforcement.

Louise is not alone in her frustration with the seemingly arbitrary rules applied by staff. Field notes from Haven reveal an incident between frontline staff and Alyson, whom staff identified as difficult to handle due to her relapses after attempts at sobriety:

> She wanted to get into her room and the staff wouldn't let her. She began to get very upset, quite surprising from what I've seen from her. She was still quite rational though. She said she just wanted to get into her room to get something. She knew it was against the rules but as she said: "I'm dying and all I want to do is get into my room." She was very frustrated with staff, saying that she was not doing well and she was just looking for some flexibility.

My interactions with Alyson were always pleasant and courteous, but the power imbalance between Alyson and staff created a hostile environment where she felt that her needs were subjugated by shelter bureaucracy. Alyson's distress was so acute that she cried out "I'm dying" and begged for "some flexibility" on the part of staff. Although Alyson's participation in detox programs is a sign of her potential redeemability, her continuous relapses left staff with compassion fatigue and they were unwilling to soften the rules for her. Once again, Chico's advice that "I don't like to rock the boat ... Therefore I've had no problems" rings true. Although Alyson was not as openly defiant of staff as Louise, her opposition to "black and white" rule enforcement as described by Seamus is a small act of resistance that brings to the fore the hidden voices of those who are often unseen and unheard. In her plea for flexibility, Alyson articulates what is obvious to most shelter residents – that the rules are flexible for some, but not for others. In this way, frontline staff members maintain authority during these everyday struggles for power through their ability to grant flexibility.

Conclusion

Emergency shelters act as unique spaces meant to encompass a social welfarist ideology, while in practice emphasizing security and surveillance, in large part due to the sheer size and magnitude of the homelessness crisis. Shelters exist as part of a complex and heterogeneous network of institutions that regulate allegedly risky populations through their freedom. In this way, shelters share many of the same characteristics as traditional total institutions: the strict regulation of space; the regimentation of time; and the demarcation of power between staff and residents. Shelters differ, however, in that their ability to engage in social control exists in tandem with the socio-political environment that limits alternative arrangements to shelter living and that positions people experiencing homelessness as voluntary subjects in their institutionalization.

While there is a distinction between traditional total institutions and the shelter as their neoliberal counterpart, these places also share important similarities. Total institutions are places of mortification and identity loss. By characterizing the shelter as a kind of total institution, we can recognize the ways in which people experiencing homelessness are excluded from the mainstream social body and are thrust into the moral career of the homeless person. Institutionalization takes a neoliberal form by inculcating its subversive power within the parameters of choice and autonomy. The people I spent time with described the ways they felt institutionalized given their dependence on the shelter for a warm place to sleep, food to eat, and, as many highlighted, the opportunity to work on the project of the self. That homeless shelters exist within the wider (transcarceral) net (Cohen, 1985) of neoliberal governance demonstrates how total institutions have transformed in the twenty-first century. As a neoliberal total institution, the shelter exists in and among downtown condominiums, high-end restaurants, and shopping malls as a site of exclusion. While it is just as visible as any other building, the distress, marginality, and pains of homelessness remain invisible to the included citizenry who occupy the space around it. Those who reside in a shelter may be free to leave during the day but they cannot so easily escape the homeless identity or the poverty, racism, and discrimination that often go along with living on the margins.

4

Identity Management: Identity Making in the Context of Marginalization

A tension exists in the way identities are actively and consciously created and performed within the confines of marginality. Rather than seeking an "authentic" or "true" identity, identity construction is a performance undertaken within social, cultural, and historical parameters (Butler, 1990; Gergen, 2000; Goffman, 1963; Roseneil & Seymour, 1999). Discursive constructs, such as mental illness diagnoses, are tools used to illustrate particular subjectivities that resonate with some individuals (Ussher, 2003). In this way, a diagnosis or a label, such as depressed or alcoholic, does not offer a definitive "truth," but acts as an identity descriptor that comes with specific meanings and constraints. People experiencing homelessness engage in identity performance, but their status as homeless directly affects the types of identities that they perform and the effectiveness or believability of these performances. By understanding how identity performance works within a broader social system, we can highlight the intersection of individual and socio-structural factors shaping people's experiences and the complexity of what it means to adopt, negotiate, or resist the homeless, mentally ill, and/or addict identities.

How people experiencing homelessness manage their identity is predicated on how they make sense of their marginal status. Social norms dictate how someone who is excluded should relate to the self, such as having a sense of shame and accepting the distance between themselves and the mainstream social body. This sense of self builds the homeless, mentally ill, and addict identities. Most participants consciously and unconsciously attempted to achieve and maintain a redeemable status by negotiating these identities, although some cast themselves, or are cast by others, as irredeemable. In keeping with Goffman's dramaturgical approach where identity is constructed as a performance, research participants negotiated particular identities as a way to situate themselves as redeemable and worthy of services and support and to distance themselves from the irredeemable.

Technologies of freedom manifest not only in the context of institutional mandates and program policies, but also in the very shaping of who we are and how we understand ourselves. Identity develops at the intersection of individual biography and social forces. Personal identity conceptualizes the self as quintessentially unique. Our individuality must be, in some respect, differentiated from others and from this perspective, we shape our biography. Personal identity is closely bound to social identity – that is, how we present ourselves to others and what behavioural expectations the social world bestows on us based on our personal characteristics. We are constantly trying to deduce what others think of us based on our presentation of self (Goffman, 1959, 1963).

Materiality moulds our identity. External constraints such as racism, classism, sexism, ableism, heteronormativity, colonialism, and other oppressions limit people's freedom to identify as they like, which goes on to shape their social identities because these discriminatory perspectives influence how others view them (Bauman, 1988). For example, ask a woman firefighter about the kinds of narratives she heard from people in her life and the public at large as she chose and began her career – women are not strong enough, women firefighters are inferior to men firefighters, etc. – to understand how it may be that women come to self-identify as too weak for the job or that they do not belong. Meanwhile, firefighting equipment does not always fit women's bodies and fire halls have historically not been designed to include women firefighters, highlighting the structural factors that can impact one's sense of identity. The way our identity changes based on others' perceptions of it parallels Lemert's (1979) secondary deviance, where deviance is understood as the outcome of being labelled so. When the social world constantly tells people experiencing homelessness that they are lazy, disturbing, and unwelcome, it is no wonder that they begin to feel like this must be true and self-identify in this way.

In order to be free in the neoliberal era, it is up to the individual to produce an identity that aligns with neoliberal projects, such as self-actualization and self-fulfillment. We do this by performing our identity in particular ways, sometimes intentionally and sometimes unconsciously. Performativity gets at the ways that we move about the world, present ourselves, and interact with others. In this way, it is useful to consider how people experiencing homelessness "do" their mental health status in the same way gender scholars consider how people "do" gender. To do gender means to invoke "a complex of socially guided perceptual, interactional, and micro-political activities that cast particular pursuits as expressions of masculine and feminine 'natures'" (West & Zimmerman, 1987, p. 126). Doing gender implies that people are constantly assessing normative conceptions of gender in their social relationships and activities so that they are always acting out their gender identity (Dej, 2018). The social and cultural configurations of identity performance (Butler, 1990; Goffman, 1959) capture the complexity of identity creation – that identity is flexible, situated within the specificity of time and space, built from pre-existing norms, and contingent on how others perceive the performance. These tensions between personal conceptions of self and socially constructed meanings ring true to how those experiencing homelessness "do" their mental health status and to how we all attempt to make sense of ourselves. We have some, but limited, awareness and control over our positionality and subjectivity in the world around us and in this space we can assert, negotiate, or resist dominant identity markers. Temporal, cultural, and social understandings of homelessness impact identity expression. At the same time, people use some self-governance techniques and reject others as tools to perform mental illness, wellness, or something in between. Experiences of social exclusion mediate the opportunities, or more commonly limitations, of identity performance.

In the sections that follow, I describe the various arrangements of people's perceptions and presentations of self and demonstrate that people experiencing homelessness are active participants in their own identity construction, within the exceptionally limited parameters of their marginalized status. These very limitations exemplify what exclusion looks like in practice. With the exception of necessary explanatory remarks, this chapter is organized around different ways identity management plays out rather than on each identity marker (i.e., homeless, mentally ill, etc.). This is because identity components blend with and detract from one another in ways that cannot be described in isolation. Still, at times I rely on terms such as "homeless identities" or "mentally ill identities" to describe specific elements of an identity marker. This is not to reduce someone's personal and social identity to a single entity, but rather to demarcate thematic similarities and points of analysis between identities and to complicate common narratives about what it means to be "a homeless person" or "someone who is mentally ill."

Of Shame and Otherness: Marginalized Identities

The Shamed Poor

Expressions of embarrassment and sadness are common narratives from people experiencing homelessness. These sentiments permeate their sense of self, their relationships with family and social networks, and how they move about the world. By *shame*, I mean "a painful emotion responding to a sense of failure to attain some ideal state ... In shame, one feels inadequate, lacking some desired type of completeness or perfection" (Nussbaum, 2006, p. 184). The lack of self-esteem and sense of place in the world is in keeping with the neoliberal expectation of individual accountability, often leaving those who receive public assistance feeling dehumanized, excluded, and Othered for their reliance on state support. Of course, we all rely on the state in one way or another – to remove snow from the road, to teach our children, and to provide health care, for instance. Using these public services does not invoke shameful discourses, but using other supports – those typically accessed by people with a low income – does. There is an expectation that people receiving social assistance, whether it be financial assistance, housing, child protection, or shelter, demonstrate humility and gratitude, lest they be deemed the "bad poor" (Castel, 2003). The poor must "earn" assistance by exhibiting the "shamed poor role" (Allen, 2000; Chunn & Gavigan, 2004; Katz, 2013) and will only be considered redeemable if they adhere to inclusive goals such as adopting normative ways of being, finding employment, and being able to self-govern. Should they fail to do so, they are expected to remain unhappy and unsatisfied while living an excluded life.

Participants used a range of narratives to articulate their sense of shame. Daniel recalled his hesitation to enter a homeless shelter because he considered it "the end of the universe," while Karla described her unhappiness with living in a homeless shelter: "That's all I want. I just want to be happy, I'm not happy. It really says something about your life when you're fucking happy while you're living in this hell over here." For Karla, homelessness is a negative, crippling, and lonely experience. Karla, a 32-year-old white woman who describes suffering from depression and anxiety, identifies as coming from a middle-class family where each member is employed and contributes to the family and broader community. Karla remarked on the shame she felt when she was arrested for drug dealing because her cousin is a police officer, and feeling abandoned by her family due to her charges: "My cousin doesn't talk to me now. He's like, 'I can't believe you got a record.' He goes, 'you know both sides, why would you ... I can't ... conflict of interest, I can't talk to you until you're off all your conditions.'" Karla was unsure whether it is truly a conflict of interest for her cousin to maintain a relationship with her; rather, she felt the stigma of her criminalization had, by extension, shamed her family.

Karla's sense of shame was not unique. Many who came from stable families lamented their decline into social and familial exclusion. Julien called himself "the black sheep" of his family because, unlike him, his sister is employed and does not use drugs. Matilda compared herself to her children: "Like if I had it all together I wouldn't be here. My daughter has it all together, she just became a social worker. My son is going to college taking business. They have it together. I don't have it together." As a result of her shame, Matilda tried to hide her homelessness from her children and limited her contact with them to avoid their questions. Shame is a powerful instigator for isolation and loneliness. This sense of shame causes many people experiencing homelessness to pre-emptively exclude themselves from public places, feeling as though they do not belong. But as Matilda's experience demonstrates, some will also exclude themselves from private spaces and personal relationships. Matilda wanted to avoid the sense of abandonment that Karla experienced by distancing herself from her children first. DeOllos (1997) suggests that extended experiences of homelessness distances people who are homeless from relatives and friends, in part because the family cannot relate to their excluded lives. Furthermore, there is a sense of embarrassment that stems from being unable to repay friends and family for charitable acts, such as financial support or being allowed to sleep on a couch for a few nights.[1] Matilda's narrative reminds us that the notion of inclusion and exclusion are not simply abstract theoretical tools but instead shape the spatial, social, and emotional distances of Otherness.

Like Matilda, Mustang felt a great deal of shame when comparing himself to his family. Although he acknowledged that he grew up in a "dysfunctional family" mired in addiction and egregious physical and sexual abuse, Mustang contrasted his life with his siblings' success:

> I have a brother. I have two older sisters. They're all doing well. None of them struggle with the addictions I am. Everybody's married, everybody's got a home, kids, etc. I had a rough childhood and for some odd reason I chose to grow up living rough and this is where I sit today.

Mustang describes his bipolar diagnosis, alcohol dependence, and homelessness as a choice he made that his siblings did not. Although Mustang expresses shame, he later suggested that his siblings are also emotionally dysfunctional, and he finds solace in the fact that he is aware of his self-described abnormality and has "more peace" than his siblings. Despite this assertion, Mustang's narrative of difference, similar to Karla's, Matilda's, and Julien's, is imbued with a sense of shame.

Shame fills the corners of the spaces where people experiencing homelessness reside and acts as a governing technique to maintain docility. Emergency shelters swell with quiet voices and bowed heads, where residents must ask staff for their dose of psychotropic medication, shampoo, or a pair of socks. The loss of dignity felt by some is palpable. I visited Crossroads on the day of the annual Christmas dinner service for residents, which includes appearances from politicians and camera crews from local news stations. We sat, hunched over the few grey plastic folding tables that filled the common room, and watched the preparations unfold outside the glass doors of the dining room. Several residents told me they were not going to attend the dinner, despite the feast awaiting them and their being served rather than having to line up cafeteria-style, because they did not want their faces shown on TV. Although Crossroads is careful not to allow news agencies to film anyone who does not give express permission for them to do so, the presence of camera crews dissuaded some residents from partaking in the meal. The political process and shelters' constant fundraising needs due to investment shortages co-opts a dinner, meant to act as a source of dignity and celebration for those experiencing homelessness, and turns it into a voyeuristic spectacle and inductor of shame.

Shame is also undoubtedly gendered. From my field notes:

> I learned today that women have to ask for a [menstrual] pad each time they need one from front desk staff (sometimes from male staff). They are only allowed one pad at a time. One woman who I've never seen before shuffled over to the staff counter. She was obviously embarrassed to ask and was almost whispering it to the woman staff member through the glass partition. When the staff member figured out what she was saying she jumped up and loudly said they have some, ignoring the woman's desire for discretion. The woman told the staff that she thinks she won't have to ask for too many more.

Dignity – the feeling of self-worth – is not a possession, but rather an ontological manifestation of humanity. Shame is the vulnerability that comes from the outside world witnessing one's inner world (Nussbaum, 2006). Policies and practices aimed at managing homelessness rarely address dignity and substantive inclusion, given immediate concerns around shelter, food, and clothing. This stands in contrast to the fact that many of those experiencing homelessness are deeply concerned about their sense of self-worth. Miller and Keys (2001) found that interactions with staff, program structure, and rule enforcement all influence people's sense of dignity when they are experiencing homelessness. In the instances described above, even seemingly innocuous encounters have the capacity to invoke a sense of shame among those experiencing homelessness. Not only does the woman asking for a sanitary napkin have to manage the shame that comes with being a member of the excluded class but also, given the rules and bureaucracy of the shelter, her shame is turned inward and exerted onto her body. That women are socialized to feel shame toward their bodies is not new (Bessenoff & Snow, 2006; Butler, 1990, 2004b; Ussher, 1991), but it is further complicated when women experiencing homelessness are not afforded privacy and discretion. Women's bodies are a site of contention. Many women's experiences are that of hidden homelessness – staying in motels, couch-surfing, or entering into or remaining in unsafe relationships because being visibly homeless in public is unsafe. Here women's bodies are concealed and thus ignored, as are their experiences of homelessness and housing precarity. In contrast, the bodies of women who are street entrenched exist almost permanently within the public gaze because they have no home, bathroom, or bedroom for solitude. This state of being always visible is even more problematic when we consider the physical and sexual abuse histories for many women experiencing homelessness (Asberg & Renk, 2015; Schmidt et al., 2015).

Because dignity is intimately connected to one's sense of humanity (Seltser & Miller, 1993) it is troubling that individuals experiencing homelessness encounter sites of shame and dehumanizing interactions on a daily basis. Butler (2004a) suggests that shame's de-subjectification is a technology of control: "one way of 'managing' a population is to constitute them as the less than human without entitlement to rights, as the humanly unrecognizable" (p. 98). Indeed, the sense of shame that participants exhibit relates directly to the assumption that people who are homeless are largely "undeserving" of dignity (Chunn & Gavigan, 2004; Katz, 2013). Positioning those experiencing homelessness as unworthy and irredeemable reduces or even eliminates the public's obligation toward those in need, unless they can prove themselves worthy of the public investment.

Vince's story offers a glimpse into the assumption that to be homeless is to be irredeemable. Vince is embarrassed by his addiction and homeless status, causing him to disconnect from supportive people and programs when he is actively using drugs:

> When I'm clean I still have this support network, but ... Whether I choose to reach out ... which I'm not using all my support network right now. Some of those reasons are because of some shame and guilt I have for relapsing and not showing up at meetings.

Vince situates himself as a member of the "undeserving poor" and does not believe he is worthy of assistance and support when he relapses. He qualifies those services as only available to those who take responsibility for their actions – something he did not feel he could do at the time. Vince uses the rhetoric of "earned assistance" (Rose, 1999), where only those who demonstrate their worth and seek redeemability merit social supports. Although Vince characterized himself as irredeemable at the time of the interview, this does not preclude him from adopting responsibilization techniques in the future and gaining the redeemable status. Because exclusion exists along a continuum, the redeemable subjectivity requires constant maintenance and negotiation. Governing through freedom includes encouraging the hope that people like Vince have, that they can once again become redeemable; however, maintaining hope for inclusion is exceptionally difficult for those who are repeatedly separated and rejected from the mainstream social body.

Living as an Other

Awareness of one's own precariousness is essential to the operation of exclusion as a method of social control. Only when someone recognizes their excluded status can they begin to work on positioning themselves as redeemable. Otherness – being distinctly different from the dominant social group – is shaped by settler-colonial, racialized, classist, sexist, ableist, and heteronormative ideals of normality. Jamie explained his definition of normal:

> JAMIE: This isn't a life. I've said I can survive here. That's really it, survival. It's basic instinct. It's shelter, food, clothing provided for you. It's easy.
> ERIN: What's a life then, if this isn't, what's a life?
> JAMIE: Uh ... a house, two cars, 2.5 kids, you know what I mean [laughs]. No, uh ... I guess people would call it being productive in society.

When I probed further about what he meant by being "productive in society," Jamie said that it means being normal, but admitted to hating that word: "Well, define normal. But in today's society that's what's expected of you, and I'm not trying to make blasé of my situation here." Jamie, a 35-year-old white man who has lived on the streets for half his life, has a critical perspective of normalization but accepts its dominant discourses. He juxtaposes the inclusionary ideals with his experiences in youth and adult shelters and prison, and concludes that "this isn't a life" because it does not live up to the norm.

Jamie's portrayal of the stark contrast between being an included or excluded member of society does not account for the myriad of ways in which otherwise excluded people may feel included. Other research participants claimed a sense of inclusion from various sources: positive relationships with friends or family; volunteering at the community-based organizations that they frequent; and being connected to community resources. The power of social services as community-builders and spaces of inclusion is often missed or downplayed by funders and even the social services themselves, but is vital to people's well-being. Jamie's dichotomous thinking on exclusion likely comes from his isolation and lack of ties to people or places. A self-described "loner" with no familial contact, Jamie goes out of his way to keep distance from his peers. He never stays in a city for more than a few months at a time and frequently moves between emergency shelters. Jamie characterized himself as "institutionalized" in that he learned skills to "get by" but does not set down roots anywhere. It is no wonder that Jamie regards inclusion and exclusion as binaries given that his narrative is one of complete separation from the community, indoctrinated from years spent in jails, shelters, and self-imposed exclusion to cope with his depression.

Several participants situated themselves as separate from the community as a result of prevailing heteronormativity (Schilt & Westbrook, 2009). Gaston, who grew up in the 1950s, claimed that from a young age he knew he was different because he is gay and as such has always felt isolated and alone for failing to be "normal": "I don't know what it is, but I know I was different. I know it was different chaos in my head. I didn't fit in." Gaston's introduction to the mental health system came from his parents' concern with his sexuality. The formal and substantive modes of oppression facing LGBTQ2S+ people are well documented, but the dual status of homeless and gay left Gaston particularly vulnerable (Abramovich, 2017; Ecker et al., 2019). Gaston continues to avoid making friends because of his perception of the homeless population as homophobic and his fear of victimization. Other service users felt similarly to Gaston. Tom is a 54-year-old white man whose experiences as a popular actor in gay pornography films in the 1970s and '80s led him to deduce that he can never be normal. He too hides his sexual orientation from others who are homeless for fear of victimization but is out among his friends and family.

Gerry expressed shame because of his lack of sexual experience, stating:

GERRY: Well maybe it's just because of a deeper problem, because being a virgin is a problem.
ERIN: Why is it a problem?
GERRY: Well, if it wasn't a problem and if I was happy with my everyday life I wouldn't be stuck, I wouldn't have come here [the shelter]. I would have just kept working for McDonald's forever.

Gerry noted that because he does not know other 34-year-old virgins he must be abnormal, which causes chaos in his life, such as quitting his job at McDonald's unexpectedly because he was "bored by it," as he described to me. Gerry subscribes to the discourse that he should be happy with "everyday life," irrespective of the conditions of that life. For example, encouraging the working class to thankfully and uncritically accept precarious, underpaid labour out of an ingrained sense of productivity is part of the neoliberal mechanism that governs poverty – policies and norms that Wacquant (2009) refers to as "desocialized wage work." Gerry internalizes and individualizes his dissatisfaction with his previous employment as resulting from his self-described "abnormality," exemplified through his failed attempts to find a sexual partner.

While Gerry is deeply ashamed of his "abnormality," he briefly departed from the shamed poor script to question whether he wants to be normal:

GERRY: The whole being happy, like trying to do what everyone else is trying to do, make it to retirement and be happy with money and stuff. It's kind of boring. The whole, do the same thing over and over again, forever. The same job, the same life, the same roof for thirty years. It's a long time.
ERIN: So why do you want to be normal then?
GERRY: Well you don't always have a choice, you just have to, you know, suck it up and just play it out.

Gerry sees no alternative but to strive for standard norms in order to be an included member of society despite his reservations and the lack of resources to be included. Gerry has difficulty maintaining a job, securing housing, and having a sexual relationship, but he perseveres through (so far unsuccessful) attempts to earn his General Education Development (GED) diploma (high school equivalency) and using counselling to try and improve his prospects at having an intimate relationship.

Besides Jamie's and Gerry's expressions of ambivalence toward normative ways of being, only one other participant described resisting the standards of normality. In fact, unlike Jamie and Gerry, Lenny was emphatic in expressing no desire to become "normal":

> I'm finding people who are normal by society's definition of the word are very unhappy. They spend their lives just replacing their TVs and replacing their cars and watching mindless television and complaining about the way the world is and I don't see any happiness there whatsoever. I just see this, you know, what Thoreau says, "the mass of men who live in quiet desperation," and I think that's exactly what's happening.

Lenny firmly rejects middle-class consumptive expectations. However, he may be more apt to do so than many of his homeless peers because despite his critique, he has a relative abundance of human and social capital. Human capital refers to acquired skills and knowledge such as education and employment (Reisig et al., 2002) and social capital is the combination of real and potential resources associated with strong relationships built from a shared network (Bourdieu, 1980). Lenny's position as homeless leaves him unable to fully participate in the bonds of social capital, but he continues to have strong relationships with family and friends, an education, and long history of work experience. Linking social capital – the notion that individuals will forge alliances with those who have more status or wealth to leverage resources – provides Lenny a sense of hope and opportunity. The prospect of maintaining these social bonds and reinvigorating his social capital allows Lenny some flexibility to speak critically of normative standards and cultural values while maintaining a "redeemable" status.

Lenny's response was unique. Other participants spoke predominantly of their isolation, describing the shelter specifically and the broader homeless population as existing within, but separate from, the world around them. I knew Daniel for a little over a year when we sat down for a formal interview. Knowing a bit about me (a middle-class, white, educated woman), he made

Identity Management

the distinction between my life as representative of the included and his life in a homeless shelter:

> Because, you know, I'm put in a different pile, you know that's you guys over there and these rules and opportunities are there for you and everybody else is frolicking in the meadows and I'm stuck in the urban jungle, just trying to survive on a day-to-day basis.

Daniel echoes Jamie's description of homelessness as survival rather than truly living. Having previously had a successful career, owned a home, and been married with two children (read, included), Daniel is also acutely aware of the symbiotic relationship between rules and opportunities that are available to those who govern themselves appropriately. When Daniel suffered a self-described "breakdown" because he felt like he was "a slave to work and taxes" he said he "stepped out of the machine," but by abandoning adherence to the rules he also lost the opportunities that come from following them.

Likewise, Jon, who stayed at Crossroads, witnessed his Otherness when he compared his poverty to the neighbourhood's gentrification: "You know, you've got all this money there to throw around on condos but you're looking at us ... as nothing. We don't exist. We're not a part of this community. We're alcoholics. We're drug addicts ... Well, so what? We're human beings. We do have feelings." Jon's perception of the division between "us" and "them" is borne out by local examples, such as when a business owner in Ottawa's downtown core launched an anonymized petition calling for one of the nearby shelters to be shut down. The petition referred to those experiencing homelessness as "a cancer which is now terminal for those residents and businesses in their vicinity," blaming shelter residents for property damage and violence in the city (thanks to widespread backlash, the petition was taken down a week later) (Osman, 2018). Jon's comment echoes Ruddick's (1996) notion of "social death" whereby people experiencing homelessness are disenfranchised from the included group. Jon is acutely aware of the public perception of homelessness and expressed a desire to speak to politicians and advocate for people experiencing homelessness as worthy of human dignity but does not have access to key stakeholders.

In a similar vein, Otto used the term "bottom feeder" to describe his disassociation from, but reliance on, the included world:

> There are people like myself and if I call myself a bottom feeder I don't think that I can't fall any farther. I mean, I know there's plenty more space

down there for me to go. My success or failure is dependent upon the whims and generosity of the rest of society at this point. If society were to turn around and chop me off and I don't get welfare and my rent's not going to be paid, I don't get free meals ... maybe, maybe I would get off my sorry ass and go out and get a god damn job and make something of myself. Maybe I'd become a crook. Maybe I'd kill myself. Who knows what would happen.

Otto is well aware of his exclusion, situating himself as a "bottom feeder," but he also understands that his exclusion is part of a continuum, as described in Chapter 1. Otto considers himself a redeemable excluded subject because he knows that others experiencing homelessness face even greater marginality. Otto had recently begun taking an interest in the ADHD diagnosis he had received a year previously (he consciously disregards his bipolar diagnosis) and was set to meet a mental health specialist a week after the interview. He exhibited shame for his dependence on public services to house, feed, and clothe him, and to provide mental health and addiction support, saying "I'm not proud of where I am in life." Having witnessed the suffering and death of his homeless peers (primarily from illnesses related to addiction such as liver failure and AIDS), for Otto, maintaining his status as a redeemable subject who is deemed worthy of services is a matter of life and death.

Otto's narrative captures the essence of his felt exclusion. For someone to access services in the neoliberal era requires them to demonstrate that they are capable of change and worthy of assistance. In this case it means taking up and demonstrating an enthusiasm for the services and programs offered by the mental health system in the homelessness industrial complex. Interventions include taking psychotropic medication and attending AA/NA meetings, anger-management classes, and a variety of educational and work-ready programs. Arguably, the exception to this demonstration of worthiness is the Housing First (HF) model, where those who have the most acute needs and who are most deeply entrenched in homelessness are eligible for the program. However, Phillips's (2016) research reveals that some HF programs fail to engage with people deemed "hardest to house" or with the "most complex needs" and that even those who do receive no-barrier housing continue to be street-involved and depend heavily on services provided by the homelessness industrial complex.

The alternative to demonstrating one's worthiness is to be considered impossible or irredeemable and become further separated from the mainstream social body, as Vince described above. Bauman (1988) articulates the depravity of the excluded identity: "Society would be much better off if the poor just burnt their tents and left. The world would be that much more pleasant without them. The poor are not needed, and so they are unwanted" (p. 91). These are harsh words meant to provoke, but with significant cuts to social assistance (Prince, 2015), the dismantling of Canada's social housing policies (Suttor, 2016), the criminalization of poverty (Hermer & Mosher, 2002; O'Grady et al., 2011), and the moves by several communities across Canada to disband homeless encampments, it is apparent that excommunicating the "bad investments" (Bauman, 1988) is not merely hyperbole. Indigenous Peoples and people of colour face the brunt of these exclusionary tactics, reinforcing the historical and ongoing colonization and racialization of marginality in Canada (Freistadt, 2016; Maynard, 2017). For exclusion to be acceptable in a civil society, however, the structural and systematic inequities facing people living in poverty are buried within discourses of individual failure and inadequacy. It is easy to cast Jon, Otto, and their peers into the irredeemable camp given the unfounded but popularized notion that those diagnosed with a mental illness are unmanageable, incurable, and exceptionally dangerous (Elbogen & Johnson, 2009) – in essence, to define the mentally ill as unworthy. It is intriguing then, that many marginalized people attempt to perform marginalized identities to align themselves with the ideals of the included group. To do so requires that they acknowledge their thoughts, behaviours, and environment as disordered and demonstrate a willingness to be disciplined in an effort to become normalized; however, conceding to one's exclusion runs the risk of further entrenching the excluded status and adopting responsibilization techniques that require accepting social problems as individualized and decontextualized.

Situating Exclusionary Identities

Those experiencing homelessness are often acutely aware of their exclusion, and true to the internalization of normative ideals, most situate themselves as "shamed poor." By bearing witness to their own exclusion and marking their status as inherently negative and necessarily shameful, we begin to see how marginalized individuals can, at least in some ways, consciously perform their identities so as to present themselves as redeemable and to distance themselves from irredeemable subjects. The homeless and mentally ill identities act as performative tools to achieve the redeemable status.

Not Just "Rubby Dub" People: Homelessness as Heterogeneous Identities

The common identity marker among participants in this study was their status as homeless or precariously housed. Participants had experienced homelessness for an average of four and a half years, but the length of time varied, from three months to over fifteen years. When I carried out the interviews, everyone but Max had experience living in a shelter. Max had moved between jail, hospital, and subsidized housing; while he did not live in a shelter, he depended on their services to meet his daily needs (i.e., food, clothing, companionship). Within months of the interview, however, he lost his housing and began staying at Crossroads. Despite their deep entrenchment in homelessness, participants forged their own unique sense of what it means to be homeless.

The stereotypes about homelessness relate to people's level of "deservedness" of assistance: slackers (lazy and framed as undeserving); lackers (lacking competency to care for themselves through no fault of their own, often pathologized and considered as more deserving); and victims (seen as being the most deserving of all) (Rosenthal, 2000). However, this simplified categorization does not hold up to the reality of the homeless experience. Rick, a support worker in one of Ottawa's homeless-serving agencies for over thirty years, remarked on the changing nature of the homeless population over time:

> When I started working in shelters it was really traditionally hobo, like your rubby dub people. Tended to be older guys and just before I left in the mid-'80s you started to see more youth and new immigrants. It was very homogenized thirty years ago, it was white. It was predominately … you have more women now also on the streets. Or perhaps because there was no woman's shelter in Ottawa before, I think probably, it was '86, '87 before [a women's shelter] opened, you didn't have women come into the shelters. So there's a diversity of people here.

Rick is able to reflect on the changing dynamics of homelessness in Ottawa over the last three decades, especially as neoliberal ideology began to reshape the social assistance and social housing landscape beginning in the 1980s and '90s (Gaetz et al., 2014). Rick articulates what Pearce (1978) describes as the feminization of poverty, whereby the increase in women-headed households, the decrease in the income level of these households, and the destruction of the welfare system coalesce to create housing insecurity and homelessness for women and their children. The invisibility of women's poverty is most acute among women of colour and Indigenous women (Maynard, 2017; Walsh et al., 2016). Although most of the participants responded with indifference when I asked about gender dynamics among the homeless population, Karla offered insight on the specific challenges facing women:

> I think women have more to deal with if they're living in a shelter because they've got their mental health and their physical health and they don't know whether they're going or whether they're coming, you know? So they're struggling. People are just coming from living in apartments for years and just coming in here and it's hard. Like, I think men can adjust easily because they don't deal with everything. They just keep plugging at it and then one day they blow up and they start beating everybody up, you know? So it's a lot harder for women. There's a lot more emotions and everything else.

Karla expresses the familiar trope that women are more emotional and thus less stable than men (Kendall, 2000; Ussher, 1991, 2010) and characterizes men as more aggressive and prone to violence. She also alludes to the reality that women are often solely responsible for the family and the home, whereas men "don't deal with everything," both in terms of emotionality and domestic responsibilities. More than this though, Karla notes how segments of the population cope with homelessness differently. Not only are experiences of homelessness heterogeneous in terms of coping mechanisms, but so are the structural impediments for women trying to manage homelessness. For example, Wanda found a lack of support specifically for single women:

> There's no help out there for us and there's a lot of women in here that need it, mentally, I mean really mentally, they talk to themselves. There's another few women that need a roof over their head but they need counselling to talk to. There should be more beds or there should be more shelters. The women only have this one and the one on [names street]. There's a few other ones but when I did call they were for abused women or kids.

Segments of the homeless population access services and experience homelessness differently; single women in particular are limited in terms of the programs and assistance available to them, especially with respect to emergency shelter beds, the bulk of which are designated for men. The emphasis on providing resources to families represents Rosenthal's (2000) "lacker" category, where children are usually regarded as the deserving poor. Single women, often presumed to have lost custody of their children, are generally characterized as undeserving.

Not only is poverty gendered, it is also highly racialized. The historical and contemporary structural racism that disproportionately impoverishes people of colour in North America (Maynard, 2017; Rankin & Quane, 2000; Wacquant, 2002) and the cultural genocide, genocide, and ongoing colonization that perpetuates the oppression of Indigenous Peoples in Canada (Kendall, 2001; NIMMIWG, 2019; Wilson & Macdonald, 2010) are well documented. Giles is a 51-year-old Black man who came to Canada from Rwanda as a refugee in the 1980s. He described his childhood as being without a place to call home. He does not consider himself Rwandan; rather, he feels he has roots in Canada. Giles finds a sense of home in a country where he has spent much of his time homeless. His precarious status as a refugee left him continually feeling at risk of being displaced:

> When I was in Montreal, I had a lawyer but, they seem to be interested in me. They said you cannot do anything, you cannot work, we send you back to Africa. Why they did that? So I didn't work, I had nothing to do. They didn't like ... they didn't let me work or do something.

The threat of being "sent back to Africa" was unsettling for Giles who has never considered Rwanda home. Giles identifies as schizophrenic and struggles to communicate his needs to others. He had difficulty finding support in the homelessness sector because of his legal, cultural, and social context. As Rick mentioned, homelessness was historically framed as a white problem, perhaps because of the sense that white people are entitled to housing whereas it is a privilege for racialized minorities (Hogan & Berry, 2011; Wacquant, 2008).

The disproportionate rate of Indigenous Peoples in the homeless population does not demystify racist and colonialist attitudes, but instead perpetuates colonialist explanations of homelessness. For example, Chico, a 50-year-old white man, suggested that Inuit people do not deserve assistance from frontline staff: "But still there are guys here who treat [staff] like shit. It's usually the ... well I know not to say it but it's usually the Inuits and stuff, you know, and I mean they get right rowdy at them. But they beat the crap out of each other too." Ottawa has the largest Inuit population in Canada outside of the North and Chico's comment that "I know not to say it," implies that he was aware of the racist and unfair characterization, but he said it anyway. Chico's statement suggests that Inuit residents are not

Identity Management

worthy of assistance because of his perception that they are disrespectful, violent, and dangerous: a perception that is rooted in harmful historical settler-colonial stereotypes of "the savage" (Harding, 2006). Racialized, colonized, gendered, heteronormative, and ableist discourses pervade assessments of redeemability and interpretations of worthiness, including among people who are homeless themselves.

Resisting the Homeless Identity

The diversity of research participants' identity narratives exemplifies the heterogeneity of the homeless population. Indeed, some individuals experiencing homelessness reject the homeless identity outright. For example, Jon problematized his felt sense of home at Crossroads: "Well, see I'm not homeless. I have a home. I call this home right now, but I shouldn't because when you call this place home then you're getting a little too comfortable." As described in the previous chapter, shelters offer the material conditions of home but lack its symbolic significance. Jon is aware that emergency shelters are not meant to be a home. Shelters are designed and operate as a temporary intervention, despite the chronic shortage of affordable housing in Canada resulting in people staying in shelters for months or years. The homelessness crisis that we face today exists in part because we have used short-term crisis measures, such as the shelter, as if they were long-term, sustainable solutions. This response has led to, at best, managing homelessness, or at worst, supporting its proliferation; it has not led to the overall reduction and elimination of homelessness. A homelessness prevention and Housing First orientation that positions shelters as pivotal in the shift to ending homelessness is necessary to develop solutions rather than management techniques.

Jon was not alone in his complicated feelings of the shelter as home. Chico, who also resided at Crossroads at the time of the interview but who had stayed at countless shelters across Canada, suggested that he was not homeless:

> CHICO: I've been homeless man, I mean I've slept in a park. This is not homeless. Being at [another large shelter in Ottawa], that would be friggin' homeless. That would be absolutely scary homeless to me. Because I can't live with people like that. I'd get myself a tent and move up to [Rockcliffe] Park or something [laughs].
> ERIN: So why isn't this homeless?
> CHICO: Because I know some of the people in there and that's one thing that's scary because I leave and I'm gone for six or eight months and

the same guys are still there and that's another reason why I never get any [flak] in there because I come for two months and I leave for two, three years sometimes, and then I'll come back. The only time I've ever got a letter on my bed, to go for the interview to see what my plans were and she said, "what are your plans?" and I said "well my plans are to get out of here today" and she said, "yeah, you know how often I hear that?" And I said "I guarantee you by noon I'll have a place and I'll be out of here." And I went out and got a room and I came back at noon, had my promise on time and she was like, "you're the only person I've ever ... " and then I had a place down on [a residence run by another shelter]. That was four years ago.

Chico demonstrates that his sense of home comes from the people who live at the shelter rather than the building or the shelter system itself. It is the same shelter that pressured him to leave four years prior, and despite his pride in being able to secure housing (albeit from another shelter), he considered his most recent stay at Crossroads a return home.

For Chico, homelessness is living on the street or in a shelter where he does not feel safe. Security is the hallmark of a sense of home. The definition of precarious housing includes homes that are deemed unsafe, either because buildings do not meet safety regulations or because occupants do not feel a sense of safety (often because of a lack of privacy, inability to lock doors, location in a high-crime neighbourhood, or living with people who jeopardize their safety, especially for women and members of the LGBTQ2S+ community). Although both Chico and Jon reject the homeless identity, they qualify their rebuttal with an acknowledgment that their living situation is not ideal and is certainly not meant to be permanent. Moreover, their narratives demonstrate the degree to which they resist or reject the homeless identity and instead perform the worthy and redeemable subjectivity, in part by expressing appreciation for the support offered by the shelter.

Mental Illness as Identity

The vast majority of the research participants identified as experiencing mental illness (84 percent). Out of those, 13 percent were self-diagnoses of depression, anxiety, OCD, ADHD,[2] and bipolar disorder. Self-diagnoses are likely facilitated by the heavy reliance on psychotropic medication as the pre-eminent mental health intervention in the community, which is often prescribed without a corresponding official diagnosis. Mark, for example, identified as suffering with "a bit" of ADD and "extreme" OCD. Further probing revealed that he only uses the OCD construct when he acquires a lot of money: "Like when I got my income tax return, I blew it. I don't even know where I was for a week. And then I ended up [at Crossroads], shaking pretty bad." Whether Mark's distress meets the criteria for OCD according to the *DSM-V* (2013) is not especially important. What is more interesting is that Mark, and others in the study, use psy-language, and in turn adopt a mentally ill identity, to describe their actions. This suggests that people who are homeless actively reframe diagnoses to make them useful in the context of homelessness. This redefinition is reminiscent of Hacking's (1995, 2004) "looping effect." For Hacking, identities are fluid and as individuals engage with and shape identity, by accepting or resisting mental illness labels for instance, the social understanding of the identity changes. Those who are homeless use, negotiate, and resist mental illness labels, fostering a unique discourse that comes from both social conceptions of mental illness and individual identity construction.

The proliferation of psy-rhetoric in everyday discourse is not limited to the homelessness sector. Terms such as OCD, schizophrenia, anxiety, and depression are used in everyday vernacular as hyperbole to emphasize a chaotic or atypical characteristic or situation. It is not uncommon to hear someone say "I'm totally OCD" with reference to something as benign as being annoyed by dirty clothes on the floor. Media representations of OCD are particularly misleading, using the term to characterize a broad array of qualities, including being infatuated with a potential lover (Fennell & Boyd, 2014). In turn, film and television portray OCD as endearing more so than as causing distress. The flourishing of psy-language is common in the neoliberal era (Rimke, 2000) but has distinct qualities when referring to people who are homeless. Here mental illness is more often regarded as dangerous than quirky.

The finding that many people experiencing homelessness embrace psy-discourses comes up against the literature that suggests people's reluctance to adopt a mental illness label because of its stigmatizing effects (Hansen et al., 2014; O'Reilly et al., 2009). Evidence from this project calls for a more nuanced explanation for how and why some individuals experiencing homelessness adopt psy-discourses. In some ways, embodying the mentally ill identity can align with the included ideals of self-improvement and allows otherwise excluded individuals to be framed as redeemable (but rarely redeemed or included) subjects. How individuals negotiate the mentally ill identity is essential to understanding this complexity.

Because professional and self-diagnoses are commonplace in the homelessness sector, some people I spoke with normalize mental illness and reject its common tropes as abnormal and stigmatizing. For example, Courtney characterizes mental illness as universal but more evident in and problematic for some: "Everybody's got mental problems, but some are just worse than others. Like a lot of people actually have depression and not realize it." Normalizing mental illness may be a method of stigma management among a highly stigmatized group that is otherwise considered abnormal (Goffman, 1963), but as Jamie described, the pathologization of late modern life (Rimke, 2016) is evident in society as a whole:

> But is there a stigma attached [to mental illness]? There still is. It's a thousand times better than ten years ago. You told somebody you were seeing a shrink, even if it was just for something like minor depression or something or hell, just for dealing with life, it's like, you were looked down upon. But that's changing. You see it every day. Now it's almost the *in* thing. "Oh yeah, I'm seeing a shrink!" It's swung the opposite way. I think it's almost like, are you normal if you're not seeing ... like how are you dealing with life if you're not talking to somebody about it?

Jamie's reflection articulates the anxiety and uncertainty of the late modern period (Gergen, 2000; Giddens, 1991) and the notion that a responsibilized subject will have the common sense and resources to seek treatment to cope with the constant unease brought on by contemporary life. Interestingly, Jamie uses his mental illness as an identity marker to position himself along the included end of the exclusion continuum by normalizing mental illness as part of living within (as opposed to outside of) modern society. "Just dealing with life" requires professional assistance. Presenting the mentally ill identity as normal and in keeping with the included social body who also struggle to "deal with life" works to minimize the difference between inclusion and exclusion. However, those experiencing homelessness or precarious housing face different and often extreme sources of stress, such as challenges securing safe, suitable, and affordable shelter, accessing nutritious food and warm clothing, and being vulnerable to threats to their personal safety. That people experiencing homelessness have limited financial and social capital to mitigate insecurity and marginality magnifies the anxiety brought on by the rapidly changing modern world.

The Mentally Ill and the Addict Identities – One and the Same?

Like mental illness, most of the research participants (89 percent) identified as being addicted to a variety of licit and illicit substances. As described in Chapter 2, most participants spoke about addiction and mental illness interchangeably. I suspect that the two converge, not because of an abundance of concurrent treatment in the homelessness sector (of which, as noted below, there is little), but because of the *lack* of treatment options. Because mental health treatment in the homelessness industrial complex consists almost exclusively of psychotropic medication, those experiencing distress turn to the widely available addiction group therapy programs for advice on coping strategies and support. Likewise, outpatient addiction treatment programs commonly discuss PTSD, ADHD, depression, and bipolar disorder, acting as a kind of informal concurrent treatment program. Therefore, frontline workers, counsellors, and individuals in distress regard addiction and mental health treatment as part and parcel of one another.

Many people I encountered subscribed to the substance-induced model, where substances are thought to cause or exacerbate psychiatric symptoms, or the self-medication model, where individuals use substances illicitly to manage or cope with psychiatric symptoms (Vorspan et al., 2015). Toby, a 48-year-old Two-Spirited[3] Inuk woman who was in an intensive substance abuse treatment program located at Haven, connected her bipolar diagnosis to her cravings for alcohol:

> Maybe it's crazy to want to drink all the time. I don't know. For some people, yeah, but for others it's like, because they enjoy it. Like their body enjoys being drunk. And those are the ones who have fun when they're drinking, not like [makes screaming noises].

Many times, I witnessed Toby screaming and acting out when she was heavily intoxicated. She claimed that her body does not enjoy being drunk and so she regards her cravings for alcohol as being "crazy" and in need of mental health treatment and management. Toby's understanding of her body as failing to enjoy being drunk carries the weight of the "drunken Indian" myth. The stereotype that Indigenous Peoples are genetically predisposed to alcoholism and/or that they all binge drink dates back to the first colonizers who used alcohol as a weapon to control and dominate Indigenous Peoples (Vowel, 2016). The myth's potency influenced and can be linked to the Sixties Scoop, where Indigenous children were taken from their families by child protection services and adopted out, often into white families, as well as the continued overrepresentation of Indigenous children in child protection agencies (Blackstock, 2014). Tragically, the myth is also embedded in many Indigenous communities: "Many Indigenous Peoples have internalized the stereotype, believing alcoholism is something genetically impossible to avoid" (Vowel, 2016, p. 151). Toby believes that her desire for alcohol means that she is mentally ill. She regards her substance use as a personal failing, stripped of its colonial context. Toby's story is an example of how distress is materially experienced and of how mental illness and addiction are often rendered as indistinguishable in someone's personal narrative.

Despite the paradigm shift from a treatment first model to integrated treatment for mental illness and substance abuse, in practice, stark divisions remain. Staff in the homelessness sector voiced their frustration at the lack of coherency between the public mental health and addiction systems:

> Even if he goes to get assessed, often mental health professionals will say "well look you've been using then I can't assess your mental health issues." [Everyone nods in agreement] You can't separate what the difference is, what your symptoms [are and] if [your] symptoms are related to your drug abuse or if they're related to your mental health. So there's so many outs for somebody not to be assessed. (Chuck)

Not only does Chuck, a frontline worker at Crossroads, note the "silo effect" (Mental Health Commission of Canada, 2012) of mental health and addiction services, he also regards the inability to assess someone's mental health status as an "out," suggesting that practitioners in an overburdened mental health system use addiction to lessen their workload. Hartwell (2004) found that because dually diagnosed individuals are less likely to be accepted into programming, they are at greater risk of homelessness and, not surprisingly, criminalization. Vince remarked that in the addiction programming he's encountered, mental health care is lacking and people need to take it on themselves to seek counselling: "But if you're working with [different addiction programs], you're going to look at your mental issues. You still need to follow that up with, like, there's professionals here in addiction but not necessarily in mental health." This research reveals that although for many people with a dual diagnosis their experiences, symptoms, and identification with mental illness and addiction are blurred, the two are still often managed and governed separately.

Addiction treatment relies heavily on self-help and talk therapy. With the exception of treatments like methadone maintenance and Suboxone (a synthetic opioid), there are few pharmaceutical interventions to treat addiction, relative to the array of psychotropic medications on the market. Participants in this research project attended predominantly outpatient group therapy run by the shelters and community health centres. The Canadian Mental Health Association (CMHA), for example, runs a weekly concurrent disorder therapy group, the only one of its kind I heard about in my years in the community. Many had also experienced in-patient treatment programs ranging from thirty-day to five-month intensive programs offered by public, private, charitable, or for-profit organizations. Hospitals such as the Royal Ottawa Hospital (ROH) and the Centre for Addiction and Mental Health (CAMH) in Toronto also provide in- and outpatient addiction treatment.

In contrast, there are few programs available strictly for mental health. Some programs exist, including ones for anger management and The Men's Project (now Men & Healing); however, they do not address mental illness specifically. When asked about mental health treatment, only two research participants noted specific mental health programs. Giles, who uses many mental health services to cope with schizophrenia, attends group cognitive behavioural therapy (CBT) run by the ROH. Doug was the only other interviewee to mention a mental health program in the city, the wellness recovery action plan (WRAP), which teaches self-management skills to help people manage and decrease psychiatric symptoms (Fukui et al., 2011). At the time of the interview, Doug had not yet attended a WRAP meeting because he was unsure whether the program required participants to be sober, a criterion he felt he could not meet. Instead, and as I explore in depth in Chapter 6, psychotropic medication is the only mode of treatment available for the vast majority of people who are homeless. Most of the people I spoke with were taking some form of psychotropic medication (66 percent) with over half of those who disclosed the types of medication taking two or more daily. Less than 5 percent of the sample had no experience taking psychotropic medication. These divergent approaches to mental illness and addiction demonstrate the disjuncture between discourse and practice, and the ongoing challenges people experiencing homelessness face in accessing appropriate treatment of their choosing.

Managing Marginalized Identity Performances

While mental health and homeless identities are as personal as each individual, common themes emerge. Many adopt the stereotypes and warped expectations of being visibly homeless and/or being diagnosed with a mental illness, such as feeling shame for living in poverty and inadvertently participating in their own Othering. Some resist the identities, such as those who find a sense of home in the shelter system and those who normalize mental illness. These identities are consciously and unconsciously created and performed as those experiencing homelessness navigate personal relationships, negotiate system and institutional arrangements, and find space in the broader social world.

The Limits of Identity Performance
Each of our abilities' to manipulate and transform identities depends in large part on our social and human capital. Financial resources, knowledge and education, and our corporeality (including factors such as gender identity, race, ability, and sexuality, among others) influence identity performance (Bauman, 1988; Butler, 1990). Many individuals experiencing homelessness and/or distress are limited in what identities they can effectively perform. For example, it would be extremely difficult for someone living in an emergency shelter to perform the role of CEO of a successful company. The traits that commonly accompany such an identity – well educated, an influential network of friends, and opulent displays of wealth – cannot be translated to someone who is homeless. Indeed, attempting to perform an identity for which one is not well equipped is often characterized as a delusion and considered a symptom of mental illness.

People from all walks of life become homeless, including those who were previously financially secure. Despite having access to this knowledge, staff members are often surprised by these past identities because they are incongruent with the stereotype of the homeless and mentally ill as permanently excluded, as evidenced by a discussion during the focus group:

> RICK: I have a client from Bangladesh and he was a GP [general practitioner]. Just for me, even with all the years I have, it just blew my mind, how can someone end up in a shelter who's a doctor?
> CHUCK: We had a client recently who was an OPP [Ontario Provincial Police] officer in southern Ontario for twenty-one years ... [gasps all around] ... and there was a guy who had an MA, he was staying here. I mean it's shocking sometimes with what background some guys have.

It is arguable that the shock over the fact that someone with a graduate degree can become homeless is attributable in part to the realization that those who are included (such as some of the participants in the focus group and I) are not immune from descending into exclusion. The awareness that the inclusive status is unstable is evidence that the included and excluded groups are not differentiated by moral absolutes. The reaction from the group to Chuck's story of a former police officer living in a homeless shelter draws attention to the limits of identity performance. Those who present a history of a previously successful life are viewed as anomalies. Although, as Goffman (1959; see also Roseneil & Seymour, 1999) articulates, identities are created and managed, the types of identities available to those experiencing homelessness and/or distress are limited by their marginality.

Shadow, a 43-year-old white male who identifies as having depression and bipolar disorder along with an addiction to alcohol, uses his social capital as evidence of his included status, despite his lengthy criminal record and the fact that he currently lives in a rooming house and is dependent on shelters for his food and clothing:

> So I went through St. FX[4] ... learned some things there. I did a year with [a province] as [a] coordinator to their first family court. I was kinda like a prosecutor. I had a career that covered several departments including security. And Brian Mulroney who also carries a ring for St. FX made me downsize. I was babysitting political appointees from [another province] and I said no way. So I stopped being a babysitter. I took my money. I went into the [ByWard] Market [downtown Ottawa] in the '80s. I spent a year at Innes Road [OCDC], did trial like Conrad Black. I was resigned to a time with the feds, which I did receive. I was there for a couple of years. Came back to Ottawa, ended up here. First my contacts, rebuilt my credentials and got a place with [a housing provider].

Shadow positioned himself as educated and intelligent with a great deal of power on account of his intellect and personal connections. He alluded to the idea that he reported directly to the prime minister and when accounting for his time spent in prison he likened himself to Conrad Black[5] as an identifier of his status. Shadow's presentation of self could be characterized as misrepresentation, as he displays a status that he cannot adequately perform given his vulnerable social positioning (Goffman, 1959). Whether Shadow has such powerful allies is irrelevant to his identity construction. What is important here is that he equates himself with prominent members of the included society, and as someone experiencing precarious housing he will likely be considered an "imposter" (Goffman, 1959) by professionals, para-professionals, and his homeless peers. Perhaps at one time Shadow was able to perform this identity authentically. Now, however, Shadow must re-identify himself within the social framework of homelessness, otherwise his performance may be assessed as a symptom of mental illness that further entrenches his excluded status along the continuum. It is likely that Shadow's presentation as fully redeemed within the homelessness context would be viewed by professionals and service providers as an impossibility and as a personal failure to take up the project of the self required of all neoliberal subjects, especially those receiving public assistance.

Identity is flexible and malleable only within the specificity of time and space built from pre-existing norms, and contingent on how others perceive the performance. Daniel's conflict with staff over his self-identity illustrates how identity is actively managed by individuals but constrained through structure, in this case the rules of the emergency shelter:

> Craig is my first name. And when I showed my ID here, well, Craig. So they've been calling me Craig for two years. They refused to call me Daniel because we have to go by your first name. Well that causes a whole detachment thing. That's not even me, that's some Craig guy. Imagine somebody asks you your name and you tell them but they refuse to call you that. They're calling you something else. Like, who am I then? That's actually pretty detrimental thing. Of course people are, "hey Daniel," this and that, so [frontline staff] says, finally, "well what is your name?" Well "my name is Craig Daniel. I'm Daniel." "Oh, I'm going to start calling you Daniel now." And, ahhhh!

Daniel's struggle to convince staff to use his preferred name is characteristic of the structural impediments to identity management. A person's name is fundamental to their sense of self (Hook, 1984). To deny a name on account of bureaucracy is to invalidate self-identity. While filling out government forms using a given name may be of little consequence to members of the included group, Daniel encounters this mismatched identity on a daily basis because of his reliance on public assistance. His homelessness sets parameters to his self-identity not experienced by housed individuals. Although none of the participants in this study identified as transgender, the effect of misnaming and/or mis-gendering trans people is incredibly harmful. The oppression trans people face in the homeless population and the criminal justice system demonstrates the severe physical and psychological trauma that results from the structural denial of the self (Kirkup, 2018; Lyons et al., 2016). Daniel's story illustrates Butler's (2004a,) contention that demands on our identity often come from elsewhere: "What binds us morally has to do with how we are addressed by others in ways that we cannot avert or avoid; this impingement by the other's address constitutes us first and foremost against our will or, perhaps put more appropriately, prior to the formation of our will" (p. 130). Butler refers to this formation as obligations that come from specific identity types. For Daniel, his unwillingness to submit to shelter policies regarding given names reminds us that where there are limits to identity production there are also spaces to contest, resist, and shape identity.

Goffman in Practice: Impression Management and Distancing
In *The Presentation of Self in Everyday Life,* Goffman (1959) sets out the dramaturgical method of impression management. In *Stigma* (1963) he expands on impression management to include how people manage undesirable characteristics, such as being identified as mentally ill and/or homeless. One strategy they use is to create distance between "us" and "them"; in essence, to other members of the same group. Young (1999) suggests that marginalized people essentialize others who experience similar oppression because people who are excluded face a greater sense of ontological insecurity than the included group. For example, in Stuart's (2016) ethnography, he found that punitive policing practices compelled some residents of Skid Row to ensure police officers took notice of especially vulnerable people as a way to deflect attention (and the very real threat of citations or arrest) from themselves. When people experiencing homelessness and/or distress create and position themselves within a hierarchy it acts as a strategy to situate the self as redeemable by characterizing others as irredeemable.

In describing his favourable relationship with police, Gerry stated: "Well I try not to think of myself as better than anybody else but, in a way I am because I don't cause any problems, you know? I just try to be good." Gerry "tries to be good" by refraining from substance use and not engaging in criminal activity. Gerry also expressed great concern that a catastrophe is soon going to strike the globe and that he will be responsible for forming a new civilization among the survivors who will look to him as their leader. He uses these premonitions as motivation to hold himself to a higher standard than his peers. He sees his difference and exclusion from others as characteristic of his leadership abilities: "Like if I did the same thing as everyone else it might lead to tragedy. What's the point of being the same as everyone else if you're supposed to do something to *help*, maybe even survive the whole thing?" As described above, Gerry feels he is "abnormal" because of his impulsive decision making and his lack of sexual experience. I got to know Gerry over the course of two years and in that time he spoke about himself almost always in self-deprecating terms. A timid, quiet-spoken man, Gerry was friendly and respectful to me and others, but whenever the conversation turned toward himself there was always sadness there, where he fixated on his inadequacies with education and women. It is because of this history that I was so struck by Gerry's comment on his potential for greatness. His comment demonstrates the complexity of identity construction and management. In this instance at least, Gerry transforms his "abnormality" into a distinguishing characteristic that will lead him to success in a post-apocalyptic society.

In an attempt at identity management, Chico distanced himself from other alcoholics: "I was never like sparky in the cage there[6] or drinking Listerine or shit like that. If there's not a beer, I'm pretty much not going to drink. I wouldn't get to that because I seen people drink aftershave and I just, that doesn't compute to me." Chico identifies as an alcoholic but considers other manifestations of substance use abhorrent. To accept oneself as a member of a stigmatized group is to adopt the "unworthy" status of that group (Bauman, 1988; Goffman, 1963; Rosenthal, 2000). Chico characterizes himself as a worthier addict than individuals who ingest mouthwash, thereby situating himself as more redeemable than others.

Impression management can take the form of performing an idealized presentation of self grounded in dominant social norms. For example, some of the women in this study spoke about pregnancy and motherhood as a site for identity construction. This is not surprising given that motherhood is constituted as a fundamental component of a woman's identity, and this also explains why few men spoke about their children. When I asked Christine about her children she became agitated and said she did not want to talk about them; however, when I tried to quickly move on to the next question to avoid making her upset Christine continued, saying she wanted me to know that despite her current addiction, she successfully abstained from drugs and cigarettes during her pregnancies. Although losing custody of her children was obviously painful for Christine, she made sure to present herself as a good mother. Louise shared a similar story:

> It was hard for me being an addict and all of a sudden being pregnant. And they'd say just quit, you're pregnant and, I can't believe you're pregnant, and you're having that child. And I felt bad about it, although I'd just have one beer. You know, sometimes the doctor says one glass of wine won't hurt, and I was trying to justify, but it was extremely difficult for me to stay clean until the end ... which I did for the first three months for each child, where I heard that's the most crucial time.

Louise gained a great deal of satisfaction from abstaining from drugs for the first trimester of both of her pregnancies. Like Christine, Louise is deeply aware of the importance of motherhood as an identifier and presents an idealized version of herself as a mother, despite her actions failing to live up to the expectations for neoliberal motherhood (Douglas & Michaels, 2004; Kilty & Dej, 2012).

Tom's narrative provides an example of overt impression management. When Tom called me to sign up for the interview he told me that he had a story that I would never forget; his past experience as a gay pornographic film actor was a source of great pride for him. He insisted I bring a laptop to the interview, it turns out so he could show me online photos of cassette covers of the videos he was in. He named several high-profile celebrities that he had relationships with at that time. Several times during the interview, Tom sought reassurance that his was indeed the most shocking interview I had encountered. Tom performed a carefully crafted and well-rehearsed presentation of self so as to create the impression that he is unique, sensational, and above all, "not like the other people here." Like Gerry, Tom transforms what might otherwise be a stigmatizing trait into a unique and interesting characteristic that makes him memorable. Given the homogenization of homelessness in the public imagination Tom uses his difference to set himself apart from the typical homeless identity. In this way, Tom articulates being "abnormal" as a positive quality.[7] Distinguishing themselves from others who are homeless was a key identity management strategy for most participants.

Creating a "Second Skin"
Besides distancing themselves from other marginalized people, another method of impression management some participants adopt is creating a facade to cope with the anxiety, vulnerability, and loneliness of being homeless. Giddens (1991) and Gergen (2000) argue that the lack of an authentic identity in late modernity means that we all create a facade.

The "masks" (Mick) to which some participants refer are much more consciously employed than those described in the literature. For example, Sheela referred to the persona she builds to survive in the homeless shelter:

> Sometimes it can be very frightening in here. You have to build a persona. My daughter's noticed that too. She goes, "if you're gonna live on the street you have to wear a coat that changes you, who you are, and sometimes you have to act a little bit more crazy than what you are to keep people away from you." And I think a lot of us women do that here to protect ourselves. We have to build ourselves up more than what we're accustomed to, to keep these other people away. It's tiring and sometimes you find that you even carry it when you're away from here.

Interestingly, Sheela's daughter suggests that her persona consists of acting "a little more crazy than what you are" in order to isolate and protect herself. The seriously mentally ill identity is thus othered and characterized as something to be feared among the homeless.[8] Sheela's description of the "coat" she wears is demonstrative of Goffman's (1959) disguise. However, she notes how difficult it is to remove the coat. The autonomy to decide when to use the persona in lieu of the "true" self becomes blurred. Here, Butler's (1990) explanation of identity as dependent on social and cultural constructs is useful. Sheela consciously creates a mentally ill persona but the frightening and violent surroundings of the emergency shelter and the vulnerabilities facing women experiencing homelessness in particular require her to be continually vigilant and to don the coat regularly, perhaps explaining her decision to seek out a depression diagnosis.

Like Sheela, Jamie reported creating a facade as a "passing mechanism" (Boydell et al., 2000; Goffman, 1963) to hide his depression from others. He offered that the jokes and cheerfulness he exhibits during activity nights at the shelter are part of this facade: "That's not me but that's the façade I put off." Jamie described in detail the tension between choosing to create a facade and losing his sense of self within this created identity:

> It's second skin. It is. For me it's just another piece of clothing I put on every day. It's things like that, it's a façade I put on that is so much a part of me now that it's, once again, it's who I am. Honestly, right now it would probably be a lot harder for me to get better, for lack of a better word, today than it would have been ten, fifteen years ago, just because so much of who

I am today is built around my experiences, my mental health up 'til now and what I've had to do to make it through some days.

Interestingly, Sheela creates a persona of a mentally ill woman to mitigate her vulnerability. Jamie, on the other hand, uses a facade to conceal his depression. The mentally ill identity, then, can be characterized as both a stigmatizing trait and a tool for identity management, although both interpretations see the facade as contributing negatively to their mental health and well-being. Jamie continued, stating:

> It's who I am. Late at night when I'm lying in bed, but I won't even think of it that way because, like with this, in this relationship or dealing with the staff here or dealing with the people at the library, dealing with somebody, somebody who's not a serious, close relationship is like, that's who I am. Maybe that's the outer layer of me, like an onion. You start peeling back an onion, there's different layers there, but that is who I am.

Like Sheela's description of donning a coat, Jamie uses the metaphor of peeling an onion to depict the facade as a second skin that is a consciously created artifact, but one that is difficult to distinguish from his "true" self. While Jamie is certain that he embodies a separate identity for those he is close to and that truly "know" him, his whole self is a combination of the facade and this "authentic" identity. Also, given that Jamie is a self-described "loner," the temporal and relational conditions brought about by his homelessness make him unable to reveal this "true" identity. Developing a "second skin" as a form of identity management is a deliberate and conscious act but given the constant stress and vulnerabilities experienced by those who are homeless, the facade soon becomes a permanent fixture in an individual's identity construction. This reality complicates Goffman's dramaturgical approach, blurring the boundary between conscious and unconscious identity performance.

Conclusion

Identity management can be simultaneously conscious and deliberate while also shaped by underlying social and structural factors that limit the types of identity that are available to be effectively performed. This tension creates the conditions where someone may permanently adopt a facade. The quality and nature of the marginalized identities reflect the complexity between intentional identity construction and the pre-existing social constructs that unconsciously inform that identity. For all the variances in identity performance exhibited by those experiencing homelessness, the research participants all attempted to manage their excluded status in some capacity. Some participants mitigated their exclusion by presenting themselves as redeemable subjects. They did so by selectively choosing the types of identities they embraced and carefully reconstructed what it means to be homeless and/or mentally ill. For example, Chico's account of his addict identity as superior to others demonstrates that while these identities are vilified, they may still be performed in a way that maintains a hierarchy of marginalization. Sheela and Jamie's descriptions of their facades revealed a multifaceted approach to identity construction – one that is unique to each individual's performance, but that is also highly constrained by the homeless environment. The paradox between the medicalization of distress and responsibilization discourses further complicates the mental illness identity among the homeless.

5

Taking the Blame: Responsibilizing Homelessness

In Chapter 2, I noted that mental illness and addiction have a complex relationship with the disease framework as they hold strong associations with moralistic and normalized understandings of behaviour and are often considered less legitimate than physical health concerns. Still, the *DSM-V* regards both issues as biologically driven, manifesting from pathologies located within the brain, genetic code, and nervous system. This complexity foregrounds the challenge presented in this chapter – how mental illness and addiction discourses constitute medical problems as deriving from biological anomalies while also holding individuals accountable for their recovery and exit from homelessness. There is a seeming incongruence between biological determinism – the notion that all behaviour is caused by biological forces – and responsibilization techniques that rely on narratives of choice as the solution to homelessness. In its purest form, biological determinism is fatalistic, suggesting that those who experience chronic homelessness, in particular those identified as mentally ill, are victims of their own body and mind, which make them incapable of change. Arguably, this would position people in distress as having no accountability for their actions and thus being blameless for their circumstances. However, it became very apparent throughout this project that biological understandings of mental illness and addiction do not negate personal feelings of blame, thus allowing responsibilization logics to take hold.

Rather than them being incompatible, I argue that biological determinism and responsibilization discourses are intimately linked in understanding and managing mental illness and addiction in the homelessness industrial complex; that is, they both rely on the individual as the site of the problem and the source of the solution. The production and perpetuation of these discourses by those working in the homelessness sector are rarely intentional. The medical model is primarily designed to address the individual body as the site of intervention (with social determinants of health scholarship broadening the scope) and as such, there are virtually no tools available to funding-dependent, resource-limited social service organizations to produce alternative responses that address the structural and systematic causes of poverty and distress (Wilson Gilmore, 2007). The only frameworks and techniques at the disposal of these organizations are those that rely on self-regulation and personal accountability to respond to the perceived causes of homelessness (mainly personal factors). The effect then, is one of individual responsibilization. This is important to reflect on because this analysis does not refute the positive impact some individual interventions have on people's lives. Instead, the argument here is that individualized mental health responses are positioned as *the* solution to distress, poverty, and homelessness without grounding the challenges people face within an exclusionary social and cultural context. Achieving housing, mental well-being, and social inclusion within these oppressive and harmful conditions is extremely difficult and an unfair expectation to place on marginalized people.

To flesh out the unlikely kinship between biological determinist and responsibilization discourses we must first establish the medicalization of distress and its adoption within the homelessness industrial complex and by people experiencing homelessness. Many people experiencing homelessness come to identify a "true" and "untrue" self to distinguish their bio-bodies from their felt identities, and a small but vocal minority resist biological explanations of mental illness. When I explain my research to people within and outside of the homelessness sector, a common response I hear is that people experiencing homelessness likely take on the mentally ill identity as a way to avoid blame for their circumstances. In fact, the opposite is true, with most participants in this study expressly refusing to use the medical framework to allay their personal responsibility for their distress, addiction, criminalization, and homelessness. As a result, the homelessness industrial complex often takes up the responsibilization discourses and strategies that borrow from biopsychology to emphasize how people can take ownership over their lives and rewire their brains to recover and become included members of society. The overwhelming obstacles to creating a normalized healthy lifestyle while experiencing homelessness and/or housing precarity rarely makes its way into the narrative. The notion of "taking the blame" is deeply entrenched among those experiencing homelessness, so much so that those who use mental illness and/or addiction to explain their marginality are often vilified by their peers for failing to take ownership of their circumstances. In fact, demonstrating accountability for one's distress and rejecting broader structural issues is characterized as a form of empowerment.

"The Island of Broken Toys": Medicalizing Distress

The Biological Imperative

The medical model is a tool used to explain the root causes of homelessness. People experiencing homelessness adopt, and in some cases resist, biological explanations for distress as a way of making sense of their status as mentally ill, addicted, criminalized, and marginalized. Szasz's (1989) notion of "problems in living" describes the myriad ways that challenges people face, and emotions people feel, are characterized as medical problems. Distress is understood and remedied from a biological perspective, or what Foucault (1988) calls "medicine of the mind." This is not to say that those who subscribe to the medical model ignore external circumstances, but environmental factors are often regarded as "triggers" to an underlying biological issue. People experiencing homelessness overwhelmingly define mental illness and addiction as biological in nature. Most participants with a mental illness diagnosis, and many without a formal diagnosis, are prescribed medication by a physician, psychiatrist, or nurse. Most addiction treatment programs described by research participants teach from a medical model, which characterizes genetics, biology, and family lineage as common explanations of the cause of mental illness and addiction. Pam (1995) points out the faulty logic inherent in presuming that family members pass on their distress through genetics, ignoring intergenerational poverty and oppression, or that because symptoms respond to medication, they must be biologically derived. Still, participants commonly referred to genetics and chemical imbalances to situate their distress within a biological explanatory model. For example, Sheela was extremely concerned that she might have passed on a mental illness gene to her grandchildren:

> I have a fear of mine that it's going to go to my grandchildren. I have a fear that it's going to pass on to the next generation, the mental illness. So I'm

scared of that. But I know if I can stay and live my life to whatever fullness that I can find and happiness that I can find that will give hope for my grandchildren, for those that are coming. "If she did, I can do it, I can live and I don't need this unhappiness to bring me down and destroy my life."

Sheela previously struggled with disordered eating, is self-diagnosed with depression, takes psychotropic medication, and has attempted suicide several times. She was caught up in the child welfare system, experienced sexual abuse as a child, and was cut off from her First Nations culture. Although her grandchildren have not experienced this kind of trauma, Sheela is worried that they will inherit her mental illness because of its biological nature and so the best she can do is act as an example of how to carry the burden of inevitable "unhappiness" by not letting it "bring [them] down." The intergenerational trauma caused by colonization practices certainly has long-term, devastating impacts for Indigenous Peoples, families and communities, languages, and cultures. But just like the idea that blame for homelessness rests with individuals, the belief that Indigenous Peoples pass on mental illness or addiction is yet another form of discrimination and colonization:

> Obscured behind these discourses are the historical processes and narrative prejudices practiced by the Canadian state and settler society that have produced Indigenous homelessness. Discourse about these processes disappears into myths about flawed Indigenous individuals: mental "illness," substance abuse, recidivism, delinquency, and other myths. (Thistle, 2017, p. 7)

Sheela rests the blame for over five hundred years of settler-colonialism on her laden shoulders, a sentiment perpetuated by the medical model's dominance in mental health and addiction treatment. Such beliefs have real life, lamentable effects. Sheela has vowed not to visit her grandchildren until she can act as a proper role model for how to cope responsibly with distress. Feeling it is her obligation to stay away from her family, and in so doing depriving them of her love, wisdom, and teachings, is evidence of the durability and longevity of colonial practices that attempt to keep Indigenous families apart with the aim of cultural genocide.

Sheela was among many participants who took the medical model of mental illness to heart. Max also framed mental illness as strictly biologically determined and used a heartbreaking analogy to explain the origins of his depression:

> I don't think it's as complicated as some people make it out. I mean, you ever see the Christmas cartoon, the little puppets are shown every Christmas, it's Santa Claus and the Island of Broken Toys.[1] I'm just a broken toy. Sometimes, who knows why, a million units come out fine and one of them's broken. And I think it's just I'm broken somewhere. And I've also not helped that brokenness by years of drug addiction and alcohol and depression and not dealing with it and just running through life. That of course, I think I probably had a lot to do with it. I think I'm just ... you know, I own this. Maybe a chemical imbalance, I don't know.

Max articulates his decades-long cycle of distress, addiction, homelessness, and criminalization as coming from a fragmentation in his biochemical makeup. While he explained his brokenness as a sort of biological determinism, he was also quick to point out that he exacerbated his depression by using drugs and "not dealing with it," asserting "I own this." Although Max claimed that mental illness can be explained simply, the description of his distress is tangled, whereby he is at once a victim of his biology and responsible for the thoughts and behaviours that led to and/or aggravated his depression and subsequent criminalization and homelessness.

Part of the sense of accountability for distress comes from the understanding that substance use exacerbates mental illness. Like Max, Milan connected the two: "I think a part of it is in my genes but I think that all the alcohol abuse must have triggered something. I'm sure about that. All the alcohol and drug abuse and not sleeping and neglecting my body, I'm sure it had a big part to do with it." Milan reaffirms the perceived association between mental illness and addiction discussed in the previous chapter, but he also pivots the conversation around mental illness being both biological and grounded in individual decision making. Milan equates his substance use, party-going lifestyle, and lack of self-care as triggering a biological response that led to his distress. Participants framed addiction as partially responsible for their distress and primarily interpreted addiction through a medical paradigm. Gaston described mental illness and addiction as intimately connected through their similar biological foundations:

> I define it as a disease. I define it as something chemically different inside the brain. It's almost like, alcoholic – that's me – I find that it's almost like

alcoholic is a mental illness, it's almost in itself because it's chemically different than most other people.

Gaston described mental illness as a comparative biological condition. He went on to equate addiction with diabetes and allergies, both organic physiological conditions. Many of the outpatient addiction programs frequented by those experiencing homelessness teach the allergy model, popularized by AA/NA groups, which resonated with some participants. Vince explained:

> For myself I believe in the allergy concept. A normal person can have a drink, or two drinks, or three drinks, and shut it down. Whereas with, we're calling it the disease addiction, and I know for myself, maybe one, or one day I can have a few drinks. Maybe even the twelfth time I can have a couple drinks, but eventually it's gonna get me because I do have this allergy, where, eventually I'm not going to be able to shut it down. I can't stop at two drinks more often than not and it's this, "I need another drink, another drink, another drink."

The allergy model makes sense to people because it situates addiction as an illness rather than a moral fault and creates a "sick" addict identity (Miller, 2010; Valverde, 1998). The twelve-step AA/NA programs are built on the premise of powerlessness. Step one requires an admission of powerlessness over the addictive substance. Because of this lack of power, the programs tout that one will forever be an addict but may learn to manage addiction (if responsibilized). In this way, mental illness and addiction are similarly constructed in that they are both seen as chronic incurable diseases that may be managed by responsibilized subjects who actively govern their thoughts, desires, and actions.

Given the implication that mental illness and addiction are permanent, surveillance, professional guidance, and the search for self-governance become tools, used in varying combinations, to regulate people long term. Whether it is through medication or group therapy sessions, treating mental illness and addiction as chronic illnesses, similar to HIV or Parkinson's disease, connotes an ongoing relationship with medical institutions and professionals. Kathy, a public health nurse, found it useful to compare mental illness to physical chronic illnesses to emphasize its permanence and thus the necessity of lifelong medication compliance:

> That's how I explain [mental illness] to clients, because there's so much stigma around it, that just like you treat hypertension and you have to take

medication every day for hypertension, if you have depression you have to take medication every day for depression. And just like hypertension you need to eat well, exercise, do things in your environment to help manage your hypertension. Same goes for depression. So I think seeing it like that for me is important, not only for reducing the stigma but also in helping people understand this is something you have to take care of for the rest of your life. And that sucks for people, right? A question you always get is "am I going to have to take this medication for the rest of my life?" Probably. Some people don't, but most of our clients will have to take it for the rest of their life just because ... most of them have had such chaotic lifestyles and terrible lives that the likelihood of them not needing medication is very, very slim.

Kathy not only equates the need for lifelong psychopharmaceuticals as medical treatment but also implies that medication is necessary to govern "chaotic lifestyles." People commonly require long-term medical care for various physical and mental illnesses and this is not a marker of exclusion on its own. However, Kathy firmly roots the need for ongoing intervention for her patients within their marginalized status, stating that they will likely have to take medication for the rest of their lives "just because" of their "terrible lives." In this way, medicalized intervention and supervision are not designed strictly to manage illness, but are also disciplinary tactics used to manage particular people, especially those who are more likely to be identified as irredeemable.

Resisting the Biological Model
Biological explanations of distress are not universally accepted. A few participants took an overtly critical position on psychiatry, mirroring the critical psy (Conrad, 2007) and mad movement literature (Burstow, 2013; Laing, 1960, 1967; Shimrat, 1997; Szasz, 1974, 1989). Daniel, for example, questioned treating distress with psychotropic medication when he did not think it was biologically derived:

The thing is to get your head above the water just from talking and some counselling and not through medication because, I mean, depression is psychological. It's not psychiatric. It does not indicate any pharmacology needed, it's just to get everything in line. Make sense out of those self-destructive ideas that are floating around in your head, you know. No drug is going to change that self-talk I mean it's only self-talk, you know that will change it.

Daniel called for increased access to counsellors and group therapy programs, mental health care treatments that are sorely lacking in the homelessness sector, and he was reluctant to take medication for depression. Daniel regarded his low self-esteem and feelings of isolation as cognitive distortions rather than biochemical problems (Fennell, 2004). Daniel blames his thoughts and feelings for his depression rather than his biological makeup.

Lenny finds the medicalization of addiction problematic; he suggested that different explanations and treatments of addiction are trendy rather than rooted in evidence:

> I don't believe in alcoholism as a disease. I believe it's a result more of situational and environmental [issues]. I think that's the whole problem with a lot of people's recovery is they're being told they have this disease and the whole disease concept of alcoholism is nothing more than a model. The disease model is exactly that. It is a model. In 1990 there were nineteen different models, you know, and here we are. Twenty years later, I don't know how many more models are out there, I just stopped reading them.

Lenny strongly opposed harm reduction models such as safe consumption sites and managed alcohol programs because the sheer number of program models he has experienced through his interaction with the mental health, addiction, and correctional systems over the years nullifies their validity. Lenny is homing in on the sordid history of managing addiction through different philosophies and sectors over the past century. Interpretations of addiction from religious, moral, deviancy, medical, and ethical perspectives have produced varying, and sometimes competing definition of addiction, its cause, and its subsequent treatment. This being the case, Lenny is cynical of AA/NA's disease approach, which he sees as pseudo-scientific and too focused on the neoliberal project of the self,[2] which fails to account for the "spiritual sickness" that he regards as the root of addiction.

Finally, both Giles and Al offer that their distress derives from racism and oppression rather than a biological imperative. Giles accepts his schizophrenia diagnosis, but claims that the onset of his distress was social rather than biological:

> My illness is caused not by natural things but by harassment from people, from the police. Harassment from the police, harassment from bureaucrats. That time I lived [in a refugee camp] was stressful so I become ill. But when I arrived here I was ok.

Giles suggests that the trauma of coming to Canada as a refugee triggered symptoms associated with schizophrenia. Although he attributes his distress to illness, he does not see its cause as "natural." Psychiatrists would almost certainly associate his feelings of being followed by the police as paranoia and as a symptom of schizophrenia, but as Laing (1960) suggests, regardless of whether the police are in fact following Giles, his perception of being targeted on account of his migrant status is significant in its testament to the widespread implications of over-policing racialized communities (McLeod et al., 2019).

Similarly, although Al does not identify as having a mental illness, he finds that the systemic racism he encounters negatively affects his mental well-being. Al recounted multiple events where he experienced overt racism. He described an incident where he claims a police officer killed his friend because he was a Rastafarian, of being unable to walk around downtown Ottawa holding hands with a white woman for fear of being assaulted, and of being hit by a taxi and left for dead on account of his race. In the latter instance, Al felt completely abandoned by society: "When he just ran me over and left me like that, it just made me really worthless as a person. Like to not even have rights. Like even a dog they would have picked up off the street." Al suggests that the cumulative emotional effects of these events led to his poor mental health:

> I think you grow up with that, like your mom telling you, "you have to work twice as hard to get half as far," and people are like abusing you for certain things. And I'm not saying I was an angel but that played a lot, over the years it just festers and festers and festers so it got to the point where I was like, I mean I'm like not killing somebody or killing myself, I was just like "I didn't know how to deal with it anymore."

Systemic racism impacts Al's sense of self-worth and he pinpoints a racist police culture as particularly harmful following several negative and abusive encounters with the police. His comment echoes the sentiments of the Black Lives Matter movement that was triggered by the multiple fatal shootings of unarmed Black men in North America (Rickford, 2015), the deep-rooted oppression of Black communities and people of colour by state actors and institutions in Canada (Cole, 2020; Maynard, 2017), the overrepresentation of Black People in Canadian prisons (Office of the Correctional Investigator, 2013), and the heightened police presence in spaces frequented by the homeless (Bernier et al., 2011; Stuart, 2016). Al does not dismiss a biological foundation for serious mental illnesses but believes eliminating racism and discrimination will improve his mental health, not taking medication.

Finding the "True" Self

While there were a handful of outliers, the vast majority of participants accepted the medical model of mental health and illness. Biological determinism can be personified by characterizing mental illness and addiction as objects unto themselves that hijack bodies and so do not represent the person's "true" self (Maruna, 2001; Pollack, 2005). Embodying mental illness as its own subjectivity within the body shifts blame away from the core self onto another, "untrue" self. Contrary to common assumptions, however, this strategy does not eliminate personal responsibility; rather, it provides hope that there is a true self that is governable.

Mia, a 57-year-old Métis woman, was clear about the biological transformation that takes place when her bipolar disorder "kicks in":

> Somebody else is taking over my body and I really want to hurt the person but me, I don't want to hurt the person. I'd rather walk away but I can't because of this bipolar that took over my body. I can be talking to a person really, really nice and if they make me mad, get me angry and I can't fight the anger that's when it kicks in and that's when it seems like this other person is in my body and they're, they're fighting. Not me. I told [my sister] that and she said "yeah, Mia, that is one part of your brain."

Although Mia is in poor health and is often weak, she regularly acts aggressively and is known to hit and punch other women at Haven. At the time of the interview, Mia's arm was in a cast from an altercation she had had with another woman who derided Katie, whom Mia affectionately calls her daughter. Mia causally links her short temper to her bipolar diagnosis and explains that it feels like something or someone is taking over her body and states that her sister, a medical doctor, explained that her brain has two sides. She told conflicting stories of how her bipolar disease originated, once citing a concussion as an infant and then later suggesting it was a result of giving birth to her children. In both scenarios, Mia sees a direct physiological connection between her lack of self-control and her mental health status. When referring to another situation where she hit someone, Mia said that her bipolar disorder "flared up" in the same way many people refer to arthritis. Mia feels disembodied from her true self when this happens and no longer in control of her own bodily movements.

Mia describes the experience of an untrue self overriding her decision-making capacity. The untrue self is embedded within Mia's body and, while separate, cannot be easily parsed from her "core" self. The fatalistic quality of Mia's account of bipolar disorder was contrasted with her excitement about beginning an anger-management program at a shelter she moved to the week before the interview. Mia often referred to the impossibility of managing bipolar disorder because it is like attempting to assert dominance over a completely different person, but she remained open to learning how to try to gain control over her thoughts and actions.

Mia's account of her mental illness as a completely separate entity was clear in its polarization of the true and untrue selves. More commonly, participants referenced a true self that is hidden by mental illness and addiction and explained shameful behaviour by citing biological influences, especially the physiological effects of substance use (Maruna, 2001; Pollack, 2005). Mac claimed that his alcohol and drug use transformed him into someone else: "It's not who I really am." Similarly, Otto talked about substances "overtaking my personality," which he used to explain his absence as a father, following a similar narrative to substance using mothers (Kilty & Dej, 2012). J. J. told the story of how his understanding of his true self kept him from committing suicide when he was using:

> You know what one of my sponsors said to me? He said to me, and this is when I was contemplating stopping using, I was still using, and I was in and out type of deal of the program and of sobriety. He said, "you know, J. J., people who are using or are in early recovery should not consider suicide because the person they're killing may be a stranger." Now think of that wisdom. You're right, we're so miserable, we don't even know who we are or why we're killing ourselves.

J. J. told me this story many times throughout my fieldwork in the shelters and during our formal interview. The advice he received from his sponsor had a positive impact on his outlook on addiction, mental health, and his sense of self, and ultimately saved his life. Echoing Mia, J. J. argues that committing suicide while heavily addicted is tantamount to murder because the addict self is disembodied from the true self. For these participants, the body consists of two separate entities, the sober and mentally well self, and the "miserable" addict self. J. J.'s explanation reveals the strength of the true self/untrue self-narrative, providing him a way to envision his self-worth beyond his status as an excluded, homeless, drug addict and giving him hope for a brighter future where his non-addict self dominates.

There is evidence that similar narratives take shape in prisons where prisoners differentiate their core self from their behaviours as part of their redemption script (Maruna, 2001; Maruna & Ramsden, 2004). The working hypothesis is that prisoners identify with the medical model of distress because it acts as a "shield" to protect them from taking responsibility (Pollack, 2005). Kathy, a public health nurse, agreed with the assertion that framing distress as a disease works to downplay individual responsibility:

> I had a guy who was hospitalized, who was drinking his own pee for, he thought it was helping him get well. Got him into the hospital, came out, came back to us. He was doing really well. The voices went away, but he got depressed, because there he was an herbalist, a doctor, he was working with doctors in the hospital, saving all these people and now he's a guy living in the streets that had a really abusive wife, his kids in the shelter, like, it's insane, right? So that's part of mental illness that people don't think about. You know, it gives people meaning in their life. Like it's a lot easier to be grandiose when I'm the queen of England than see, oh shit I'm living in a shelter.

The nurse suggests that cognitive distortions can sometimes be preferable to facing the reality of living life on the margins, providing insight into the depths of harm caused by social exclusion. The argument goes that mental illness acts as a kind of escapism from the degradation and humiliation of being homeless. However, findings from this research do not align with the notion that those in distress use mental illness to deflect blame. In fact, the opposite was true. People experiencing homelessness carry the weight of living in poverty, suffering with distress in many forms, often facing trauma and violence, and do not allow themselves to unload that burden onto anyone or anything.

The self-reproach those experiencing homelessness feel for their distress and exclusion is an exercise in contradiction. Biological determinism, although touted by the mental health and correctional systems, would appear antithetical to the attempt to discipline and responsibilize subjects (Maruna, 2001). Still, correctionalist discourses emphasize prisoners' choice-making as central to their rehabilitation, which aligns with neoliberal responsibilization discourses. How these two frameworks coexist in institutional practices and the broader public imagination is rarely acknowledged;

however, it is imperative that we flesh out this discursive relationship because people experiencing homelessness continue to take the blame for their marginality, despite their belief in a biological foundation for mental illness and its impact on their quality of life. This quandary highlights the surprising alliance between biological determinist explanations and the neoliberal late modern insistence on accountability, self-governance, and individual responsibility.

Responsibilization: Fixing the Flaw

The medical model of distress is commonly used in mental health and addiction services and programming. Calls for marginalized people to be accountable for their homeless and mentally ill identities appears counterintuitive to biological determinism. Those marked as mentally ill and who must face its accompanying stigma are subject to what Parsons (1975) describes as the "sick role," where pathologized individuals are regarded as helpless victims of biology. If mental illness, its symptoms, and its potentially deviant behaviour are *destined* through bodily makeup, then the individual is blameless and guilt-free, but hopeless. In their efforts to reduce stigma, many professionals and para-professionals working in the homelessness sector rely on the biological framework to deflect blame for people's homelessness and distress. As cited above, Kathy compared hypertension and mental illness as examples of chronic illness. Similarly, Anthony, part of the management team at Crossroads, compared mental illness with a broken arm: "We would not hesitate to seek medical attention if we broke a bone, and would not be judged for doing so, and the same should be said for mental illness." While broken bones rarely carry much stigma, physical illness is not immune to judgment despite obvious biological foundations. Individuals are often blamed for their physical ailments because they do not manage their risks properly, take preventative measures, or adhere to suggestions offered by health promotion discourses. Lupton (1995) differentiates fatalism, static risk factors such as a genetic predisposition, from "lifestylism," those factors that people can alter with lifestyle changes, such as diet and exercise. The two are often conflated, thereby positioning individuals as accountable for their physical illnesses. For example, literature on self-perception among cancer patients indicates that people experience tremendous guilt and shame for their diagnosis (Else-Quest et al., 2009). Lung cancer carries significant stigma because of its association with smoking cigarettes, which society regards as a poor lifestyle choice. Even among those with lung cancer who do not smoke, the level of felt judgment and shame by association is reportedly high (Chapple et al., 2004). The responsibilization of lung cancer patients comes from an assumption that individuals make bad choices and are thus at least somewhat deserving of their illness.

In an example concerning homelessness specifically, Jesse Thistle (2015) recounts how doctors were frustrated by his inability to keep an open wound on his leg clean, with one doctor exclaiming: "Do you know how sick you've made yourself?" (p. 43). Jesse's leg was infected and became affected with gangrene in large part because he was staying at an emergency shelter that was not designed for residents to heal from injury. Jesse describes how within four days of returning to the shelter his suction pump for improving circulation and antibiotics were stolen and the aftercare nurse did not visit the shelter. Jesse's living conditions made it nearly impossible for him to recover from his injury, but he was ultimately held responsible for his poor physical health.

Even among those mental illnesses linked to physical markers, stigma remains high. Schnittker (2008) found that biological explanations of distress do not necessarily reduce stigma. In fact, the fatalism of the medical model can have the opposite effect, where the public is more fearful of the potential dangerousness of those diagnosed with a mental illness (particularly schizophrenia) because individuals are perceived as difficult or impossible to treat. If we can assert, then, that a biological explanation of illness does not ipso facto eliminate blame, we can consider how self-governance discourses coexist within a medical model framework.

When the Cure Lies Within
Treatment programming in Ottawa's homeless industrial complex relies on a version of biological determinism that asserts that distress can be reformed with appropriate environmental and lifestyle changes. Indeed, this paradigm is necessary to avoid falling into the fatalist trap described above. How can there be treatment without a belief that the biological factors that create mental illness can be altered? To bridge the biological determinist and responsibilization divide, treatment discourses must do two things: first, they must be grounded in medicalized language that leans on the credibility of the medical model to justify their approach; and second, that same medicalized language must be mobilized to legitimize thinking around the ways that individuals' actions and their surroundings impact these biological processes, for better or for worse. The effect of aligning these two frameworks is that neoliberal modes of self-governance are situated as

appropriate responses to mental illness and addiction by fixating on the individualization of the perceived physical impairment.

To find that balance, many of the treatment programs offered in Ottawa rely heavily on biopsychology literature, in particular Gabor Maté's work. Maté is an internationally renowned physician who spent most of his career in Vancouver's Downtown Eastside, one of Canada's most impoverished neighbourhoods. Biopsychology contends that there are a variety of biological and environmental factors that influence both mental illness and addiction. But that, at their core, they are a manifestation of an abnormality in the brain caused by undeveloped or impeded dopamine receptors in the cerebral cortex – the part of the brain responsible for rational decision making and emotional control. More than genetic predisposition, Maté focuses on how gene expression takes shape in pre- and post-natal environments. Considering addiction specifically, Maté (2008) questions an addicted person's ability to make informed choices:

> People choose, decide and act in a context – and to a large degree, that context is determined by how their brains function. The brain itself also develops in the real world, influenced by conditions over which the individual, as a young child, had no choice whatsoever. (p. 174)

Maté contends that the brain's development in utero and in childhood is highly malleable, and trauma can lead to permanent cognitive, behavioural, and emotional problems. An unstable home environment, whether due to political unrest, discrimination, poverty, social circumstance, or some other cause, leads to poor self-regulation, which can account for symptoms of mental illness and addiction. From this perspective, one's neurophysiological development is conditioned by social and environmental factors and vice versa.

Treatment programs in the homelessness sector emphasize the neurological aspect of mental illness and addiction, situating recovery within environmental and behavioural changes that can directly affect the body and reprogram the brain. Herein lies the crux of adopting the biological determinist framework while rejecting its fatalism. The use of scientific evidence that the brain's internal environment can be manipulated contributes to the political economy of hope (Novas, 2006; Rose & Novas, 2005). Neuroplasticity, the brain's lifelong ability to rewire its neural connections, provides the basis for situating individualized responsibilization strategies for managing distress. Maté (2008) argues that people diagnosed with OCD can override their brain's neural connections if they are exposed to an "enriched environment." An enriched environment can be as simple as doing puzzles to ward off dementia or as difficult as reorienting the salience attribution in the brain that prioritizes love, happiness, and safety over the feeling of being high. Similarly, with reference to treating ADD, individuals can engage in "self-parenting," where they create for themselves a physical and emotional space where they feel safe, healthy, creative, and open to self-insight in order to form new neural circuits that process emotions in a "healthy" way (Maté, 1999).

While the benefits of creating an enriched environment are undeniable, in practice the strategies have a decidedly neoliberal leaning in that they rely on individuals to acquire the financial, social, and cultural capital to develop these recovery tools themselves. Westernized perceptions dominate the conceptualization of enriched environments as individually constituted and managed, and a failure to decolonize these understandings means inflicting colonial violence that is detrimental to Indigenous Peoples and communities (Allwood & Berry, 2006; Firestone et al., 2019; Kral et al., 2011). There is an opportunity here to consider how structural change, social inclusion, and community-building shape our collective environment, particularly by drawing from and prioritizing Indigenous knowledges. However, to date, the emphasis remains on how individuals construct their own environment.

Borrowing heavily from the AA/NA paradigm, Maté (2008) highlights the powerlessness of those suffering from addiction but suggests that through the brain's reconfiguration, an individual can regain the freedom of choice:

> Life, until now, has created you. You've been acting according to ingrained mechanisms wired into your brain before you had a choice in the matter, and it's out of those automatic mechanisms that you've created the life you have now. It's time to re-create: to choose a different life ... In place of a life blighted by your addictive need for acquisition, self-soothing, admiration, oblivion, meaningless activity, what is the life you really want? What do you choose to create? (p. 361)

Here the addict subject is at once a complete victim and the site of the solution. Maté does not make light of the immense difficulty that comes with creating an enriched environment or the ability to self-parent. Given his work with arguably the most marginalized neighbourhood in Canada, Vancouver's Downtown Eastside, he is keenly aware of the personal, economic, and social impediments his patients face. Maté is a staunch supporter of Insite,

Canada's first legal safe injection site, and has called for an end to the war on drugs, recognizing that the criminalization of addiction and the dearth of public health approaches are enormous barriers to personal and social wellness. Maté and other biopsychologists' work provides hope – hope that the brain can be changed if those in distress can seize enough willpower to make good choices within, and indeed despite, their social exclusion. From this perspective, those who suffer with mental illness and/or addiction are victims, but victims who can achieve freedom through responsible choices, often with supports, including medication. Because it's their brain that requires changing, the individual ultimately remains responsible for their own freedom.

The biopsychological framework carries tremendous weight for many people experiencing homelessness in Ottawa who take ownership over their distress based on its teachings. Many individuals who participate in outpatient addiction treatment programs re-narrated their past on learning about brain development. This discursive shift is another example of Hacking's (1999) looping effect, whereby people conceptualize life events in an entirely different way than when the event took place, creating a substantial narrative shift in their life histories. The biopsychological model allows people who are homeless to reconfigure past events as triggering biological effects. Mick explained: "Growing up as a kid in a stress environment, or stress caregivers, um, the brain circuits don't form properly. But the brain is very plastic, eh, this stuff can be fixed." Mustang explained the etiology of mental illness in the same way: "[Mental illness] is brought on, from my understanding, is brought on from the environment that's exposed to me from birth to ... however long. So however I gone through stressors, trauma, whatnot, I believe something got interrupted while the brain was being formed or as it's aging or whatever." Participants add a biological component to their childhood experiences of abuse and neglect. More than this, though, the addiction programs use this framework on both mental illness and substance abuse to provide the sense of hope necessary to "fix" the brain:

> Gabor Maté empowers you. He says that if you acclaim it to genetics then nobody's responsible and you might as well give up because you're an addict and you have no hope of recovering, right? But if it's from an experience, right, what does he call his something, L P [left prefrontal hemisphere] brain, it's the malleable brain that you can, it can form new pathways, L P whatever, I forget. So basically in time, and that's where I had hope, in

time these brain patterns or whatever, connections, will no longer be used because I'll no longer be using so they'll create newer ones that will be relevant to my new lifestyle. (Ron)

Ron is a 41-year-old white, bisexual man who is diagnosed with a raft of mental illnesses (including PTSD, bipolar disorder, depression, and antisocial personality disorder) and who actively uses cocaine, crack, heroin, and alcohol. At the time of the interview, he lived in another homeless shelter in Ottawa and had a long history of incarceration. In short, Ron's situation can easily be described as hopeless. Alternatively, he uses the material provided in the addictions programs as a source of hope through which to write his redemption script. Ron seizes on the biological model of mental illness and addiction to make sense of his brain and provide a pathway for well-being – namely through self-regulation and forging a "new lifestyle." Maté's work gives Ron hope and a sense of control over his life but when the model is used in the absence of adequate social supports, it provides little recourse to address the structural barriers Ron and others face.

As the framework unfolds, it becomes Ron's responsibility to adopt a normative lifestyle and to create an enriched environment to grow new nerve cells; through this discourse, Ron is simultaneously pathologized and responsibilized. Ron explained that the knowledge he needs to create a new life for himself gives him hope: "Now I know so I know, even if I have to run with a thousand pounds on my back around the block every day, at least I know that's what I have to do. Whereas before ... it's hopeless." Ron did not elaborate on how he can lift this "thousand pounds" – securing safe, affordable, and permanent housing; finding counselling; becoming sober; staying out of jail; accessing food, clothing, and transportation; dealing with past trauma; and building positive relationships – off his back. There is a disconnect in Ron's narrative, and the broader treatment discourse, where discussions of how the socio-structural reality of living on the margins can be transformed into an enriched environment is either ignored or described simplistically as emerging from the ability to make better choices. In this instance, we see how some marginalized people are framed as redeemable. If they are willing and able to fix their brain by adopting a normative lifestyle then it is possible for them to become socially included, which affords vulnerable people like Ron a degree of hope. This hope provides the necessary motivation for them to take responsibility for their distress. But this hope belies the tremendous challenge people experiencing homelessness face in seeking to self-parent under conditions of extreme poverty, limited personal autonomy, and a lack of access to supports for well-being besides those offered by the mental health system. Despite this tension, a dominant narrative among those experiencing homelessness is that they expect themselves and their peers to be accountable for their exclusion.

No Excuses: Taking Responsibility for the Mentally Ill and Addict Identities

So far in this chapter I have scrutinized the complex intersection of biology and responsibility commonly used as an explanatory tool for distress among those experiencing homelessness. But what of those narratives that do not adopt this framework? Many people who are homeless place tremendous significance on accepting blame for their social circumstances. In some instances, this includes deriding others for making excuses for their distress.

Taking the Blame
The cornerstone of governing through freedom is an individual's ability to make autonomous, rational decisions. Freedom comes with obligations to choose correctly, mitigate risk, and live with the consequences of our choices (Bauman, 1988; Rose, 1999). Many research participants situate the mentally ill and addict identities within the medical model while adhering to the the notion that they can fix their brain through a responsible lifestyle, which gives credence to self-government discourses. Although I did not ask participants directly about their history of trauma, most people volunteered information about the physical, sexual, and emotional abuse they endured as children and adults. True to Maté's focus on early adversity, many understand this victimization as a causal feature in abnormal brain development, but this does not diminish their felt responsibility to self-govern in a way that aligns with socially accepted norms. To perform simultaneously the shamed poor and responsibilized citizen roles, those who are identified as mentally ill and/or addicted must hold themselves accountable for their current "unenriched" environment as well as be responsible for creating an enriched environment conducive to neurological, psychological, and emotional growth. As Maruna (2001) notes, individuals seeking redemption are expected to assume "complete and unmediated blame" (p. 132) for their marginal status. Accepting this unequivocal blame is the only way for them to exhibit the necessary shame to be considered redeemable and thus worthy of services and positive interactions with staff and professionals.

Participants commonly told me that, notwithstanding the biological nature of their condition(s) or the context of their childhood and current circumstances, they must assume responsibility for the state of their lives if they want to escape homelessness, manage their mental illness, and/ or become sober. For example, Christine takes full responsibility for her depression, OCD, and bipolar disorder diagnoses as well as her addiction to crack. When I asked her how living in a shelter affects her mental health, she replied: "No matter where I am, I can't blame the environment because that would be me being in denial." Christine uses psy-language like "being in denial" to explain why she cannot acknowledge the negative impact living in a homeless shelter has on her mental health. In this way, Christine judges herself through psy-language and internalizes external distress factors as part of her responsibilization narrative and redemption.

Karla uses a similar narrative to take ownership of her addiction: "My addictions started because I liked it, so I'm not blaming nobody and I'm not screaming telling the government to pay me because you had me addicted for two years, you fucked my life up. I fucked my own life up. I chose to take the pills. It was up to me not to take them." Karla was prescribed opioids to manage pain when she escaped an abusive relationship and has since become addicted. Still, she blames herself for her addiction and depression. Part of Karla's responsibilization narrative is to be clear that she only accepts the social assistance that she absolutely requires – shelter, food, and mental health care, which enables her to differentiate herself from the irredeemable who take advantage of the system and fail to take responsibility for their circumstances. Her claim that she is not "screaming" at the government establishes that she is not demanding compensation or care to which she feels she may be entitled. Instead, she only uses the most basic services and entrusts the rest of her recovery to her own willpower.

Like Karla, Jon spoke at length about the importance of taking ownership of his anxiety and addiction. When asked how mental illness might mitigate this responsibility, he adamantly denied its relevance:

> Well I don't see too much difference with that. Well a little because if I'm taking care of myself, and I'm being responsible, if I'm in recovery and I'm taking care of myself and being responsible for my actions, and my negativity ... If I'm doing that, that makes me that much more happier, and happy for being in [addiction] recovery.

Jon feels mentally well when he is participating in an addiction recovery program, noting that it is his responsibility to access and remain in the program. Being in distress, therefore, is a consequence of his inability to "choose correctly" between following the rules set out by the para-professionals in the programs and following his own inclinations. On the morning of our interview, Jon was ecstatic when he told me that he had just been admitted into the first stage of a three-tier process of a publicly funded in-patient addiction treatment program. In this way, Jon is performing the redeemable identity. He is aware that he cannot govern himself but, ironically, his willingness to be managed in the disciplinary sense is an act of responsibilization necessary to be admitted into the addiction program.

"It's Weakness": Rejecting Common Explanations for Distress

Those who took ownership of their distress were subsequently critical of others who use mental illness, addiction, or histories of trauma to explain their marginalized status. Maruna (2001) contends that individuals who use negative experiences to justify their behaviour are actually embracing normative values and positioning themselves as victims of illness or circumstance rather than seeing their core self as being irredeemable. In this sense, using an excuse is indicative of a desire to be included. The participants in this research project would disagree with this premise. The paramount normative value in the neoliberal era is self-responsibilization, one that programming in the prison and homeless industrial complexes emphasize. Self-governance is a coveted trait that stands in contrast to making excuses. As the participants claimed, using excuses does not allow you to perform the redeemable identity, which calls for uncompromising responsibilization.

Seamus was frustrated by those who use mental illness as an excuse for their marginality:

> I think a lot more of it is done by choice or by decision. Sorry, not by choice by decision. They make a bad decision at one point and it maybe snowballs, and then they end up making more bad decisions. And those decisions may very well be based on a mental illness. It's 'cause I always thought, growing up, always, even though I was mid-twenties, I'm like, "these guys are just weak." They could have got help before if they needed [it], they're not that bad, they were just lazy.

This discourse harkens back to the vagabond typology, which presents the homeless as manipulative and lazy. On further probing, Seamus remarked that despite recently becoming homeless himself, he maintains his opinion that homelessness is equated with weakness. His assertion that "they're not that bad, they [are] just lazy" exemplifies the continuum of exclusion, where avoiding the "bad guy" identity does not mean the "good guy" status is necessarily achievable. Seamus's thoughts on addiction are similar; for example, he recounted an argument he had with his brother:

> I said no it's a choice. Sure it's a disease, they call it a disease. It's a choice. Every morning you decide whether or not you're gonna have a drink that day. "Well it's not that easy for ... " I know it's not that easy. I didn't say that. I said they still decide at some point during that day that they're going to have a drink or they're going to smoke a joint or do some crack or whatever. They decide that. It's a decision. It's a conscious decision. So, this, "but it's a disease, people can't control their diseases." Well I disagree. I do, and again, I'm not saying it's easy for people. It'd probably be the hardest thing they do, *but* every day they do make that choice. They decide. They make a conscious decision whether or not they're going to go to the liquor store and get a drink, or go to their dealer and get some weed, get whatever they're on. It's a decision they make that day, every day, and every time they do it.

On several occasions during the interview, Seamus referred to the distress that other people experiencing homelessness face because of their unwillingness to act responsibly. Seamus did not identify as having a mental illness or an addiction, although he admitted that his drinking was a factor in losing his wife, children, and home and that he lost several bartending jobs because he drank too much while working. Seamus has trouble identifying himself as a "lazy" and "weak" homeless person but recognizes his increased exclusion comes from his poor decisions. While Maté would disagree that an addict's decisions are conscious, Seamus considers reference to any mitigating factors beyond immediate decision making to be making an excuse for inappropriate behaviour.

Unlike Seamus, Max believes his past trauma contributes to his mental illness and addiction but feels he cannot let that deflect from his accountability:

> I was raped by men. It wasn't in prison, this was when I was younger and several times. And I've a really hard time blaming my life and my addiction on something that happened forty years ago, but everybody says, that's what people say, "no that's what you need help with," but to me that's too

much of an excuse, that gets me off too easy. You know 'cause I don't think there's anybody without problems. Some I think it's a factor but I don't think I can let myself off that way.

Max, who has participated in countless mental health and addiction programs over the years, believes in the disease model of mental illness and addiction and is aware of the impact that trauma can have on brain development, but like Seamus, feels his past victimization cannot excuse the daily decisions he makes to drink and use drugs. He attributes his crippling depression to his inability to be assertive, stay motivated, and be content with everyday life. In Max's case his victimization as a young man caused distress, and he used illicit substances to cope. In turn, he was criminalized for this behaviour, which further entrenched his social exclusion. This evolution of marginality can begin to explain how a series of events forty years in the making affects Max's decisions today. Max's contention that framing his distress as a consequence of past trauma "gets me off too easy" retains the individualization of neoliberal governance arrangements. Rose (1999, 2000) defines "anti-citizens" as those who fail to manage their own risk. In this sense, and echoing Seamus, Max feels complicit in his own marginality for getting himself into risky situations.

A number of participants felt that there are people who waste time finding excuses for their marginality rather than using that time to transform themselves. Milan lamented that the people he lives with at Crossroads complain too much:

Well instead of complaining all day long make steps to improve your life, you know? All there is, is complain, complain, complain I hear. Just go and change your life, do something about it. If you want to be here, or if you don't want to be here, just don't complain about it.

Milan takes pride in his father's graduate degrees and his emphasis on intellectual pursuits during his childhood. He recently enrolled in a university program and saw his desire to learn and study as a characteristic of a redeemable subject. For Milan, people who place blame elsewhere are missing key opportunities to work on the project of the self to establish and/ or reinforce their redeemable status.

Interestingly, it was predominantly men who voiced intolerance for using excuses to explain their marginality (Dej, 2018). Although women in this study judged other women for their drug use (especially if they were mothers), cleanliness (or lack thereof), and attitude (rudeness, aggressiveness), among other issues, there was a general acceptance that their histories of trauma and structural and social contexts impact their distress. Women accepted personal blame but were less likely to project that blame onto other women. For example, although Matilda does not feel safe at Haven and is concerned about some of the aggressive and unpredictable women who live there, she has a great deal of sympathy for them:

> So I just, you know, they're doing the best they can but there's people that are not conscious of their behaviour, how they hurt other people. That can be upsetting because you never realize how sometimes people are hurting, eh? And it makes you realize just how hard it is.

Like Seamus, Matilda does not identify as having a mental illness or an addiction, but unlike Seamus, she sympathizes with women in distress and contextualizes their conduct as being related to their mental illness and/or addiction. I offer two reasons why this might be. First, women are socialized to take on the caregiver role, bringing a kind of solidarity among women in the shelter not found among their male counterparts. Examinations of gendered socialization practices suggest that women seek attachment and sustained relationships and thus demonstrate a more established ethic of care than men (Gilligan, 1982). An ethic of care is deeply entrenched in the normalization of womanhood, for example in the essentialization of women within their role as mothers. Women often internalize these sentiments and can refrain from judgment and possess a general concern for others' well-being.

Second, women experiencing homelessness are more likely than housed women to be victims of violence and assault as a cause, and consequence, of homelessness. Intimate partner violence is among the leading causes of women's homelessness and women experiencing homelessness are three times more likely to be victims of sexual assault than women who never experience homelessness (Baker et al., 2010). Indigenous women in particular are three times more likely to experience violence than non-Indigenous women, regardless of their housing status (Brennan, 2011). Situating violence against Indigenous women experiencing homelessness within the context of missing and murdered Indigenous women and girls – which is the result of gender-based genocide where Indigenous women are disproportionately victim to all forms of violence, including murder – reveals the unique and horrific forms of discrimination and ongoing colonialism

Indigenous women face (NIMMIWG, 2019). Because of the high risk of victimization, coupled with normative gender practices that allow women to acknowledge and respond to this victimization differently than men, it is arguable that women experiencing homelessness have a greater appreciation for how trauma and distress impact other women's social conditions. Having greater sympathy and empathy for another woman's history of violent victimization provides important context to the mentally ill and addict identities among women experiencing homelessness, enabling them to recognize the degree to which individualization fails to account for the lasting effects of trauma.

Becoming Empowered through Responsibilization

Although many women recognize the historical and social causes of marginality, this context does not fit within individualized responses to distress. Given the prominence of self-blaming discourses revealed above, it is not surprising that participants identified with individualized treatment approaches aimed at boosting self-esteem and encouraging people to adopt a responsibilized lifestyle. Cruikshank's (1999) interrogation of empowerment reveals that while many efforts to empower people are well intentioned, neoliberal rationalities regarding self-judgment, normalization, and individualized strategies persuade people to seek out socially acceptable goals and to look to themselves to realize these ambitions. Daniel offered compelling insight into how his one-on-one therapy with an addiction counsellor and participation in an outpatient drug treatment program reinvigorated a sense of responsibility that he had lost when he "stepped out of the machine" (read, fell down the exclusion continuum):

> I'm breaking myself down to nothing and I was really given the opportunity to assess who am I? Do I want to? You know and without any pressure, no inner fear or persuasion. It's all up to me. And that's one thing for sure. So I can say "ah those guys aren't doing this and this" but really it's all a choice. Life is all choice. Every day, you know as soon as you open your eyes you make a choice. That empowers you when you realize that everybody in life is exactly where they've chosen to be. But you constantly have to take responsibility, take ownership, over your choices and realize that nobody did this, nobody caused that. It was the way I reacted. Instead of responding, you know and on and on and on. Then it becomes empowering because you click, I'll choose different next time.

In this passage, Daniel fuses the notions of self-blame and responsibilization discussed throughout this chapter. For Daniel, empowerment comes from being the cause of, and solution to, his homelessness and distress. If he "broke" himself, then arguably he can "fix" himself too. Daniel's comment that he is "breaking myself down to nothing" exemplifies the reflexive self-objectification of self-help programs (Cruikshank, 1999; Vaz & Bruno, 2003) that encourages him to treat his mind as a transformative project. The responsible, objective, fearless Daniel will mould and build a new self. In keeping with self-governance strategies, he engages in self-scrutiny in the hope that he will not have to rely on professional surveillance in the future.

While Daniel finds the freedom of self-government empowering, the more prominent discourse among interviewees was that their sense of empowerment comes from a restraint on their freedom. Responsibilization and disciplinary strategies merge as participants gain a more positive sense of self when they cede their decision-making capabilities to authority figures, thus positioning themselves as redeemable, but not redeemed. For some participants, there is such a thing as "too much freedom." Mick suggested the freedom he gained when he separated from his spouse was his undoing: "I guess 2004 I separated. 2006 I started getting really bored of my free life. I was hanging around bars more. And I never did that before, like I was a drinker but I never hung around bars." Mick associates the lack of restrictions on his time that stemmed from the dissolution of his role as husband and active parent with his increasing propensity to drink excessively. Minimized responsibility in one part of his life led to irresponsibility in another, allowing him to conclude that he requires other people to structure his life. Jon recounts his anxiety on his discharge from an in-patient addiction treatment program because he felt he did not have the willpower to stay sober without the structure of an insulated treatment environment: "I knew I was going to pick up because I had that freedom. I had no one there to say, 'don't do it.' About two or three days later I picked up." Bauman (1988) argues that people who are controlled are made to be incapable of being free. Jon situates his recovery journey within responsibilization discourses that position his acquiescence to disciplinary control as recognition of his shift toward self-governance.

Similar arrangements play out in prison. With few chances to exercise freedom, some individuals become weighed down by disciplinary technologies and lose the motivation and self-assuredness needed to practise freedom (Bosworth, 2007; Kilty, 2012; Pollack, 2009). Disciplinary regimes can exclude people to such an extent that gaining independence no longer seems viable or preferable. When marginalized people are deprived of opportunities for self-determination and self-fulfillment for long enough, disciplinary discourses and practices come to inform their ideas of what responsibility and self-esteem look like (Rose, 1996). Mick and Jon, both of whom had spent years in jail, treatment centres, and emergency shelters, do not feel capable of navigating their lives independently and making decisions that are conducive to securing housing, managing distress, and maintaining sobriety. In keeping with responsibilization discourses, Mick and Jon see their potential failure as an individual fault rather than as affected in part by the governing techniques that smother acts of freedom. In this case, empowerment, and in turn the redeemable status, come from being accountable and self-aware enough to defer decision-making ability regarding housing, time and money management, and treatment options to authority figures. Achieving the redeemable status requires acknowledging that an individual cannot meet the ideals of inclusion without professional support.

Interestingly, J. J. is the only participant who spoke directly about his personal sense of freedom, or lack thereof:

> Freedom is a good thing or a bad thing. You can have so much freedom that we get to pick our own poison. You know what I mean? We have too much freedom in this country sometimes. So don't abuse that. Find some balance in you, in your decisions. Your freedom is your decision to make, but it's also your consequences to suffer. So freedom is a good thing if you don't abuse it.

J. J.'s comment parallels Bauman's (1988) take on freedom:

> One is free to pursue (and, with luck, to achieve) one's aims, but one is also free to err. The first comes with the second, in a package deal. Being free, you can be sure that no one will prohibit the actions you wish to undertake. But you are not offered any certainty that what you wish to do, and do, will bring you the benefit you expect, or benefit at all for that matter. (pp. 1–2)

Both J. J. and Bauman describe the obligations of freedom. After years of mental health and addiction treatment, J. J. found that it is in his best interest to give up his freedom to others to make day-to-day decisions regarding his routine and lifestyle. He has expertly navigated the system to acquire services and support that many others experiencing homelessness struggle to access. His support system is made up of a Canadian Mental Health Association (CMHA) worker, counsellors in the shelter, his AA sponsor, and the counsellor who runs a trauma group, among others. J. J. uses these authority figures, all of whom are tied up in these neoliberal projects and strategies that emphasize individual responsibility, to instruct him on how to manage his feelings and change his behaviour. Combined, these para-professionals are responsible for his housing, psychotropic medication, and time management. As per Jon's and J. J.'s narratives, it is ironic that to be considered redeemable people must have enough self-discipline to know that they need assistance to govern themselves appropriately.

J. J. identifies himself as a redeemable subject because he adopts self-help discourses. When asked why he has success accessing services when so many others are unable to find resources or are kept on wait-lists for counselling or housing for years,[3] J. J. replied, "I got with the program. I got with the program where I was becoming one of the poster child[ren]." J. J. quite literally became several organizations' poster child, having his story featured in promotional material and his art hanging in their offices. By obeying the programs' rules, regulations, and recommendations, J. J. earns high praise among professionals and para-professionals. His sense of self-worth comes from his openness to being managed by others. He is a "true believer" in that he unquestioningly accepts the disciplinary strategies invoked by the various mental health and addiction programs. In their study of drug treatment courts, Moore and Hirai (2014) found that even among those participants who internalize the responsibilization discourses touted by its programs, they remain excluded because those same strategies that seek to empower them also call on them to acknowledge and cement their excluded status. The same can be said for J. J. His prospects for becoming fully included are small; indeed, the disciplinary tactics he engages in do not align with how mainstream society understands inclusion (i.e., full autonomy). J. J. has lived in subsidized housing for years but continues to rely on shelters and other service providers to meet his basic needs. There are wonderful stories of people who have beaten the odds and become fully independent (in the mainstream sense of the term) and achieved included status. These stories are without a doubt inspiring and should be celebrated. The homelessness industrial complex and recovery industry often position these stories as pillars of the individualized, medicalized model and use them as examples that everyone can escape homelessness if they just work hard enough. However, many people, like J. J., remain excluded but can strive to be among the most redeemable of the excluded, a subject explored in detail in the next chapter.

Conclusion

The purpose of this chapter is to provide a counter-narrative to the claim that people experiencing homelessness adopt a medicalized understanding of mental illness and addiction as a way to deflect blame for their circumstances. Findings from this research reveal that this is not the case. While there was a small but vocal segment of participants who are critical of the medical model, most could be described as "true believers," embracing a medicalized understanding of their situation. At its most simplistic, biological determinism connotes futility in trying to offset the effects of biologically pre-determined behaviour, but when combined with responsibilization discourses through the biopsychological model, it creates a powerful discourse that establishes distress and addiction as medical issues that can be ameliorated through individual accountability. "Fixing" the brain through disciplinary tactics becomes part of the overarching governing rationale through which people experiencing homelessness can move toward redeemability, and for some, feel empowered by the hope that comes with having a way forward. Rather than trying to avoid blame, people in this study overwhelmingly expressed culpability for their homelessness, mental illness, addiction, and criminalization because, ultimately, they felt accountable for their circumstances.

Most participants felt such a strong sense of personal responsibility that some vilified others who explained their homelessness as deriving from mental illness or addiction. Some people regarded their peers who adopted the medical discourse but omitted responsibilization logics as "making excuses" and failing to take ownership of their lives. This negotiation between various discourses provides further evidence that adopting the medical model does not deflect blame. Rather than acting as a justification for people experiencing homelessness, as members of the public regularly suggest to me, people experiencing homelessness who adopt the medical model but do not couch it in responsibilization techniques garner more contempt from those around them than if they had disregarded the medical model altogether.

Merging biological determinist and responsibilization narratives drives solutions to distress and homelessness toward empowering people to make "good" choices in order to rewire the brain. These solutions individualize, and therefore minimize, the reality of living on the margins and the immense difficulty of escaping homelessness. This leaves little space to explore the structural and systemic limitations within which people must make these choices. Emphasizing personal responsibility for social marginalization and solutions to homelessness leads some participants to situate themselves as homeless mental health consumers as a method of demonstrating their redeemability.

6

The Homeless Mental Health Consumer: Managing Exclusion through Redeemability

Throughout this book I have examined various ways people experiencing homelessness are managed and their responses to these forms of social control. While I have pointed to sites of negotiation and resistance, strategies that limit personal autonomy dominate. There are copious examples of disciplinary techniques that curtail freedom: for instance, curfews, expectations of sobriety to access certain services, and the criminalization of panhandling and tent cities. Still, people who are homeless find ways to assert control over their lives. A sense of dignity, purpose, and autonomy comes from achieving the *redeemable* status – that is, positioning themselves and being looked on favourably by staff and professionals as working toward inclusion by engaging in self-surveillance and responsibilization strategies. Mental health resources are valuable tools for those wanting to attain redeemability that allow people to work on their project of the self, empower them, and aid them in self-discipline. The mental health system can situate those experiencing homelessness as included within an otherwise exclusionary environment.

Inclusion, exclusion, and redeemability exist within the modern capitalist system where spending power demarcates someone's worth. People without the financial capital to participate as "true" consumers can position themselves as consumers of public systems, fuelling the homelessness industrial complex. In this way, many people experiencing homelessness are active in shaping their lives and claiming their identity and are not merely passive recipients of charity or treatment. Those who use the mental health system to establish themselves as *homeless mental health consumers* must accept the pathologization and individualization of their circumstances with the implicit promise that, through self-improvement, social inclusion is possible. However, the programs and services available in the homelessness sector almost always target individual rather than social problems, and rarely lead to social inclusion, leaving many people permanently redeem*able* but never fully redeem*ed*. We also must consider the fate of those who cannot or will not play the homeless mental health consumer role and who are thus cast as *irredeemable*.

Rags Where Riches Are Required: Poverty and Homelessness in Consumer Society

Consumption, as a concept, is benign. To consume is to use up. Consumption is reframed as consumerism when the ability to appropriate an ever-expanding list of desirable items becomes the driving force in developing and maintaining the social fabric. We are now a society of consumers where consumption has become an end in and of itself. In a consumer society, our social identity is intimately associated with our consumptive habits (Bauman, 2007). We understand who we are through what we consume – be it the model of phone we have, the kind of food we buy, or the neighbourhood we rent or purchase our home in. The freedom of the neoliberal era goes hand in hand with the rights of the consumer. Consumption also becomes our responsibility. Our obligations as good, neoliberal citizens rest on our willingness to consume. For example, during the 2008 global economic crisis, governments and central banks throughout the global North stressed citizens' obligation to spend money and created incentives like low interest rates to encourage people to buy big-ticket items like cars and houses. We see similar economic strategies emerging during the COVID-19 pandemic, which is unfolding at the time of writing.

Consumer society promises to fulfill our desires, empower us, and allow us to gain individual autonomy. This leaves consumers in a perpetual state of want. We are told that we must be continuously happy, never feel discomfort, sadness, longing, or pain, and that the only way to avoid these experiences is through ongoing consumption (Bauman, 2007). The happiness industry (Ahmed, 2010) tells us that purchasing products and services is the (only) road to fulfillment. Bauman (2007) contends that it is too simplistic to argue that consumerism brings happiness;

rather consumerism builds on the political economy of hope where the prospect of personal well-being is monetized. In order to ensure continual consumption, people must remain unsatisfied. The contentment someone feels by acquiring the latest iPhone quickly dissipates when a few months later a newer, flashier model is released, rendering the "old" product obsolete. The promise of happiness, coupled with the reality that products and services are not designed to create long-term feelings of satisfaction, allows consumer society to propel itself forward without ever reaching an end.

Given the political economy of hope that is ensconced in consumer society, it is no wonder that consumerism is positioned as a method for realizing the neoliberal project of the self. To properly work on the self necessarily means to consume. "Caring for the soul" (Rose, 1999, p. 84) is branded by the psy-discipline as purchasing a variety of mental health products and services. Both consumption and the project of the self rely on individuals to identify their needs and be proactive and enterprising in seeking out what goods and services will help them achieve self-actualization, be it self-help books, therapy, or psychotropic medication. The project of the self is a never-ending search for improvement that requires the continuous acquisition of consumer goods – the same goods that will inevitably be unsatisfying. This system creates a tautology whereby consuming products to achieve the best self will always fall short, requiring further self-scrutiny and discipline that results in purchasing new consumer products that are short-lived ... and so the cycle continues.

If the project of the self necessitates consumptive practices, why are self-improvement programs and services geared to those experiencing homelessness, who do not have the resources to be consumers? Neoliberal society equates the ability to consume with an individual's moral character; in a society of free consumers, failure to consume or inappropriate consumption (such as consuming substances illicitly) is characterized as a poor choice and those who do not adequately participate in the consumer culture are characterized as failures who bring about their own exclusion.

The Flawed Consumer

Individuals who fail to consume are regarded as "waste," "redundant," and, indeed, "flawed" or "failed" consumers. Those who cannot or choose not to take on the consumer role are merely spectators, passively watching others consume (Bauman, 2004, 2007; Young, 1999). In contrast, Reith (2004) outlines how addiction acts as consumerism run amok:

> The notion of addiction turns the sovereign consumer on its head, transforming freedom into determinism and desire into need. Rather than consuming to realize the self, in the state of addiction, the individual is consumed *by* consumption; the self destroyed. Whereas the consumer *chooses* to act, addicts are *forced* to do so. [emphasis in original] (p. 286)

Here, consumption is inextricably linked with the obligations of freedom described in Chapter 1. Flawed consumers do not consume products that are in keeping with normative ways of being and fail to demonstrate self-regulation through their consumptive habits.[1]

Flawed consumers are not only excluded but are constituted as enemies of consumer society (Bauman, 1998). The flawed consumer's reliance on social assistance, for example, comes at the expense of "good" neoliberal consumer citizens, supposedly limiting their ability to consume by taxing their income. As a mode of regulation, consumer society vilifies those living on the margins as "outside of the 'consuming civility'" (Rose, 1999, p. 87), and thus requiring other forms of regulation, including surveillance and discipline by the criminal justice system. Because social problems such as poverty are configured as ill-advised choices, "the poor are envisioned as lacking the necessary levels of competence, intention, and willpower to responsibly manage their daily (market) activities" (Stuart, 2016, p. 13). Despite the dominant rhetoric, many vulnerable individuals do not position themselves as necessarily and completely outside of consuming society. Critical criminological scholarship tells us that rather than being separate from the consuming world, we might frame flawed consumers as clients of disciplinary systems.

Tracing the Client in the Prison and Psychiatric Hospital

Orienting the flawed consumer as a client is not a new practice. The mental health, addiction, and criminal justice sectors all rely on the client subjectivity to varying degrees. As described in Chapter 1, broadly conceived, the mad movement is made up of psychiatric survivors and consumers. While survivors tend to reject medical intervention and perceive the psychiatric system as causing violence, oppression, and coercion, consumers view their role within the mental health system as collaborators and partners

(Diamond, 2013; McLean, 2000). Framing the mad person as a consumer is a strategy readily adopted by some individuals, families, psy-professionals, mental health care administrators, and government agencies because it presents the mental health client as an autonomous, self-determining individual of the mental health system (Burstow, 2013; McLean, 2000).

Likewise, professionals, para-professionals, and other service providers constitute the addict (specifically those who use substances illicitly) and the criminal as clients looking for guidance in treatment centres, harm reduction sites, and prison programs to gain the necessary skills and competencies to become self-sufficient, active citizens (Fischer et al., 2004). The criminal justice system positions certain people in conflict with the law as clients, especially those who are characterized as damaged individuals in need, rather than inherently deviant and unmanageable (Donohue & Moore, 2009).

How subjugated individuals are imbued with the features of a consumer – that is, free and empowered – within oppressive regimes such as the prison, psychiatric hospital, or, I argue, homeless industrial complex, is undertheorized. The findings from this research make it clear that orienting some marginalized people as clients requires them to accept the pathologization and the individualization of distress. Individuals must recognize the personal failings that led to their exclusion in order to be empowered to work on the project of the self. The narrow focus on individual problems and the pathologization of social conditions, for instance poverty and structural violence related to discrimination and colonialism, fit well within a consumerist ethos that is concerned with maximizing personal gain. It is difficult to imagine consumable products to alleviate unequal and unfair wage distribution, reduce the explosive rate of young Black and Indigenous Peoples in North American correctional facilities, or eliminate gender-based violence. But it *is* easy to create products and programs targeting impulse control problems, dependency issues, and irrational cognitive patterns. To be considered a client of the social welfare, mental health, or criminal justice systems, an individual must be prepared to accept their personal failings and to consume the available remedies.

Critical criminological and mad studies scholars have begun to chip away at understanding client subjectivity within disciplinary settings like the correctional facility and psychiatric hospital. Situating oneself as a consumer of treatment and services can be positive and empowering; consumers can assess their needs and choose among the services offered for what best suits them (Prior, 2011). Of course, one must earn the privilege of choosing a program by successfully positioning oneself as redeemable (that is, demonstrating a willingness to adopt normative ways of being) (Cook & Jonikas, 2002). This approach also assumes that there are multiple products to choose from, a far cry from the programs and services available in many jails, prisons, and psychiatric hospitals[2] and in most homeless-serving organizations across the country. For those implicated in the criminal justice and/or mental health systems, there is a constant threat that their freedom of choice will be withdrawn if they fail to make "appropriate" choices. In this way, the client subjectivity in the criminal justice system recruits individuals to participate in their own punishment and correction (Donohue & Moore, 2009). The same is true for the mental health system, where patients must comply with treatment plans (primarily medication regimes) to be discharged and/or maintain access to services (Fabris, 2011; Klassen, 2016). The consumer model, when applied to marginalized groups, uses the obligations of freedom to manipulate and ultimately impede people's choice.

In a system built on the dominant discourses of professional knowledges, most notably those of psy-professionals, consumer choice and a client-centred approach often involve a tokenistic gesture, such as having a single client representative on a board or committee, rather than a genuine attempt to transform the mental health system. Instead of promoting real change, the consumer discourse veils the coerciveness embedded within institutions of social control and reimagines disciplinary tactics as a matter of choice (Burstow, 2013; Fabris, 2013). To practise consumerism is to engage in choice-making, an option that is not found among prisoners or some mental health consumers as clients. As Donohue and Moore (2009) write: "The notion that people in conflict with the law have choice or empowerment or agency afforded to them by the State is perhaps one of the greatest (if not most effective) mythologies of contemporary punishment" (p. 329). Prisoners and those identified as mentally ill may have some choice in which services they use, but it is often mandatory that they work on the project of the self in some sort of formal, expert-driven, and normalized capacity. In this way, the homeless consumer presents slightly differently than the "client" in the criminal justice or mental health systems. For people experiencing homelessness, there are strong incentives to participate in treatment programs and connect with mental health services but as neoliberal total institutions, shelters and homeless-serving agencies do not possess many of the overtly coercive elements found in prisons and psychiatric hospitals. Most individuals experiencing homelessness are not *required* to participate in programming, and a handful of research participants in this study asserted that freedom. However, there are consequences to ignoring the advice of the professionals in the homelessness industrial complex. Those whom professionals and para-professionals regard as failing to take responsibility for their situation and engage in self-discipline risk being cast as irredeemable.

Much of the consumerism literature among marginalized people assumes that flawed consumers cannot be consumers at all. Crook and Wood (2014) argue: "Because they can't be true consumers they have little incentive to try to be consumers at all" (p. 62). Among people experiencing homelessness, however, the notion of the flawed consumer is more complex. Rather than resist consumer culture, many people who are homeless practise consumerism by positioning themselves as clients of the mental health system and/or homelessness industrial complex. Many people experiencing homelessness have the freedom to choose if and how to manage their pathologies, but to be considered redeemable and reap the rewards of that status they must adopt individualized and medicalized explanations for their homelessness and its treatment.

Aiming for Inclusion

Many (although not all) people who took part in this research sought inclusion, with some taking deliberate steps to demonstrate their commitment to the normalizing qualities expected in the included society. Many individuals experiencing homelessness use the mental health system as one of the key avenues to perform the redeemable status. These methods are founded on a sense of hope that with persistence they will achieve inclusion. As noted throughout this book, inclusion and exclusion exist along a continuum and vary depending on one's position in any given local context (i.e., I feel like I belong on my university campus and in my local coffee shop, but would not be included at an elite country club or at a rave). While the nuances of the inclusion-exclusion continuum are crucial to the theoretical orientation of this book, there are also numerous instances where people experiencing homelessness spoke of inclusion as an end-game, as if there were an obvious but invisible line they might pass to feel part of the mainstream world. Just what that line looks like is different for each person and they may not know precisely what inclusion is until they get there. Generally, though, we can describe inclusion as a point in time and/or space where someone can stop living in survival mode, unsure of whether they will have food to the end of the month or their housing until the end of the year, where they are no longer regularly surveilled by social services and/or police, and where they have an overall sense of well-being.

Becoming a Better Person: Performing the Homeless Mental Health Consumer Role

The driving goal for many people in this study was to escape marginalization and achieve social inclusion. To do this, people experiencing homelessness look to reform what dominant discourses describe are the sources of their exclusion: their individual biography, personal flaws, and lack of skills (Hannah-Moffat, 2000b; Lyon-Callo, 2000, 2004). Services offered in the homelessness sector, such as mental health treatment (almost exclusively medication), addiction treatment (largely group therapy and some in-patient treatment centres and one-on-one counselling), and CBT (such as anger-management programming), are steeped within individualized understandings of distress and marginalization. There are no programs or services that highlight how inequitable wealth distribution, the low vacancy rate, or the dearth of affordable housing stock[3] impact people's personal experiences of homelessness and perpetuate the homelessness crisis across Canada.

Given the orientation of the services offered through the homelessness industrial complex it is no wonder that participants emphasized the importance of working on the project of the self to gain acceptance into the included world. Indeed, there is little alternative language, and few alternative knowledges and techniques to inform their perspectives. Programs not embedded within psy-knowledges are usually regarded by professionals as illegitimate (Stuart, 2016). Individualized discourses shaped participants' visions about what it meant to be a better version of themselves and, importantly, about how becoming the new-and-improved self would lead to inclusion. Mick explained:

> Like I look at a bigger picture ... so that I know that ok, whatever I have to do now is really key ... I'll learn to have fun again, know, meet somebody, get in another relationship, have a normal life. But I know I have to be healthy to do that ... then I can grow and be a better person and a better friend and a partner, and a worker, and a father, and a brother, and a son, you know. I'll be better at those things. I'll be healthier, so that's a lifelong journey ... I'm doing better. And that's the other thing is that I measure my progress and as long, I don't care how small the increment is, as long as it's, I'm better now than I was yesterday.

Mick was ecstatic that he was finding order and peace in his life. Based on programs that tout inclusive ideals, he saw his self-improvement as inevitably leading to inclusion. Mick stated that the effort he puts into his project of the self is part of a "bigger picture," one that he identifies as becoming "normal" and being reintegrated into the community through his personal relationships. The obligations of freedom necessary for inclusion require that an individual behave civilly, engage in self-surveillance, and make responsible choices. Mick works on himself primarily through mental health and addiction treatment. At the time of the interview Mick attended several group therapy sessions each week (AA, NA, the outpatient treatment program run by the shelter, and group therapy program) and was having his PTSD, OCD, social phobia, and ADD diagnoses reassessed by a psychiatrist.

By noting, "that's a lifelong journey," Mick reiterates the commonly held narrative that self-actualization can never truly be achieved and that the project of the self is permanently ongoing (Rimke, 2000; Rose, 1999). While Mick is hopeful that making these incremental changes will lead to social inclusion, his years of homelessness, time spent in jail, and significant distress and substance use challenges make inclusion extremely difficult given the structural and systemic barriers he faces. Mick's narrative speaks to Berlant's (2011) notion of "cruel optimism." Cruel optimism occurs when someone orients their present to fixate on a specific idea of the future. The cruelty lies in a person organizing their present life for a future that may or may not become a reality and where that organization is problematic or at times counterproductive to them reaching their goal. In this case, individualizing the causes of homelessness with the aim of full inclusion in the future can have the effect of entrenching someone in pathologizing and disciplinary discourses that can make attaining inclusion difficult. Here, I use the concept to highlight the ways that some people experiencing homelessness regard the present as continuously at an impasse until such time as they reach full inclusion.

By taking medication consistently, subjecting himself to mental health assessments, and regularly attending outpatient addiction treatment, Mick seeks services that will regulate his life and thereby enable him to achieve inclusion. These services have positive effects for Mick and likely others, but they are not designed to address the broader structural challenges that arguably have just as much, if not a greater, impact on marginalization than do individual factors, and so are unlikely to lead to inclusion. Mick and others aspire to a time when they can work on themselves independently from the direct supervision of psy-experts and para-professionals. The self as an unfinished project suits consumer society where perpetual dissatisfaction is necessary for continual consumption (Bauman, 2007). The proliferation of the self-help/self-improvement industry exemplifies the symbiotic relationship between self-regulative techniques and consumerism. In the case of people who are homeless, they gear their consumptive habits toward publicly funded mental health resources – specifically medication.

Many research participants sought out mental health services in part to position themselves as moving toward inclusion. This trajectory contrasts with the critical discourse that asserts that the mental health system is strictly a coercive and oppressive method of social control that is used against people's will (Wynn, 2006). The system can and does invoke coercive strategies, as evidenced through involuntary hospitalization and the use of CTOs to enforce medication compliance, for example. However, those seeking a path to inclusion regard the mental health system as a tool for self-improvement, accountability, and normalization through their position as homeless mental health consumers. Similar to Donohue and Moore's (2009) argument that prisoners become participants in their own punishment, some people experiencing homelessness actively engage with the strategies offered by the mental health system that inevitably lead to stricter disciplinary controls. Perhaps we can explain the voluntary acceptance of the mentally ill identity because as long as those who claim this identity maintain the redeemable status, management techniques are considered voluntary, which demonstrates an important distinction between the prisoner and homeless subjectivities.[4]

Diagnosis as Entrée into Mental Health Consumption

Obtaining a mental illness diagnosis is a popular (although not always necessary) method for becoming a mental health consumer. Many participants received mental illness diagnoses passively, through their interactions with various psy-professionals. Participants were diagnosed by general practitioners, addiction specialists, and psychiatrists visiting homeless shelters. Some were diagnosed in hospital after suicide attempts, as children, or while incarcerated. Conversely, others actively sought a diagnosis as a way to participate in mental health consumerism. Milan pursued a mental health assessment so that he could "fix" the personal flaws that he identified as leading to his exclusion: "I'm just happy that I know that, you know, I have a name I can put on and I can use medicine or exercise and I just want to move forward, just, not knowing what's wrong with your head is the worst part." Milan was diagnosed with bipolar disorder four months prior to the interview. He saw a diagnosis as the first step to becoming a homeless mental health consumer. Because he was looking to pursue post-secondary education, he felt he needed a diagnosis to perform adequately:

> I had a miniature depression two years ago and I still didn't go see the doctor, I just left for a couple of months but this time it's because I was in school and it affected my school work, and my interest went spinning with too many, thousand miles an hour, and it was affecting my school so I went to see a mental health nurse and she referred me to a psychiatric doctor and they diagnosed me with bipolar.

Given his father's emphasis on education, Milan wholeheartedly believes that a university degree is the key to escaping exclusion. Milan used his prescription mood stabilizers and antidepressants to gain entrée into included society and keep up with those who are included. By identifying his struggles as the result of mental illness, Milan adopts the homeless mental health consumer role to work on his project of the self.

Not everyone is keen to pursue a mental illness diagnosis. Christine offers one such example. After a shelter counsellor referred her to a psychiatrist, she was diagnosed with OCD. She did not accept the diagnosis and did not feel that the psychiatrist was truly interested in helping her resolve the issues she identified as leading to her incarceration and homelessness (drug addiction, an abusive relationship, and trauma from her brother's suicide): "I said, go walk in my shoes for one week instead of reading that book there, like, you're probably born with a silver spoon in your mouth ... I said, walk a week in my shoes and then come talk to me, you know?" Christine calls out the psychiatrist's class privilege to reorient the doctor/patient power dynamics and subsequently dismisses the diagnosis and medication offered. Instead, Christine accesses Clonazepam, a benzodiazepine used to treat anxiety and panic disorders, on the street. She was prescribed Clonazepam when she was twelve years old and the drug has since been found to be addictive. Christine's limited use of the mental health system can be characterized as a transgression (Bosworth & Carrabine, 2001), where she disrupts the sane/insane binary and uses the mental health system in a way that suits her needs. Christine rejected the OCD diagnosis but wanted to find a mental health worker and one-on-one counselling. She intended to use these services to develop a relationship with a confidante rather than simply accept a medicalized understanding of her homelessness. Christine embodies the client role by choosing how and what aspects of the mental health system she employs. At the same time, Christine's situation highlights the paucity of support systems available in the homelessness sector that exist outside of the mental health and addiction systems. She relies on the mental health system to manage her loneliness and isolation because that is all that is available to her. This, along with her inability to access the medication of her choice, reveals the limitations of what it means to be a homeless mental health consumer.

Hope at the Bottom of a Pill Bottle

In order to position oneself as a homeless mental health consumer one must, of course, consume something. If citizenship in the late modern era is concomitant with participating in the economic market, then those striving for inclusion must use up appropriate goods and services that have monetary worth. Because most people experiencing homelessness do not have the financial capital to participate significantly in the market, they can act out the consumer role by using publicly funded resources. In doing so, the homelessness industrial complex remains socially and economically viable. Welfarist programming is antithetical to the neoliberal capitalist agenda that decries public intervention in the market, so homeless mental health consumers must consume public products that demonstrate their redeemability and movement toward inclusion. They must counteract long-standing criticisms that they are permanently dependent on "good" consuming citizens and demonstrate that they are not "enemies" of the inclusive consuming society (Bauman, 1998; Reith, 2004). Public sentiments regarding welfarist programming tends to be favourable when services are geared toward people who are viewed as "deserving" of support, specifically people identified as mentally ill and victims of intimate partner violence (Doberstein & Smith, 2019). Taking up the homeless mental health consumer identity, then, aligns with populist notions of who is worthy of public investment. It also reinforces the pathologization of homelessness and "impl[ies] that people need and deserve assistance in the form of housing *because they are sick*. Everyone else, it would follow, should be able to get by without much public help, or does not deserve it" [emphasis in original] (Katz et al., 2017, p. 142). If the homeless mental health consumer can claim that they are a victim of their mental illness and demonstrate their dedication to responsibilized and normalized ways of being, using public resources can be considered an investment in the consumerist project.

Some interviewees remarked on what it means to be a "client" of a shelter. Referencing the power imbalance between staff and residents discussed in Chapter 3, Seamus contended:

I hate to say it but bottom line is, you know, [frontline staff] are getting paid to serve us. Really. And, they act the other way, like they're doing us a service. Which, it's kinda, another huge grey area. They are doing this huge, huge service but it's not them personally it's [Crossroads] doing us a *huge* service, a huge service. But these guys take it upon themselves and they seem to feel that they're doing it personally as, you know, if it wasn't for us where would you guys be?

Like all programs, the homelessness industrial complex requires people to fill its beds and register for its programs to receive funding (Smith, 2007).[5] Seamus reframes the homeless person's position as necessary for the continued employment of shelter staff. In this way, those using services in the homelessness sector are clients whom the industry must solicit to remain viable (for example, the City requires statistics on the number of individuals staying in a shelter each night and many grants require programs to undergo evaluations, demonstrating their outputs, outcomes, and efficiencies to renew funding). By asserting that "they're getting paid to serve us," Seamus resists the dominant discourse that marginalized people are simply passive recipients of social assistance and reorients them as clients of the industry.

The most common form of consumption in the mental health system is, not surprisingly, psychotropic medication. The pathologization of homelessness comes with the widespread use of psychopharmaceuticals in the homelessness sector as well as the public at large.[6] Kathy, a public health nurse, acknowledged that she is commonly referred to as the "Seroquel queen" for using medication as the sole method of treatment, noting: "My job is primarily to see people, assess if there's any mental health issues, if they're agreeable, and if necessary help them start on medication. I monitor them, try to treat with medication. So I don't do counselling." Medication is the first and usually the only response to distress in the homelessness sector.

Many of the research participants spoke very positively about their experiences with medication. Julien, for example, was hopeful that with the right medication he could build a new life: "There's always hope and there's better days coming." Julien's narrative speaks to Rose's (2007) conception of hope as "our gaze to the horizon" (p. 135), noting that hope for a better future is fuelled by the choices and behaviours we make today. Here again we see the ways that cruel optimism projects itself, where the present is regarded as the moment *right before* something truly special unfolds before our eyes. If it does not, we look to the next moment, and the next, as a way to protect the life-sustaining optimism within us. Julien maintains a positive outlook on his future, hopeful that when doctors find the right medication combination he will gain the privilege of acting as an independent consumer.

Echoing Julien, Mac never misses a dose of his cocktail of Effexor[7], Seroquel, and methadone treatment to help him keep his composure:

> They help with violence. They keep me calm. They help with depression 'cause I still do suffer. They help so that I can stay washed and clean, and get up out of bed. And help me to look after myself. And so, I'm doing well on them, as opposed to when I wasn't on them and I was lost.

For Mac, the medication is vital to gaining some self-control so that he can fulfill the obligations of daily life, such as maintaining basic hygiene. Mac sees his efforts toward sobriety and mental well-being as his job to become an included citizen. Remarking on the in-patient addiction treatment program where he received PTSD, depression, and anxiety diagnoses, Mac described his recovery efforts as work: "It was really hard actually, and I worked thirteen hours a day on myself ... My counsellor was on afternoons so when he would start at three o'clock, I continued to work 'til eleven o'clock at night so, I was basically working twelve hours a day." Mac associates the time and effort he spent writing his life story and participating in group and one-on-one therapy with the kind of paid work practised by those who are included, taking literally Goffman's (1961) notion of the moral "career" of the mental patient. By noting "I worked thirteen hours a day on myself," Mac positions his self as an object to evaluate, discipline, and judge under the guidance of psy-experts and para-professionals. Mac's narrative exemplifies Rimke's (2000) assertion that the self is simultaneously an object of knowledge and a subject of governance. Mac's self is a product of the recovery industry, one that he has a hand in creating, while simultaneously acting as a client of the addiction and mental health systems, consuming medication and treatment programs with the aim of bettering himself.

Mac's moral career, like that of so many other participants, involves a combination of addiction and mental health services situated within the homelessness sector that formulate a complex web of treatment and social control strategies. Only one participant, Giles, had access to group therapy specifically devoted to mental health, and Mac, Courtney, and Katie attended a concurrent disorders group run by the Canadian Mental Health Association (CMHA) and the Royal Ottawa Hospital (ROH). More commonly, mental health treatment other than medication consists primarily of crisis counselling run out of drop-in centres and community health centres, conversations with case managers and frontline service providers in homeless-serving agencies, and discussions of mental health in addiction treatment programs.[8] Indeed, as noted above, some individuals received mental illness diagnoses from addiction specialists. Research participants often spoke of learning about PTSD, anxiety, and ADHD in outpatient addiction treatment programs run by the shelters. The tools they were taught to cope with addiction, such as mindfulness and emotional control, were repurposed to help them manage their distress.

Consuming medication and using services offered in the homelessness sector can be regarded positively by people experiencing homelessness while also acting as tools to perform the consumer role and thus display their potential for inclusion. Despite the prospect of inclusion offered by many of these resources, however, the reality is that it is extremely difficult for people who are chronically homeless to escape marginality and precariousness completely and become fully included.

Redeemable but Never Redeemed: The Reality of the Homeless Mental Health Consumer

Despite its footing within a political economy of hope, inclusion in mainstream society remains elusive for many homeless mental health consumers. Some people's experiences of homelessness are recurrent, where they experience periods of housing or institutionalization (i.e., incarceration or hospitalization) followed by homelessness (Mayock & Parker, 2019; Roca et al., 2019). Not surprisingly, those with a history of incarceration tend to have less success exiting homelessness compared to those who have not been imprisoned (Kerman et al., 2018; To et al., 2016). The challenge of exiting homelessness is compounded by the subsequent difficulty to remain permanently housed. Kidd et al.'s (2016) study found that rather than citing a clear distinction between homeless and housed, young people described a gradual movement out of homelessness. In fact, those who managed to secure long-term housing often experienced a sense of hopelessness when they discovered that their quality of life did not substantively improve and that it was a constant struggle to make ends meet. For some young people their mental health declined as they had a chance to reflect on past trauma, along with experiencing the depression, loneliness, and anxiety of fending for themselves. The finding that many of the elements of homelessness – a struggle to meet basic needs, relying on social services as a means of survival, and surveillance by various organizations – continues even when someone finds housing is echoed in the adult population (Phillips, 2016). For example, one of the few forms of affordable housing in urban centres are rooming houses, where people are at risk of victimization, instability, and difficulty accessing basic provisions, such as food and clothing. In fact, the *Health and Housing in Transition Study* revealed that the physical and mental health of rooming house residents were slightly worse than their homeless counterparts given the lack of access to services and supports because they did not "count" as homeless (Binch et al., 2018; Hwang et al., 2011). This reality further complicates the notion of redeemability, where people must display norms related to inclusion to access services and supports, and have affirming interactions with staff, but not be close enough to inclusion to be deemed ineligible for services.

Unfortunately, many people who do exit homelessness cite their quality of life as low, as they remain deeply entrenched in poverty and tend to rely heavily on social assistance, especially rent supplements and charitable services, to maintain their housing (Phillips, 2016; Wallace et al., 2019). Results from Housing First (HF) programs reveal that while people's housing stability significantly improves, other outcome measures such as community integration, financial stability, and social inclusion do not (O'Campo et al., 2016; Quilgars & Pleace, 2016; Stergiopoulos et al., 2015). This is problematic because research shows that people need more than secure housing to garner a sense of well-being when exiting homelessness. Social support, people to rely on, and a sense of community have strong independent effects on individual well-being and are crucial to successfully breaking the homelessness cycle (Clapham, 2010; Johnstone et al., 2016). With HF programs and other resources stretched so thin, supporting people to build strong networks is rare, with the exception of some peer-support programs. But without accounting for and nurturing community integration, it is exceptionally difficult for people to permanently exit from homelessness. If this is the case, we must account for how the redeemable status plays out in the homeless industrial complex and consider the reasons why some individuals accept the limits of being redeemable but not redeemed.

"Just Like Prostitutes": Critically Assessing the Mental Health Consumer Role

The mental health and addiction treatment services available to those experiencing homelessness play into the political economy of hope by suggesting that through active engagement in mental health care people experiencing homelessness can become their best selves and escape homelessness and marginality. Many of the research participants in this project spoke very positively about their choices to access the mental health system and take psychotropic medication, and about their prospects for future inclusion. The fact that mental health techniques are positioned as a panacea rather than as complementary to the root causes of homelessness, including poverty, a lack of affordable housing, colonialism, discrimination, and other inequities, reproduces cruel optimism (Berlant, 2011), where the hope for a better future distorts the reality of the present. Not all interviewees were optimistic about the outcomes of identifying as a homeless mental health consumer. Otto, for example, was acutely aware of how positioning himself as a client of the mental health and addiction systems benefits the recovery industry more than himself:

> I always thought ADHD was one more little catch phrase or excuse to sell drugs by pharmaceutical companies. I think that in large part, I'm taking aside all they've done for people, addictions programs, addictions services are largely self-serving. I mean I know that for example at [the outpatient addiction treatment program], as much as I've gotten out of it and as much as I appreciate it, putting that aside, I think that in large part, if it didn't generate money for these people, for example, and I'm not saying that [a shelter] is a for-profit giant, but they make a decent salary, they make salary I would be very happy to have in life and you know, stuff like that, and it's almost a self-perpetuating need. All of a sudden, you know, you've decided to admit you're an alcoholic or a drug user, whatever the case, started going to these programs, well one common theme throughout every AA, NA, programs, is that you're always going to have to come back, or you're going to be sick. Now some people will go so far as to say, oh you might be able to make it on your own but I doubt it, kind of [laugh]. It's sorta like now that you're in you've gotta stay in or you're just gonna not get better. It's things like that and so I've had this sort of subconscious mental battle against help for that reason I guess.

Otto's remarks speak to several themes described throughout this book. First, we must note how Otto correlates mental health and addiction. He conceives of his recent interest in his ADHD diagnosis (meeting with a mental health specialist at a community health centre, contemplating taking psychopharmaceuticals) and what he has learned about ADHD in the outpatient addiction treatment program as part of an indistinguishable continuum of care offered in the homelessness sector.

Second, Otto takes a critical stance on what Mick described as the "life-long journey" toward wellness. Otto acknowledges that he and others have "gotten a lot out of" these programs and "all they've done for people" by providing services, but he is critical of the permanency of the mental illness and addiction identities and sees it as a strategic, economically motivated discourse propagated by the recovery industry (Travis, 2009) to ensure an unending supply of clientele. The notion that "you're always going to have to come back, or you're going to be sick" situates the addict subjectivity as essentially different from those who can consume alcohol, gamble, shop, or use some recreational drugs "normally" (Reith, 2004). Although Otto resists the everyday discourses of addiction, his recent interest in mental health and addiction resources serves as an example of the limited options for support offered in the homelessness sector. Otto related to me that his goal is to be stable by the time his daughter turns eighteen in three years' time but the only goods and services that he can consume in an attempt to reach this goal are publicly funded resources built on a pathologized understanding of homelessness, with which he fundamentally disagrees.

Otto's predicament is troubling because, true to his analysis, the permanency of adopting the mental health consumer role juxtaposes with the political economy of hope on which these programs are built. In a consumer society, one's consumptive practices are meant to give people the freedom to create and recreate a fluid sense of self (Gergen, 2000; Giddens, 1991). The late modern subjectivity stands in contrast to the unyielding, permanent, pathologized identity. Adopting the homeless mental health consumer role creates the impression that the person accepts the rigid conceptions of this identity and the individualized explanations for their exclusion. As Moore and Hirai (2014) note, responsibilization strategies may in fact lead to further marginalization. If the mental health consumer is a static identity that entails accepting one's permanent inability for self-control (seen, for example, in the assertion made by many interviewees that they accept that they will have to take psychotropic medication for the rest of their lives and in those who adopt AA's premise that "once an addict, always an addict"), then the standards of full inclusion – namely normalization (including appropriate consumptive practices), self-reliance distinct from publicly funded social assistance and support, and self-governance – are unattainable. Given the proliferation of psy-knowledges in everyday life, taking psychotropic medication or identifying as distressed does not preclude inclusion; rather, it is when these subjectivities are connected with a marginalized identity that they make achieving inclusion challenging.

Someone's ability to claim personal autonomy and a high level of self-governance is compromised when their distress and/or substance use management is directly associated with their ability to sustain their housing, maintain employment, actively participate in the social world, or engage in normalized personal relationships. Autonomy is also compromised for people who are at risk of, or are subject to, formal or informal surveillance by police or other criminal justice actors, child protection services, social assistance workers, or social service providers. Although Otto discursively problematizes the recovery industry, his consumption of its services renders his goal for inclusion more difficult.

Like Otto, Lenny actively resists the mental health system. Although he was diagnosed with anxiety while incarcerated, he does not perform the mental health consumer role (i.e., he does not adopt the identity, take medication, or participate in programming, etc.) because he believes that the recovery industry is strictly interested in social control:

> People that are going mental, you know, mostly due to the fact that they pump drugs by the friggin' pharmaceutical industry and I think basically that's all the recovery industry is doing too, with all their psychology. They're basically just trying to give them all pills. No, you're not taking care of them. "We can all become healthy." Stop perpetuating this bullshit on people. They don't need all their emotions drawn into a thing and being told how they should act or how they should walk through this, you know? They need to be given compassion. I see psychology and psychiatry as nothing more than just a level of prostitution. You know we go to those people, we pay these people to be loved. Just like prostitutes do, you know. Let's pay them for some physical love. Let's pay them for some mental love.

Lenny rejects the claim that mental health interventions lead to inclusion. Instead, he suggests that techniques of support, healing, and empowerment are co-opted in the name of managerialism and social control (Hannah-Moffat, 2000a; Kendall, 2000; Pollack, 2005, 2009). Lenny criticizes the mental health system for situating itself within a political economy of hope and is skeptical that "we can all become healthy. Stop perpetuating this bullshit on people." Lenny views the mental health system as manipulative because it professes benevolence and compassion, but its latent goal is to act as a system of social control by creating docile bodies. By dictating "how they should act or how they should walk," the mental health system gains "meticulous control of the operations of the body" (Foucault, 1977, p. 137).

The mental health consumer's body becomes an object of manipulation by the mental health system as well as a subject for the consumer to study and work on themselves. For Lenny, the mental health system is designed to normalize, discipline, and conduct surveillance, not to create a space for individual freedom tantamount to inclusion.

By comparing the psy-disciplines to prostitution,[9] Lenny positions mental health consumers as clients but rejects the discourse that they are empowered to choose the goods and services that will help them achieve self-actualization. Lenny's comment that clients are paying for "physical love" and "mental love" infers that psy-experts are insincere in their demonstrations of care and compassion and will not provide meaningful assistance. Just as sex workers embody the role and actions that their clients desire, Lenny suggests that psy-professionals appear to have a benevolent interest in helping the poor escape exclusion but are in fact looking to "pump drugs" into the homeless population as a way to sedate the excluded and propel Big Pharma. His contention that psy-professionals are little more than spokespeople for the pharmaceutical industry was a common theme among disenchanted homeless mental health consumers. A fundamental quality of the consumer is that they are active, empowered citizens who are able to choose what to consume in order to fulfill their desires; contrarily, psy-experts and para-professionals mediate and restrict the homeless mental health consumer role.

The Voiceless Consumer
Psychiatric survivors are often skeptical of claims about mental health consumers' inclusion at the organizational and policy levels and as equal partners with medical professionals in their mental health care (Crossley & Crossley, 2001; Fabris, 2013). Many research participants expressed this same disillusionment with the system that was meant to lead to their inclusion. While some began their mental health career with hope and optimism, the actuality that they are not "real" consumers with the autonomy to choose what, how, and when to consume mental health care left them feeling disappointed and defeated. Max described his experience with the mental health system as one of feeling invisible:

> They don't listen ... There's a lot of great doctors out there that do but I've just met so many that ... I was at the [psychiatric hospital]. I was there with my worker and sitting like this in a room having a really bad time, that's why they called him in, and all he wanted was my file, my file, my file. He kept

telling my worker my file. And I felt, I just wanted to grab him and say talk to me! You know, talk to me. I know there's information in the file that can be useful, I get that, as a guy I have respect for what intelligence he has, but sometimes I think they forget, you know, I'm not just your appointment, or a body, you know, like I just felt like getting up and walking out.

Max articulated his sense of objectification and disembodiment at the hands of a disciplinary system that was looking to manage him through an assessment of his file (Foucault, 1977; Jones, 2000) rather than respond to his own perceived needs. Self-determination, empowerment, individual biography, and recovery, recognized as the pillars of person-centred mental health care by the mad movement, were absent from Max's interaction with the psy-expert. Moreover, his CMHA worker, who is meant to act as an advocate and support person, did not intervene on his behalf at a time when Max was in deep distress and unable to assert himself. The mental health system ignores Max's personhood and he is relegated to the sum of his file.

Max attributed his voicelessness to his position as a "flawed" consumer. He has attended multiple in-patient treatment programs for both mental health and addiction over his mental health career, one of which was in a private, for-profit treatment centre. Max ascribes the higher level of care and, importantly, attention to his wishes in the for-profit program to his status as a "true" consumer:

I found that the better places that cost money, they do listen. And maybe it's because they're paid. I don't know why, but they do seem to listen to you a little more. And I understand, like [a doctor at the psychiatric hospital] doesn't have the time of some private doctor that I'm paying, 'cause he's trying to see forty addicts a day.

When the mental health client has the financial freedom to choose among a variety of treatment options, a range of top-tier mental health services are available that concentrate on responding directly to the client's needs to win business. The public mental health system, like the overall national health care system, is in crisis (Harrington et al., 2014) and must contend with a demand that it does not have the resources to meet, resulting in a lack of personal attention. But Max's comments speak to something more problematic than feeling rushed in the doctor's office. Systematically, mental health care is available to those who can participate as consumers. For "flawed" consumers who are simply playing the part of the client in a publicly funded setting, their status as citizens, and indeed as people, is compromised.

The absence of voice was most sharply felt in situations concerning psychotropic medication. Participants commonly remarked on psy-professionals acting as "pill pushers" who are simply interested in medicating, rather than helping, those in distress. Even when homeless mental health consumers were interested in pursuing medication, their voices were silenced. Like Christine's narrative above, Max and Wanda asked psy-professionals for Clonazepam to help them cope with their anxiety because they had had positive experiences with the drug in the past; however, medical professionals refused to prescribe their drug of choice because of its now known addictive properties, no doubt with concern for the opioid epidemic and fentanyl crisis:

> WANDA: No, she won't [prescribe Clonazepam]. Because it's addictive but it's not to me ... No, they won't give it out. And yet I admit, uh, there's this girl around here that sells pills and I don't like that. I'm not a pill pusher but I asked one of the girls before she moved if she had her Clonazepam and it would calm you right down. I didn't ... but I mean you're talking a good forty bucks for two or three.
>
> MAX: Because it's addictive. Again, that's makes me angry with doctors. Like, you know, it shows arrogance, you know? I know it's addictive, I've spent my life addicted to drugs, I know I'll have to take it every day for the rest of my life and probably have it filled up ... I know these things. It should be my choice at some point, you know?

Both Wanda and Max take a unique perspective on their inability to attain their medication of choice. Wanda was frustrated with her lack of physical and mental health care because she does not have a family doctor with whom to build rapport and who may then prescribe her the medication she deems necessary to cope with her anxiety. Although clearly ashamed, Wanda considered buying Clonazepam on the street as a way to manage the distress, but the high cost of street drugs and her absolute poverty made this option unviable.

Unlike Christine and Wanda, who claim that their past experiences with Clonazepam did not result in addiction, Max takes a different approach, stating, "I know it's addictive" but citing his expert knowledge as a longtime addict to argue "it should be my choice at some point." Max's statement represents the subjugation of the homeless mental health consumer's experiential knowledge. Kathy, the mental health nurse who prescribes psychotropic medication on a regular basis, addressed the issue of not fulfilling her clients' requests:

> We don't prescribe benzos[10] because of their addictive nature and it's not best practice. So that's what I say "it's not best practice, we're not doing that." Like they'll come in and they're like, "I need to be on Celexa," which is an anti-depressant and I'm like, "you're not looking depressed at all." And they're like "I've been on anti-depressants since I was eighteen and I need to be," but you know they're using, they're all over the place and you kind of think, you need more mood stabilizers, so we have that discussion.

Although not privy to Kathy's conversations with her patients, comments from research participants raise doubts about how much flexibility exists in discussions between health care providers and people experiencing homelessness. Dominant psy-knowledges subjugate the opinions of those experiencing distress. Subjugated knowledges are those voices and ways of knowing that are deemed as less-than. They are invalidated and characterized as lacking objectivity, logic, or broad applicability (Foucault, 1980b). Psy-discourses prevail over the insights of those who have anxiety or struggle with substance use. Kathy's comment that "but you know they're using, they're all over the place" reinforces the mentally ill and addict identities as irrevocably out of control (Reith, 2004), situating the individual as unable to make "good" decisions about their care. The homeless mental health consumer will rarely qualify as a full-fledged included consumer, even if they gain the financial capital, because they cannot adopt the self-regulative qualities associated with appropriate consumption (Bauman, 2007; Rose, 2000). Dominant psy-knowledges constitute what normalized self-governance looks like and while those experiencing homelessness may be able to exhibit some responsibilized qualities, such as complying with their medication regimes, participating in programming, and checking in with professionals and para-professionals, often they are constituted as permanently unable to engage in self-control without professional surveillance.

Inclusion among the Excluded
In Chapter 1 and throughout this book I have described the elements required to achieve the redeemable status. The majority of the research participants in this project can be characterized as being at the "redeemable" end of the exclusion continuum. Although 84 percent of interviewees had some

experience with the criminal justice system, with 18 percent identifying as having spent time in a federal correctional facility, their considerable length of time out of prison distinguishes them from the "monsters" (Garland, 2001), "impossibles" (Spitzer, 1975), and irredeemable (Rose, 2000) who are beyond hope. For people experiencing homelessness to gain and maintain redeemable status, they must individualize their problems and demonstrate their willingness to work on their project of the self. I describe these practices throughout this book: showing deference to authority figures; adopting the homeless/mentally ill/addict identities; accepting responsibility for their circumstances; and taking it on themselves to "solve" their mental health and homelessness problems. For those willing to "play the game," redeemability has its perks.

To an outsider, the privileges of redeemability are not immediately visible. Unlike some shelters in the United States where gang-like membership dictates authority in shelters (DeOllos, 1997), the hierarchy of Ottawa shelters is not nearly as obvious. None of the interviewees described a firm subculture in any of the shelters, although some did note that they pay deference to those who have been homeless for a long time. Seamus explains:

> Oh there's a whole hierarchy ... You just know, you can tell the guys who've been here for, you know, since Christ decided to grow his hair long, kinda thing. They've been here a long time anyway, so they know everything and, and they're the guys who butt in line and they're the guys, you know, it's the stupidest little miniscule thing but you can tell the guys who've been here a long time and, they don't run the place but ... it's, one of those intangibles that, you just know, you know? And it's got nothing to do with big burly mean guys or anything else, it's just you know that these guys have been here and they, "whoa whoa whoa, no, I go before you," or whatever else.

Seamus explains the complicated power dynamic found among shelter residents. Foucault (1980b, 2005) contends that people, structures, or the state do not possess power; instead, power is ubiquitous and exists in a pervasive and fluid manner that (re)produces dominant forms of knowledge and our common reality. The diffusion of power throughout the social world substantiates the ways that marginalized people, who are generally regarded as powerless, exert power in the locales they frequent and the interactions in which they take part. Seemingly insignificant actions such as cutting the lunch line or getting first dibs on the snack tray carry tremendous symbolic value. Housed people ignore, ridicule, and even victimize people experiencing homelessness, but some marginalized individuals gain a sense of worth from being the most seasoned and knowledgeable. Seamus is clear that "they don't run the place" but that residents pay deference to those who have "been here a long time" and who "know everything" about how to survive in what can be a hostile environment. Perhaps surprisingly given the high level of insecurity and victimization in the homeless population, power is not achieved through physical dominance and being "big burly mean guys,"[11] but by having the wherewithal to navigate the complicated array of services and bureaucratic red tape that make up the homelessness industrial complex.

Jamie, who is unlikely to be identified as redeemable given his resistance to the mental health system and other services, could not hide his anger when I asked him about whether he thought there are consequences to forgoing programming:

> They have everything, we have nothing. Every single perk this place offers, you either must be working and even then you don't get a lot, or you are in one of the programs. The programs are the poster child for this place. [The addiction treatment programs], everything is built for them to the point where they even get to come in and be special and eat ten minutes before us. How do you think that makes me feel? Half the people, I can't say about [the in-patient treatment program], half the people in the [detox program] or in [a transition addiction program] are fucking there for the perks. They get drunk once a week, at least. I know they do, I see them do it. Oh yeah just say you're addicted to something and you want to change and you get in and you get bed rest all the time, you get to watch movies on weekends, Sundays there's absolutely nothing, the libraries during the summer are closed on Sundays, I can't even go to the library. You're in the program? You can sit in [a private room] all day and watch movies. You're not in the program, tough shit.

I often witnessed these perks during my participant observation at Crossroads. Individuals who participate in the in- or outpatient addiction treatment program run by the shelter have a designated mealtime that is earlier than the general shelter population. This ensures their meals are the warmest and they get first choice of where to sit in the dining room. At the time of my observations, the rule granting permission only to individuals in programming to watch movies on weekends was flexible. Over time, however, the shelter became more scrupulous, locking the door to those not permitted. We should not underestimate the significance of watching movies undisturbed. The communal television is only turned on at six o'clock in the evening. Even then, frontline staff determine what everyone will watch. Given the reality of living within the strict rules of the shelter, we can begin to appreciate the luxury of having the autonomy to choose a movie, being able to pause it for smoke breaks, and the sense of privacy that comes with watching television with only a handful of people.

Only those participating in programming are afforded these distinct advantages. An example from Stuart's (2016) study reveals a similar narrative. Police stopped three men on Skid Row and asked for identification. Two men showed their driver's licences while one man gave his badge from the local shelter/service provider. The officer subsequently wrote the first two men citations for a crosswalk violation and let the latter man go. In Stuart's debrief with the officer, he revealed that he let the man staying at the shelter off the hook because by engaging with these services he was demonstrating his openness to take responsibility for his situation, saying: "Right there you saw one who is at least trying, while the rest are just full of excuses" (p. 106). The police officer did not know the nature of the man's rehabilitation efforts, nor did he find out what the other two men might be doing to improve their situation outside of the shelter services. Simply possessing the badge demonstrated redeemability in the eyes of the officer. Similarly, although Jamie and some other participants called into question some participants' dedication to sobriety and self-improvement, what matters is that those who participate in programming are seen as willing to accept responsibility for their marginality and display their intention to work on their project of the self by engaging with services and programs. Whether they are successful (i.e., become sober, manage their anger, find gainful employment, etc.) is secondary to their continual consumption of mental health and treatment resources that distinguishes them as deserving reward. Shelter administrators conceive of bedrest and structured leisure time as conducive to recovery; but for those who do not get access to these advantages, they resemble favouritism and exclusion.

Jamie notes that homeless mental health consumers receive more perks than individuals who reside in the section of the shelter set aside for residents who work. In large part because of stigmatization, those experiencing homelessness are often limited in the kinds of formal employment opportunities available to them. Much of this work is temporary, physically intensive, insecure, and low-paying through single-day contract employers (Williams, 2009) and does not provide the financial stability for people to be able to make ends meet, let alone become members of the included society. Contrary to intuition, the homeless mental health consumer has stronger consumerist potential than many of their working counterparts. Whereas the working homeless do not have the financial resources to engage in much meaningful consumption, by relying on the public system, the homeless mental health consumer can consume an unending supply of psy-based goods and services. Not only is the mental health consumer framed as a better consumer but also, because consumerism is so profoundly connected with self-regulation, the mental health consumer is able to demonstrate their commitment to, and efforts made toward, self-responsibilization and individual improvement (albeit under the guidance and surveillance of psy-experts and para-professionals) and thus their desire for normality. The working homeless have limited, if any, availability to engage with services and supports that occur during work hours and are unable to afford private counselling and treatment centres. In this way, the homeless mental health consumer's redeemability is more apparent and is thus deemed more deserving of reward than that of the working poor. While the mental health consumer and working homeless identities are not mutually exclusive, none of the participants in this research project who were heavily involved in programming were engaged in formal employment and those who participate in in-patient treatment do not work. The labour involved in working on the project of the self, as described by Mac in the previous section, is so time consuming and labour intensive that it leaves little, if any, opportunity for employment.

Identifying as mentally ill can provide benefits outside of the shelter system as well. Although I did not ask interviewees specifically about their financial situation, nine research participants volunteered that they receive Ontario Disability Support Payments (ODSP) rather than the standard Ontario Works (OW) social assistance. Most were eligible for ODSP based on both physical and mental disabilities. Only Vince, who receives ODSP for his PTSD and severe clinical depression diagnoses, was candid that his original interest in receiving a mental illness diagnosis was financially motivated: "I knew what depression was about but to me that was ... Well what that looked like to me is, now I can get on ODSP. It's just about getting on the system and collecting this x amount of dollars a month because, even then I wasn't going to get clean." In 2018 a single person living in Ontario received $436 more per month on ODSP than those on OW.[12] The discrepancy in assistance between those who are deemed simply unemployed and those who claim disability leads to the medicalization of poverty where accepting a pathologized subjectivity becomes a strategic means for navigating a system that so acutely distinguishes between the "slackers" and the "lackers" (Rosenthal, 2000; Werth, 2012). Using the mental health system to access greater funds through ODSP can be characterized as a form of resistance but as Hansen et al. (2014) conclude, this act of resistance should not overshadow the very real distress that many people face that compels them to use the system in this way. Instead, it demonstrates the wherewithal that many marginalized people have to situate their narrative within psy-discourses in order to access resources; but in doing so, it also reasserts the tired dichotomy between the deserving and undeserving poor.

The homeless mental health consumer comes out ahead in the homeless population: greater entitlement to counselling through programs; small but meaningful perks such as early access to meals and clothing; and improved chances of receiving subsidized or supportive housing, through Housing First programs for example. These privileges, however, do not necessarily lead to redemption and subsequent social inclusion. Instead, redeemability can act to solidify one's status as excluded. As Bauman (2001a) contends, "even a modicum of mobility feels like unbridled freedom" (p. 121). The opportunities and rewards that come with the redeemable status help those experiencing homelessness "bear the hardships of a precarious life" (p. 121) rather than leading to substantive inclusion. I cannot overstate the importance of perks that help people experiencing homelessness endure the "pains of homelessness." Small rewards act as symbols of care, worthiness, and dignity, attributes hard to come by among the homeless. Choosing where to sit or what to watch on television amounts to a "modicum of mobility" and provides individuals with a sense of freedom, however minute. Nonetheless, much of the guidance provided by professionals, para-professionals, and many of the programs available through the homelessness industrial complex do not lead to inclusion. Instead, they assist people in becoming included among the excluded. Endeavours focused on "fixing" individual shortcomings maintain the lingering principles of social citizenship exalted by the welfare state by helping willing participants manage their exclusion without having to dismantle the structures and ideologies that create marginalization.

As described above, many of the research participants in this project sought out the mental health consumer role in the hopes of inclusion; contrarily, a few interviewees spoke candidly about their more modest goal of becoming included among the excluded. Otto explains his marginality as stemming in part from the mental health and treatment systems:

> It can't just be me, so I gotta pick something. Well, I'll go with the ADHD I heard about six years ago. That sounds good. Yeah, and alcoholic too, yeah, I'll sign up for that. I get free coffee in the morning, I get to go to the clothing room on Tuesdays, I get meals, why not be an alcoholic, life's great. All I gotta do is not drink and stuff. There are benefits to those who are willing to admit their indiscretions in the mental world. But, it also boxes you in. 'Cause for the life of me, it doesn't matter what my own philosophy is. It doesn't matter what my actions are. If I were to sit down with my family right now and say you know, I change my mind I'm not really an alcoholic. Oh! You're in denial.

Otto describes both the advantages and pitfalls of situating oneself as a homeless mental health consumer. He acknowledges the rewards that come with the role, such as coffee and first access to donated clothing, but notes that to receive these perks he must be "willing to admit [his] indiscretions in the mental world." Otto's reluctant adoption of pathologized explanations for his situation acts as the key to accessing privileges but also plants him firmly in the excluded realm. According to Young (1999), the inclusive ideals touted through consumer culture subsume the excluded. Attempts to adopt inclusive norms, such as Otto's quest for self-governance, ultimately highlights and reinforces his Otherness. As described above, given its relationship with the twelve-step model, the alcoholic identity reinforces the lifelong master status and any resistance to recovery discourses is characterized as a symptom of the pathology (Reith, 2004). Having been homeless for six years, Otto considered the benefits of being included among the excluded to outweigh the costs of being permanently tied to overtly disciplinary systems.

The Hopeless

Not everyone who is homeless can perform the mental health consumer role. We must also consider the other end of the inclusion-exclusion continuum: those identified as irredeemable who are subject to more coercive disciplinary tactics. The irredeemable are those who do not or cannot engage in self-disciplinary techniques required to live up to the standards of normality and civility (Bauman, 1988, 2004; Rose, 2000; Young, 1999). In emergency shelters the irredeemable are those who sit outside of the typical homeless population; they are the excluded among the excluded. Snow and Anderson (1993) qualify some of their research subjects as "severely impaired psychiatrically" because their conduct is "so bizarre and situationally inappropriate that it would be likely to be construed as symptomatic of mental illness by most observers" (p. 66). During my participant observation, I witnessed many people exhibiting these behaviours, such as those who pace manically, mutter to themselves and sometimes call out, and argue or laugh with the empty chair beside them. The irredeemable classification is largely made up of those overcome by distress; however, this is not to suggest that the irredeemable constitute the "true" mentally ill. In keeping with the critical orientation of this work, I do not assume that those who exhibit qualities typical of mental illness symptoms embody its subjectivity. It is important, however, to bear witness to the deep distress facing some of the homeless population's most vulnerable.

Whereas the redeemable status is embedded within the political economy of hope, irredeemability connotes an absence of hope. The irredeemable are not offered words of encouragement (however unsubstantiated they may be), the promise of a brighter future, or the opportunity to consume mental health and treatment resources of their choosing. Instead, they are met with the heavy hand of disciplinary regimes, especially the mental health and criminal justice systems, to manage their risk. The irredeemable are to be contained, not corrected or empowered.

Irredeemability, as a subjectivity, is not static. In the prison, the client and offender subjectivities depend on the individual's social environment, relationships, and behaviours (Donohue & Moore, 2009). Similarly, outside the prison walls, mentally ill identities are subject to different forms of social control, depending on their perceived level of risk. Risk levels are regularly reassessed and so the kinds of services and the level of surveillance and discipline individuals are subject to are constantly in flux (Hannah-Moffat, 2016; Rose, 1998). The irredeemable status comes from assessments made by those in positions of power. Psy-authority is dispersed among psy-experts, para-professionals, and service providers to assess redeemability among those who are identified as "seriously" mentally ill in the homeless population to properly manage those who are deemed beyond hope.

Giving Up

Assessing irredeemability is not simply an exercise in abstraction; it happens in concrete, deliberate ways. Chuck, a frontline staff member at Crossroads, gave his perspective on what to do with those who cannot or will not adopt responsibilization strategies:

> I think there's also a problem sometimes with the way we prioritize, like, eventually you have to ask yourself, you know, this person has some very serious mental health issues, we've tried this method, we've tried that method, and now at this point how badly is it affecting his quality of life? If he doesn't say anything that indicates that it's negatively affecting his quality of life and we don't really perceive that he's in distress,[13] then maybe it's time to move on to somebody else and use the resources for somebody else who is maybe more acute. Prioritize right? You can always revisit.

Other professionals suggested that non-compliance with psychotropic medication and risky behaviours that justify involuntary hospitalization (forming) were two indicators that someone is irredeemable. Forming is particularly oppressive and coercive in nature. The irredeemable designation comes when someone rejects, resists, or is unable to comply with disciplinary technologies.

The excerpt above also clearly identifies the hopelessness that embodies irredeemability. As Chuck claims, "maybe it's time to move on to somebody else." Other members of the focus group concurred; for example, Anthony, a shelter manager, noted, "some ... they probably can't be helped." All of the focus group members expressed dismay at their inability to support some individuals who are facing profound and long-term distress, but they also noted resource constraints and the need to prioritize those who will accept help (read, adopt normalization discourses). In the neoliberal era of austerity measures, fiscal constraint, program evaluation, and demonstrated efficiency, program administrators look for "clients" who will properly and effectively consume mental health products and allow programs to meet measurable outcome targets (Woolford & Curran, 2011), leaving behind those who do not meet specific success markers. Even within the Housing First model that is designed to prioritize those with the most acute needs, people who are barred from homeless-serving organizations or who struggle to access services (especially women, Indigenous Peoples, racialized minorities, and LGBTQ2S+ people) will not be on the priority list or will not meet the narrow criteria for what counts as homeless for six months or more. Chuck's narrative is in keeping with Bauman's (2004) contention that some members of the underclass are constituted as beyond help and that those who cannot consume publicly funded goods and services are disposable in consumer society.

Members of the focus group were quick to point out that it is not the homelessness sector alone who gives up on the irredeemable. They expressed their extreme frustration with the lack of mental health care in the public health system, citing common problems with people being discharged from the psychiatric hospital with only a week's worth of medication and no avenue to access pharmaceuticals in the community. There is a similar lack of discharge planning evidenced in correctional facilities (Gaetz & O'Grady, 2009; John Howard Society of Toronto, 2010). Professionals pointed out that one of the most significant barriers to supporting people was difficulty accessing mental health care workers, specifically psychiatrists. At the time of the interview, the mental health nurse who routinely visited Ottawa's shelters had recently retired and had not been replaced, leaving Melissa, a case worker, to lament: "I would have a pile of referrals but I can't refer them to anybody." This leaves shelter staff to "pick up the slack" (Chuck) and manage those in deep distress within a busy, chaotic, and insecure environment. It also highlights the unequivocal reliance on the medical system, rather than building vibrant alternative methods of care, such as peer support.

Beyond "Batshit Bananas": Expanding the Psy-complex to Manage the Irredeemable

The expanding role of shelter staff as mental health providers is not new. Seamus explained that frontline staff sometimes bribe individuals to take a shower and change their clothes: "'Hey, do you want a smoke?' 'Yeah.' 'Go have a shower.' And the other guy's like, 'no no, not taking that shower.' 'Then you're not getting a cigarette.' So the guy will go and take a shower and come back. 'Nope, here's some clothes, change your clothes.' Give him the cigarettes and he'll go." According to Seamus, frontline staff intervene in shelter residents' hygiene practices to maintain order in the shelter when "other guys complain about it" more so than as a method of treatment. Still, it acts as an example of staff taking on the role of mental health care worker and is indicative of the broad application of psy-expertise among those in positions of power (Rose, 1998). It also reveals that a lack of mental health resources (and alternative supports) has the effect of downloading responsibility for managing distress to frontline staff, similar to the way police have become de facto social workers. Chuck was vocal about his thoughts on the need for frontline staff to take on a more formal role in the mental health system:

> So if we [frontline staff] had more training with basic pharmacology, terminology, how to do mental health assessment. I mean, there's no reason why front desk couldn't be doing a mental health assessment over a period of a couple days as opposed to a half-hour directed interview. Right? We could, these things could be done so that when we do possibly get a mental health nurse back in here, we can give her a file on a client saying this is what has been observed, using standard language that is respected, that is understood, that, so that when papers pass through the psych emerg they're like [claps hands] yeah, I understand what this person's saying as opposed to using words like, "this guy has gone batshit bananas." It's important to be descriptive about what's going on but again, there's a whole terminology that's used that is probably necessary for a lot of us to know.

Chuck called for a dramatic reformulation of the frontline staff role to enable them to perform the work of psy-experts. In Chuck's reimagination of shelter work, frontline staff would use their position of authority, including the panoptic gaze of the shelters' CCTV cameras and the production of a resident's "file," to observe and judge residents (Foucault, 1977) and to assess their mental health status. The medical gaze's expansion to frontline staff would further erode any semblance of privacy and autonomy for shelter residents, but as Chuck argues, transferring assessment responsibilities to staff would ease some of the pressure felt by the lack of mental health resources in the homelessness sector.

Chuck emphasized the professionalization of the frontline staff role by promoting the acquisition of proficiency in psy-language. Psychiatrists sometimes use staff observations to form distressed individuals. Chuck is looking to formalize this process by adopting a common technical, rational, and objective psy-vocabulary to demonstrate staff competence to conduct mental health assessments. Using the psy-professions' discursive formations would allow frontline staff to act as para-professionals. Chuck is seeking to translate observations such as "this guy has gone batshit bananas" into terminology that can be activated by psy-experts to assess, classify, and ultimately discipline an individual deemed "seriously" mentally ill. While translation usually refers to moving from the general to the particular – from the political regime to its application on the ground (Rose, 1999) – here translation is inversed, where the irredeemable subject's day-to-day movements and behaviours are translated into criteria for disciplinary intervention. The surveillance, judgment, and "administration of persons" (Rose, 1998) that frontline staff already conduct would be legitimized and made even more powerful through its alignment and adherence to psy-discourses.

Criminalizing the Irredeemable
Those individuals identified as "seriously" mentally ill among the homeless population are more likely to be subject to police intervention. Emergency shelters use police presence to manage people who do not engage in self-control (Bernier et al., 2011). As the focus group explained:

> CHUCK: We de-escalate them as best we can. We use our words. We try to either calm them down, keep them safe, keep the other clients safe, or we try to get them removed. Either we guide them out the door ourselves as gently as possible and as calmly as possible, ask them to take a walk, cool down, come back. Depending on the severity of the incident, they might be barred for an amount of time because, I mean, as much as we feel for these guys we can't have them ... with 200 other guys ... like if it's not during regular business hours, if front desk can't de-escalate the situation it becomes a police problem.
> ANTHONY: There's no buffer.
> MELISSA: No, there's no buffer. If there, if it's after business hours, frontline staff are on their own. If someone is going to hurt themselves or others, then, we call the police.

The criminalization of poverty acts as the ultimate form of degradation and exclusion (Stuart, 2016; Wacquant, 2000, 2009). For individuals dealing with deep distress, their interactions with police stem largely from their status as homeless. Chuck's comment that the distress of one person can disrupt the "200 other guys" at the shelter underscores the reality of experiencing distress while living in a public space and the challenges shelters have maintaining safety and security while also providing support to those who need it. Signs of distress do not automatically require police intervention, but in an emergency shelter with few or no mental health, familial, or peer supports available, staff regard police intervention as the only viable solution to maintain order. The goal of reducing individual distress is secondary to maintaining the security of the shelter (Ranasinghe, 2017). Although police are anecdotally referred to as "street-corner psychiatrists" (Steadman et al., 2000), evidence suggests that police interaction does little to relieve people's distress and often exacerbates the situation, particularly for racialized people (Shore & Lavoie, 2018). For those individuals who do not or cannot perform the consumer role "there is no buffer" and the only services available are the traditional, disciplinary, and coercive technologies of social control operating via the police and criminal justice systems.

The quote above provides another example of how frontline staff are often put in the position of acting as mental health care workers. They are responsible for managing crises and de-escalating situations. This is a problematic role for frontline staff to take on because, as noted in Chapter 3, many shelter residents view them as "bubble boys" and pseudo-correctional officers, rather than support workers. Because their role is first and foremost to maintain security, it is common practice to eject the distressed person from the premises, either briefly to "cool down" or for longer periods by having them "barred" or expelled for a certain length of time. Although not positioned as punishment, exclusion from the shelter is indeed a sanction in that it acts as a form of condemnation by authority figures who dictate normalized standards for conduct (Garland, 1990). Contrary to some other jurisdictions (Feldman, 2004; Lyon-Callo, 2004), in Ottawa it is standard practice that if someone is barred from one location, staff will find a bed at another shelter so that no one is forced to sleep outside. That being said, many interview participants commented that they would rather sleep outside than reside in some of Ottawa's shelters. Although from the shelter management's perspective being barred from one shelter is not akin to being kicked onto the streets, for many individuals, particularly those experiencing distress who are more likely to be victimized, another shelter is not a viable option.

The irredeemable are subject to disciplinary systems, be it the criminal justice and/or mental health systems, because they cannot or will not demonstrate their ability to become empowered, self-regulating, redeemable subjects. While the professionals in the focus group remarked that limited mental health resources are primarily to blame for their having to allocate supports to some individuals over others, Katz's (2013) genealogy of poverty suggests that there has always been a group of "undeserving" poor who are regarded as hopeless, whether this assessment is based on moral or biological grounds. Those who are deemed "seriously" mentally ill are among this group of irredeemable subjects (along with, and often related to, those who have spent a long time in prison) and are not afforded the same opportunities to access resources that can help them bear the pains of homelessness as are their redeemable counterparts. Instead, they face the possibility of criminalization and/or involuntary hospitalization, tools meant to manage and contain those in distress rather than support recovery.

Conclusion

In the late modern era, inclusion, exclusion, and techniques of governance must be situated within the context of consumer society. Bauman (1998, 2007) describes consumerism as the foundation for our contemporary understanding of the self, our goals and desires, because it mediates how we govern others and ourselves. But what happens to those who cannot participate in consumer society on account of their poverty? The "flawed" consumer (Bauman, 2007) is an especially problematic character because we are expected to consume goods and services that will aid in self-regulation and normalization (Rose, 1999). Because most people experiencing homelessness do not have the financial capital to act as proper consumers, some position themselves as homeless mental health consumers. In this way, they can perform the responsibilized, active, and empowered consumer role through publicly funded programs and services that primarily emphasize psychopharmacological intervention and responsibilization techniques.

The hope for inclusion that encourages individuals experiencing homelessness to accept mental illness diagnoses, treatment (almost exclusively psychotropic medication), and the individualization of problems in living is often nothing more than that – hope. The reality of the homeless mental health consumer is that their autonomy in the public mental health system is minimal and it is exceptionally difficult, although not impossible, for people to move beyond the redeemable status and into the included social world. Although this fact is discouraging, redeemability has its benefits. Homeless mental health consumers are positioned as the included among the excluded. The perks awarded to those deemed redeemable, such as earlier mealtimes and access to leisure activities, allow individuals to "bear the hardships" (Bauman, 2001b) of homelessness. These rewards are important to many who have experienced chronic homelessness and who have little prospect of escaping poverty; however, by accepting their status as mentally ill and/or addicted they reiterate their position as permanent members of the excluded circuit.

While those who reach the highest echelons of redeemability are designated the included among the excluded, those who fall closer to the irredeemable end of the continuum are understood as the always-already excluded. Typically attributed to individuals assessed as "seriously" mentally ill, the irredeemable status defines those who are thought to be hopeless. The staff, para-professionals, and psy-experts who identify them have little expectation that they will become responsible, self-governing citizens and so subject them to disciplinary techniques. Be it through involuntary hospitalization or interactions with police, the irredeemable are managed through coercive strategies to contain rather than empower them. The result is further exclusion of the most marginal and vulnerable subset of the homeless population. For those who cannot or will not participate in consumer society, even as flawed consumers, there is little illusion of hope for a different and improved sociality.

7
Moving toward Inclusion

I have used *A Complex Exile* as an opportunity to explore how people who experience homelessness perceive, respond to, negotiate, and navigate spaces and processes of exclusion, particularly as they relate to the mental health system. The mental health rationalities that orient policies and practices to manage homelessness are complex, and so we must be attuned to how people accept, mediate, and resist the experiences of exclusion that flow through these rationales. Multifarious forms of mental health intervention act as governance tools that often reinforce exclusion rather than ameliorate the structural conditions that are the root causes of homelessness and marginalization.

In an effort to suss out the complexities of exclusion, I wove together several theoretical threads that illuminate the underlying orientation for managing people who do not have a home in Canada. The notion of freedom that acts as the pillar of modern governing is complicated by the obligations that come with using that freedom correctly; that is, aligning one's freedom with normative goals and behaviours (Rose, 1999). For people who are homeless or otherwise excluded, the disciplinary regimes that seek to contain, minimize, and render them invisible are situated through and within the politics of freedom, rather than existing in opposition to it. This characterization was explored most thoroughly in Chapter 3 where I positioned emergency shelters as neoliberal total institutions. Combining Goffman's (1961) total institutions as the epitome of disciplinary arrangements with the notion of freedom and self-governance, we come to see the ways in which the homelessness industrial complex mobilizes personal autonomy to focus on homelessness as a personal failing and position those who use shelters as either working on their project of the self or surrendering to their status as excluded members of society. By unmasking the dual role shelters have taken on as purveyors of discipline within a discourse of choice (largely because of government's downloading responsibility to the non-profit sector to manage homelessness), we become attuned to how these spaces inevitably act as sites of social exclusion. This critical orientation can propel us to devise alternative responses to homelessness that claim housing as a human right and that regard homelessness as a failure of the collective state rather than of the individual (Madden & Marcuse, 2016). Until such time as we make that shift in our response to homelessness, mental health interventions will continue to be revered as *the* solution to homelessness because their discourses and practices fit within the individualized ethos that fixates on solving personal problems, without having the language or means to consider that the root causes of many people's homelessness are structural in nature.

Related to issues of freedom and responsibility, this book also explored the nature and lived experience of exclusion. In Chapter 4, I combined Goffman's (1959) dramaturgical approach and Butler's (1990) cultural perspective of performance to extend the conversation concerning identity performance beyond the true-/untrue-self dichotomy and make sense of the complexity of presentations of self within the confines of marginality. Most significantly, I eschewed the inclusion/exclusion binary, seeking to push the boundaries of how inclusionary relationships, identities, and practices inhabit otherwise exclusionary locales and explore the ways people experiencing homelessness actively make use of these spaces or create alternative forms of inclusion for themselves. These pockets of inclusion are exceptionally important for providing a sense of hope that people experiencing homelessness can move further up through the inclusion-exclusion continuum as well as offering a sense of dignity, worthiness, and purpose in a social landscape where people are often treated as undignified, unworthy, and lacking purpose. This hope is often necessary to encourage marginalized people to seek out normative aspirations despite the enormous challenges to becoming included. Using Berlant's (2011) notion of cruel optimism, this book dissected how hope can be marshalled by people experiencing homelessness and the homelessness industrial complex to create a redeemable subjectivity. Through the narratives provided by those experiencing homelessness, it becomes apparent that many of the programs, policies, and practices meant to foster inclusion instead help people to bear the "pains of homelessness" rather than lead to material and felt inclusion. In Chapter 6, I borrowed from social theorists such as Bauman (2001b) and Young (1999) and drew from critical criminological and mad scholarship to conceptualize the homeless mental health consumer as a client of the homelessness industrial complex and recovery industry who can achieve the redeemable status. Combined, these theoretical insights provide a lens through which we can understand dominant responses to homelessness as embedded within broader structural and systemic exclusionary paradigms and, with this recognition, we can deliberately work to address the root causes of homelessness in a truly inclusionary way.

My goal in writing this book was twofold. First, it was to make clear that social exclusion has an exponentially negative impact on well-being. Second and relatedly, if we are attuned to the impact of social exclusion on people's lives then we have an obligation to respond to homelessness in a way that fosters substantive hope, inclusion, and belonging. To meet these objectives, I situated the mental health system within the broader homelessness industrial complex that seeks to manage people who are homeless, in turn pathologizing and individualizing the causes and nature of homelessness, further exacerbating social exclusion. While coercive forms of management are an ever-present threat for people experiencing homelessness, the preferred governing techniques are those that work through individual freedom, encouraging marginalized people to narrow in on and take responsibility for their own faults. As a response to these dominant governance mechanisms, I argue that many (but not all) people experiencing homelessness vie for redeemability, achieved by demonstrating an openness and engagement with the norms, values, and actions promoted by the homelessness industrial complex, mental health system, and recovery industry. Seeking redeemability provides an invaluable source of hope for exiting homelessness and is also a strategic tool through which to navigate the homelessness sector.

These arguments reveal the complexity of how exclusion is produced by the homelessness industrial complex and experienced by those who are homeless, and provides the substratum for reimagining our response to homelessness in a way that provides for meaningful inclusion. First, the book expounds the obvious and obscure forms of exclusion people experiencing homelessness face and the ways in which arguably benevolent and worthwhile services and resources contribute to that exclusion. Second, despite being subject to a myriad of disciplinary techniques seeking to manage those on the margins, individuals experiencing homelessness are not passive subjects. People negotiate exclusion to allow them to gain their own sense of inclusion and spaces of acceptance in an otherwise hostile and unwelcoming world. Finally, as the homelessness landscape shifts rapidly in Canada and across the world we must recognize the power of social exclusion on housing outcomes and develop strategies to prevent and end homelessness that do not assume that social inclusion flows naturally from individual interventions, especially those that lean heavily on the mental health paradigm.

Exclusion at Every Turn

I am a critical criminologist and work in a criminology department. As such, prison segregation as a form of torture, instances of police brutality, especially targeting Black people, people of colour, and Indigenous Peoples, and the injustice victims of sexual assault face in criminal trials are common topics of discussion in my teaching and scholarly pursuits. Given the atrocities inflicted on vulnerable people by the criminal justice system, it would be easy to dismiss the subtle and opaque forms of exclusion that exist in the homeless population as innocuous or "less than" – but this would be a mistake. Seemingly insignificant policies, practices, and interactions that treat people experiencing homelessness as separate or unworthy reify their status as excluded from the broader social world. The constraints and challenges that come with staying in an emergency shelter, the protocols and inner workings that limit autonomy and institutionalize people without a home, and the difficulty in providing support with dignity and compassion while prioritizing security reflect the sense of Otherness experienced by people who are homeless. All these elements are situated within, and reinforce, a paradigm that positions those experiencing homelessness as excluded. I must be clear though: exclusionary policies are not limited to emergency shelters. All sorts of organizations and programs that serve people who are homeless contain elements of exclusion, with the important exception of most peer-led endeavours. Eligibility criteria, time limits on access to services, and strict rule enforcement impede service users from gaining the supports and resources they need to become housed and they do so in a way that undermines people's ability to navigate the included social world.

The fact that the homeless-serving system is steeped in exclusionary practices is problematic because it restricts people from exercising personal autonomy and places them in vulnerable spaces and situations that are detrimental to their security and well-being; it also moulds individuals' sense of self in a profoundly negative way. A common theme running through the research interviews and my informal conversations with people experiencing homelessness was the blame and self-disgust they internalized by nature of their circumstances. As explored in Chapter 5, regardless of programmatic discourse reinforcing mental illness as a biological anomaly, people experiencing homelessness internalize exclusionary instances and practices that further entrench their feelings of shame and unworthiness. This is incredibly concerning as it leads people experiencing homelessness to pre-emptively exclude themselves from the mainstream social body in an effort to evade public acts of humiliation and/or feelings of being unwelcome, for example when people avoid public spaces, such as parks, for fear of being harassed, moved along, or ticketed (Sylvestre, 2010b). It can also dissuade people from applying for jobs or reaching out to friends and family for fear of being outed as homeless and/or shamed for their status. In this way, exclusion becomes cyclical – the homeless population are excluded by and from the included social world, creating an environment where people exclude themselves in an act of self-preservation, reinforcing the social exclusion of people experiencing homelessness.

The homelessness industrial complex perpetuates social exclusion. Rarely is this the aim of individual actors; in fact, quite the opposite is true. Most of the frontline service providers, organizational management, policy makers, and other key stakeholders I have met over the course of my research are passionate, dedicated people who care deeply about the individuals they encounter, advocate for them, and do what they can to ameliorate the hardships faced by people experiencing homelessness. Despite intending the best, their actions, situated within this specific context, are often still exclusionary. As Moore (2011) so astutely points out, care and concern, when expressed within the confines of institutional logics, regulations, and discourses, often have punitive effects. In my volunteer work with those experiencing homelessness, I too have engaged in exclusionary behaviour. For example, on occasion at activity night I have had to ask people to leave because they were using threatening language, acting out, or making other residents fearful or agitated. I was unable to accept people where they were at and make sure they felt included because of my lack of training, limited spatial, personal, and institutional capacity, and a dearth of innovative strategies to build social inclusion among those in distress. This exclusion from activity night only furthered residents' aggressive behaviour – behaviour that is likely caused and/or exacerbated in part by the daily forms of exclusion they face. Exclusion begets exclusion. Johnsen et al.'s (2018) typology of social control includes tolerance as a type of control, where spaces and services aim to foster a welcoming and inclusive environment without trying to modify people's behaviour. While this is certainly an ideal approach, the authors note the difficulty in sharing space in this way and making sure everyone is comfortable. The homelessness industrial complex, with its purpose to manage, contain, and control people experiencing homelessness (even with the intended goal of helping someone exit homelessness) intensifies the social exclusion of the very people it is serving. This is an uncomfortable finding, but one we must be willing to confront if we hope to move toward social inclusion.

Exclusion Isn't the Whole Story

When researching and writing about people experiencing oppression, there is always a concern that in an attempt to bring awareness to social injustices we run the risk of hiding the vibrancy, resiliency, and achievements of that same group. Inadvertently placing marginalized groups into the passive victim role does a disservice to those who make up that population and ultimately fails to capture the complexity of the interactions between excluded individuals and the structural and systemic barriers they face. This challenge is what makes Spivak's (1988) question "can the subaltern speak?" continue to resonate with the intellectual community thirty years later. Are the full and complete voices of people with lived experience accurately represented? The question acts as a call for more people with experiences of marginalization and who come from oppressed communities to be better represented and take leadership positions in research. This should occur through multiple avenues, including greater financial and institutional support for community-led, participatory research, as well as diverse representation of underrepresented groups in the academy, including Indigenous Peoples, people of colour and other racialized minorities, women, people with disabilities, and LGBTQ2S+ people.

The Truth and Reconciliation Commission's (TRC's) Calls to Action (2015) provide an excellent example of how to bring awareness to atrocities without diminishing the accomplishments and pride of a group of people. Given the TRC's mandate to collect stories and develop an historical record of residential schools in Canada and provide public education and recommendations on moving toward reconciliation, most of the ninety-four Calls to Action address reparations for the monumental harms experienced by

First Nations, Métis, and Inuit peoples. But the Calls to Action also include ways to bring awareness to and build up the beauty and diversity of Indigenous cultures. For example, the TRC recommends increasing funding to Canada's public broadcaster to produce media content that includes and celebrates Indigenous languages, cultures, and Peoples. Action 87 recommends that various sports halls of fame recognize the contribution Indigenous athletes have made to sport. Among the recommendations on creating a more culturally competent and equitable health care system for Indigenous Peoples, the TRC calls for a cultural shift that integrates healers' and Elders' knowledge and expertise in using traditional healing practices. These recommendations do not in any way discount the trauma and oppression that Indigenous Peoples have experienced historically and continue to experience by the settler-colonial state, but they do provide an opportunity to bring attention to and honour the many successes Indigenous Peoples have achieved *in spite of* attempts to eliminate their culture, connections to land, language, and knowledge.

As I began to recognize the complexity of how mental health discourses and practices are used in the homelessness industrial complex, it became apparent that people experiencing homelessness are not simply resigned to their exclusion and the mental health practices that encourage, empower, and sometimes coerce particular ways of being. For many research participants, their lack of resignation meant embracing and working with the mental health system, even if it may lead to further exclusion. Others had a more cautious and strategic relationship with institutions and practitioners, while a few actively resisted normalization practices, redefining inclusion in a way that aligns with their interests and goals. Whichever tactics they employed, few, if any, people experiencing homelessness were strictly passive subjects in their own highly surveilled and managed lives. The strength and perseverance of the people I encountered cannot be overstated. This is not to romanticize homelessness – people without a home have no choice but to be courageous and self-advocate when possible given the way the homelessness industrial complex operates – but rather, it is an opportunity to pay attention to the ways marginalized people are active and engaged in their own lives despite institutional arrangements that obscure this reality.

Throughout this book I have argued that people experiencing homelessness actively negotiate and make sense of themselves and their circumstances. Theorizing redeemability has proved exceptionally helpful at uncovering the myriad of tactics people use to navigate the homelessness industrial complex. Whether people are reaching for the redeemable status, as many participants were, or eschewing normalized understandings of what it means to be redeemed and included in the social world, redeemability highlights the ways people actively participate in their own lives and rejects the common stereotype that people experiencing homelessness are apathetic and indolent. It also brings awareness to the consequences for those who cannot navigate the system on their own terms, often due to distress or physical health challenges, resulting in more coercive interventions by the mental health and criminal justice systems for those deemed irredeemable.

Mapping how those experiencing homelessness vie for redeemability also alerts us to the ways that people carve out inclusionary spaces within otherwise exclusionary environments. While being fully redeemed and welcomed into the included circuit may be the goal for some, achieving the redeem*able* status is extremely valuable yet rarely articulated. Identifying oneself and being recognized by professionals and para-professionals as redeemable provides a positive sense of self and hope that is difficult to come by when street-involved. It also comes with strategic advantages, such as increased opportunities for privacy, rule flexibility, and more favourable treatment by those in positions of power. Being excluded by the mainstream social body compels those experiencing homelessness to find people and spaces where they are included. Those who are housed do not have a monopoly over feeling included and recognizing instances of inclusion among the excluded diminishes the power of mainstream society to be the sole proprietor of feelings of belonging. The fact that people experiencing homelessness are compelled to make the best of their exclusion rests squarely on the shoulders of included members of society to challenge the status quo and the structural conditions that create and preserve the false included/excluded dichotomy.

Preventing and Ending Homelessness through Social Inclusion

Canada's federal, provincial, territorial, and municipal governments, are changing the way they respond to homelessness. As described in Chapter 2, for decades the homelessness sector was tasked with managing the homelessness crisis rather than finding solutions, and in many ways explored in this book, this is still the case. But a fundamental shift has taken place over the last decade where it is no longer deemed acceptable to provide strictly short-term, band-aid solutions. Instead, people with lived experience of homelessness, advocates, and other stakeholders are calling for bold and innovative strategies and interventions that will prevent, reduce, and ultimately end homelessness in Canada.

The *At Home/Chez Soi* project provided much-needed empirical evidence that investing in long-term solutions to homelessness involving immediate access to housing works. Housing First has become an international staple in responding to homelessness; in Finland, which offers a slightly different HF model, homelessness is consistently decreasing and rough sleeping is virtually non-existent while homelessness is rising in nearby countries (Centre for Social Justice, 2017). In Canada, the City of Medicine Hat, Alberta, has declared an end to homelessness because of their strong HF program. Housing First has the potential to dramatically reduce the number of people experiencing chronic homelessness.

The next frontier in transforming our response to homelessness is to prioritize homelessness prevention alongside HF programs. As Gaetz argues, if we focus solely on transitioning those experiencing chronic homelessness to housing there will always be new people to take their place in HF programs (Gaetz & Dej, 2017; Gaetz, Dej, et al., 2017). We must also direct our investments, innovation, and attention to support people to stay housed and avoid experiencing the potential trauma and victimization of homelessness in the first place. The typology of homelessness prevention set out by the Canadian Observatory on Homelessness (Gaetz & Dej, 2017) outlines five prevention areas: structural; systems; early intervention; eviction prevention; and housing stabilization. Including structural factors (i.e., a lack of affordable housing, discrimination facing Indigenous Peoples and people of colour, unaffordable child care, etc.) and systemic factors (i.e., restrictions to accessing services and discharging from public systems into homelessness, etc.) in the typology transgresses typically individualized interventions that dominate prevention discourses, including previous homelessness prevention initiatives. Including broader socio-structural conditions in efforts to prevent homelessness requires commitment and action from sectors not commonly involved in homelessness and housing, such as public health, education, criminal justice, and child welfare systems. Like HF, homelessness prevention is embedded within an understanding that housing is a human right and therefore we have a responsibility to ensure that people have access to a safe, appropriate, and affordable home.

As investments, policies, and practices shift toward preventing and ending homelessness, it is imperative that we take stock of how people who are homeless experience these systems, interventions, and relations with professionals and para-professionals. As a philosophy, HF positions self-determination at the forefront of all interventions; however, the arguments laid out in this book make clear that autonomy and choice are easily appropriated by techniques used to manage and contain, not empower. As HF and prevention initiatives scale up across Canada, this research cautions policy makers, advocates, and other stakeholders to be intentional about how programs and resources are delivered to people experiencing homelessness, especially mental health interventions. My call for reflection is twofold: first, we must scrutinize the unstated assumption that housing equals inclusion; and second, we must grapple with the fact that most programs, including innovative prevention and HF models, can reinforce the redeem*able* status and not actually create the redeem*ed* subject.

A common adage in the homelessness sector is "homelessness is never *only* a housing problem, but it is *always* a housing problem" [emphasis in original] (Dolbeare, 1996, p. 34). Certainly, this is true and is the foundation for the HF philosophy. Becoming healthy, finding and retaining employment or furthering education, connecting with friends and family, fostering a sense of independence, and most other goals are much more easily accomplished when housed. Given that 85 percent of those who experience homelessness do so for less than a month and do not require substantial social service intervention (Aubry et al., 2013), housing unaffordability is clearly the impetus for many people becoming and remaining homeless. The disinvestment in affordable housing by the federal government in the early 1990s substantially slowed the development of new affordable housing stock and the ability for social housing providers to maintain and repair existing stock (Suttor, 2016), playing a large part in today's homelessness crisis. The vast majority of households in core housing need struggle primarily with housing affordability and require poverty-reduction measures to reduce their risk of becoming homeless (Pomeroy, 2017). Policy shifts, such as the federal government's 2017 National Housing Strategy that includes legislation making housing a human right, is an important step toward remedying decades of insufficient investment, systems planning, and resource development.

However, there is a second part to Dolbeare's quote that is rarely repeated. He goes on to write: "Housing is necessary, *although sometimes not sufficient*, to solve the problem of homelessness" [emphasis added] (Dolbeare, 1996, p. 34). Many people who participated in this research were clear, through their words and actions, that housing was insufficient on its own to exit homelessness. Social isolation, loneliness, exclusion, and a lack of connection to community and support networks all contribute to difficulties in becoming and remaining stably housed. Even those who do exit homelessness in the normalized sense of the term (i.e., leave the streets or emergency shelters) may continue to identify as homeless because of a lack of housing stability or unsafe conditions: what Padgett (2007) calls "ontological insecurity." Many participants who no longer resided in the shelter were living in degrading conditions in run-down rooming houses or drug houses, and/or were threatened with home takeovers. Others, such as Max, faced such abject loneliness that they returned to the shelter for a sense of community and belonging. While HF relies on scattered site housing for people to live in buildings throughout the city, it is problematic to assume that people will naturally and easily create social networks outside of the homeless population. Rather, fostering social inclusion requires more deliberate and personalized support from not only service providers, but more importantly, society at large.

Housing First advocates designed interventions with an understanding that housing cannot be the sole response to homelessness, developing wraparound supports in the form of case management, addiction and/or mental health services, medical care, and related services for those who access subsidized housing. Although less developed as a broad strategy, some prevention programs also respond to issues beyond housing, such as family mediation for young people in conflict with their parents/caregivers. However, we must reflect on how far strategies, program models, and interventions go in supporting people to become socially included, rather than included among the excluded. This is not a critique of HF specifically or a systematic analysis of its outcome measurements; rather, it is a remark on all new and innovative program models seeking to solve the homelessness crisis, and a call to pay attention to the ways they may unintentionally contribute to, rather than dismantle, marginalization and social exclusion.

First, we must recognize that measures of success in housing programs remain firmly grounded in normalized, and often medicalized, understandings of stability and well-being, thus cementing the need to seek redeemability among those experiencing homelessness. For example, the original HF program, the Pathways model, sought normalized (i.e., middle-class, white, able-bodied) ways of being as an outcome of the program (that is, an "ordinary" community life that includes "ordinary" neighbours and friends) (Pleace & Bretherton, 2013). For instance, among social and health outcomes in the *At Home/Chez Soi* project, community functioning and overall well-being included a measure on how well someone accepts their psychiatric disability. Another scale determined if participants knew there were mental health services to help in times of distress, reinforcing medicalized, formalized institutional practices as defining wellness.[1]

Second, although the results of *At Home/Chez Soi* revealed some improvement in people's quality of life among those who received HF programming, the level of improvement was much smaller than housing and service use outcomes (Goering et al., 2014). Here, the focus on providing housing, while vital, obscures the material ways people exiting homelessness continue to face oppression, discrimination, and overall social exclusion once housed. Voronka et al.'s (2014) study of qualitative interviews from *At Home/Chez Soi* (both those who received HF and those who received regular community treatment) revealed the extent to which people exiting homelessness remain redeem*able* but not redeem*ed*. Participants described difficult power dynamics between themselves and service providers, where those receiving services felt compelled to show their gratitude and humility. Others described being heavily monitored and managed, with some finding that positioning medication compliance as the foremost solution to their marginalization was unhelpful and that these kinds of conditions, whether formal or informal, left many feeling like their autonomy was undermined. Most striking was the feeling of exclusion:

> This general feeling of being different, of being an outsider, was a common thread in participants' narratives. This difference was not particularly articulated as stemming from their mental health status, but rather from an assemblage of identities, for example, such as the difference of being a queer-identified Aboriginal youth adopted into a White family, or as a White male who left home early due to family instability because of sexuality. (Voronka et al., 2014, p. 265)

The authors call for a commitment to social justice in efforts to end homelessness, one that seeks to remedy issues of power imbalance, normalization, rights, privacy, and exclusion. I echo this call. Only when we render visible and undo deeply entrenched modes of exclusion can we hope to prevent and end homelessness *and* social exclusion.

Recommendations
The findings from this book provide evidence for policy and practice shifts to avoid exacerbating social exclusion and instead promote inclusion as defined by those with experiences of homelessness.

Policy
- Relevant federal, provincial, and territorial government sectors must create policies and target investments to programs that address the structural and systemic root causes of homelessness, including poverty reduction measures, anti-discrimination legislation, increased housing affordability, and the elimination of legislation that criminalizes homeless and marginalized people (e.g., anti-panhandling laws).
- Investments in social programs and community development should prioritize creating opportunities for meaningful social inclusion, especially at the municipal level and including private stakeholders. This means building community capacity and facilitating access to spaces and events of interest (i.e., providing low-cost or free public transportation, access to cultural events, community spaces, technology, etc.). These resources should ensure they reach particular excluded groups, such as the LGBTQ2S+ community, newcomers, people with disabilities, etc.
- All orders of government and various sectors (such as the criminal justice and health care systems) must show demonstrable progress in implementing the Truth and Reconciliation Commission's Calls to Action and the National Inquiry into Missing and Murdered Indigenous Women and Girls' Calls for Justice. This includes acknowledging that homelessness is a direct outcome of settler-colonialism and making reparations to address the disproportionate rate of Indigenous Peoples in the homeless population as well as other sites of exclusion and marginalization (i.e., child protection, etc.)
- Funding bodies should develop models to incentivize and support community-led research and promote research opportunities for people with lived experience of homelessness at equal pay with other research professionals.

Practice
- Housing First and prevention models must be designed and implemented intentionally to include social integration and inclusion as key outcomes, defined and measured by those experiencing homelessness, while being sensitive to culturally specific understandings of inclusion.

- Shelters must be supported to shift their focus to preventing and ending homelessness (i.e., through shelter diversion, rapid rehousing, wraparound supports for people exiting homelessness, etc.) with the ultimate goal of eliminating the homelessness industrial complex (although some kind of emergency provisions for natural disasters, personal crises, etc. will still be necessary).
- Sectors that work with marginalized populations must be required to promote a variety of services to support mental health and overall well-being beyond strictly psychotropic medication, including prioritizing and funding alternative services, especially peer-led and peer-run services.
- Investment must be made in spaces and programming for, and building knowledge capacity around, supporting people with various levels of distress, minimizing as many barriers as possible to community integration and social inclusion.
- Development of programs and intervention models should ensure that they recognize and promote personal autonomy and self-determination, especially regarding personal health and treatment.

Final Thoughts

The research contained in this book points to a single overarching theme – that Othering and exclusion have a profoundly negative impact on housing, homelessness, and well-being. Those who experience homelessness, particularly people who are chronically homeless, must grapple with institutions, systems, and interventions that maintain and potentially increase their exclusion. The mental health system holds sway in this domain, using biomedical conceptions of illness, symptoms, risk, and treatment that minimize or outright deny personal autonomy. However, there is a way forward. As housing becomes recognized as a human right, we must remedy other human rights violations that perpetuate marginalization, such as discrimination and oppression in all its forms, inequity, and barriers to Indigenous rights to self-determination. Rather than working in isolation, sweeping cultural shifts that tackle poverty, sexism and gender-based violence, racism and ethnocentrism, settler-colonialism, ableism, ageism, and homophobia and transphobia will result in better housing outcomes and less distress for those most at risk of exclusion. This is a tall order, but one that we can and must face if we are to move from social exclusion to meaningful and permanent inclusion. Solutions to homelessness must account for the homeless experience on a human level. Exclusion is more than not having a house or not being a part of the workforce. It often comes to define the core of who somebody is. Until people feel included we cannot truly end homelessness.

Notes

Chapter 1: Exploring Exclusion among People Experiencing Homelessness

1 For detailed figures see: *The Use of Custodial Remand in Canada 1988–89 to 1997–98*, http://epe.lac-bac.gc.ca/100/200/301/statcan/use_custodial_remand-e/0019885-550-XIE.pdf and *Adult Correctional Statistics in Canada 2015/2016*, http://www.statcan.gc.ca/pub/85-002-x/2017001/article/14700-eng.pdf.
2 I use the term *people experiencing homelessness* throughout the book as a form of linguistic resistance to acknowledge and affirm people's personhood beyond their housing status.
3 I use the term *distress* in this book to recognize the difficult physical and emotional situations people find themselves in while de-privileging medicalized discourses of mental health (Ussher, 1991), placing lived experience at the centre of the narrative without making assumptions as to the nature or cause of the pain.
4 For example, one volunteer I worked with serving breakfast on Monday mornings was appalled that not everyone said good morning and thank you when they received their meal. To counteract this habit, she would loudly say "you're welcome" to those who did not say thank you. I eventually pulled her aside and spoke to her about the expectations of volunteer work and the degrading and dehumanizing system that many people experiencing homelessness face. I also suggested that many individuals in the line at Starbucks likely do not say thank you on a Monday morning but are not berated for their omission. After a few months she was hired onto a police force in rural Ontario and left the shelter.
5 Pseudonyms are used for both shelters to protect the anonymity of the shelter and those who use its services.
6 Four interviews were omitted because of their brevity (lasting less than ten minutes) and lack of any kind of substantive response. I was unable to transcribe two

interviews because they occurred outside in extremely windy conditions and the recorder was unable to pick up the voices (in one of these interviews the participant was only comfortable walking in the wind while we talked). These six research participants still received their remuneration.

7 Theoretical saturation is a phase of qualitative research where no new insights emerge from the data and there is satisfactory breadth and depth to the research to allow for data collection to end.

8 These divisions are often captured during interpersonal interactions as well as being embedded in formalized practices. In *Ewert v Canada* (2018), the Supreme Court of Canada ruled that the assessment tools used by Correctional Service of Canada (CSC) to determine prisoners' security status (minimum, medium, or maximum) and parole eligibility discriminated against Indigenous prisoners. Likewise, in Ottawa, Indigenous housing service providers stopped using the VI-SPDAT (an assessment tool used to evaluate service prioritization) because it did not accurately capture Indigenous Peoples' experiences of homelessness.

9 Anti-homelessness spikes and arm rests in the middle of park benches are two examples of defensive architecture designed to stop people experiencing homelessness from existing within public spaces.

10 Jails refer to detention and remand centres for those awaiting trial and to provincial facilities for those facing convictions of less than two years, whereas prisons refer to federal correctional facilities for people serving sentences longer than two years.

Chapter 2: The Pillars of Exclusion

1 For an overview of some of these methodological challenges, see Donaldson (2017) and Frankish et al. (2005).

2 Turtle Island is the original name for North America as per the Anishinabe people.

3 ECT continued to be used past the 1960s in some cases of severe depression and bipolar disorder. It has recently gained traction as an innovative treatment for methamphetamine-induced psychosis.

4 Although there is a great deal of variation in how these terms are adopted and used by members of the mad movement, generally ex-patients/survivors are those who reject the medical model (sometimes refusing psychotropic medication) and focus on user-led alternatives. Consumers/clients/patients find fault with, but largely accept, the medical model and seek to reform the system to better include consumers in mental health decision making (Burstow, 2013; Diamond, 2013).

5 Some argue that the mental health system has co-opted the term *recovery* (Burstow, 2013). For example, the Schizophrenia Society of Canada uses the idea of recovery as paramount to its treatment programs, which relies heavily on medication compliance.

6 Between 1960 and 1976, 32,622 beds in psychiatric hospitals were closed across Canada but 4,992 psychiatric beds in general hospitals were opened in the same period, and thus 27,630 beds were lost during that time. It was not until the 1990s that the number of psychiatric beds in general hospitals also receded (Sealy & Whitehead, 2004).

7 Interacting with a police-mental health unit may allow people to avoid a holding cell or detention centre, but they are often sent to psychiatric hospitals or emergency rooms (Lee et al., 2015), thus perpetuating transcarceral modes of governance.
8 On July 27, 2013, police were called when Sammy Yatim, an 18-year-old man of colour, was threatening passengers on a Toronto streetcar with a small knife and exposed himself to a group of young women. Although all passengers were safely removed from the streetcar, Constable James Forcillo shot Yatim eight times when Yatim took a step forward, killing him instantly. In an unprecedented decision, Constable Forcillo was found guilty of attempted murder. The initial three shots that killed Yatim were regarded as justifiable but the subsequent five shots were not, thus Forcillo attempted to murder Yatim, who was already dead. Mack (2014) reminds us that Yatim's story is not exceptional and that there is a long history of police use of force against people experiencing distress and especially against people of colour.

Abdirahman Abdi died when police were called to a coffee shop on July 24, 2016, because Abdi, identified by family and neighbours as mentally ill, was allegedly groping and harassing women in the café. After a violent arrest by Constable Daniel Montsion, Abdi was pronounced dead. Montsion was charged with manslaughter, aggravated assault, and assault with a weapon. At the time of writing, the trial is still under way.

Chapter 3: Managing in Place

Epigraph: (Bauman, 2001a, p. 121). Bauman, Z. (2001a). *Community: Seeking Safety in an Insecure World*. Cambridge, UK: Polity Press.
1 The exception to a highly scheduled routine among other prisoners is if the prisoner is placed in segregation, where the absence of activity, social interaction, and communication is precisely part of the punishment (Martel, 2006).
2 In some cases, individuals will be forced to reside in a particular homeless shelter as their place of residence while awaiting trial (Gaetz & O'Grady, 2009). Ottawa shelters do not receive monetary compensation for these individuals other than the regular funding from the city for the number of beds filled.
3 The concept of the homeless consumer will be explored in Chapter 6.
4 Coercive strategies can also be used alongside persuasion strategies, especially for those who are found irredeemable: that is, those who are deemed hopeless and who are positioned as needing the traditional total institutions in the name of "public safety," such as individuals who face long-term prison sentences or involuntary commitment to psychiatric hospitals.
5 Goffman's (1961) "moral career of the mental patient" describes the phases in which someone becomes indoctrinated into a total institution, supplanting their old identity with that of the normalized, degraded, and altered subjectivity.
6 It is not clear why Mac mentions the race of his attackers but it is worth noting that he specifies only race, and not other identifiers such as gender or age. It is doubtful that he would have mentioned race had they been white (Smith, 2014). This is just one example of the regular and ongoing stereotyping and discrimination Indigenous Peoples face in the homeless population (Belanger et al., 2013).

7 Marcus does not specify what constitutes a "short stay," but in Ottawa, the average length of stay in a shelter is seventy-three days (Alliance to End Homelessness Ottawa, 2016).
8 The Men's Project, now known as Men & Healing, offers counselling for men who were childhood victims of sexual or physical abuse.
9 The Royal Ottawa Hospital (ROH) is the city's mental health care centre.
10 Seroquel is an antipsychotic meant to treat bipolar disorder but has become the drug of choice to prescribe for a wide array of issues (Kilty, 2012).
11 Louise's citizenship status and the nature of her extradition were unclear to me.

Chapter 4: Identity Management

1 This sense of shame is a Westernized construction; in many Indigenous communities it is common for people to live together, share resources, etc.
2 While ADHD is generally identified as a neurodevelopmental disorder and only sometimes qualified as a mental illness in the medical and social discourse, participants in this research who spoke about ADHD firmly placed it within the realm of mental illness.
3 Two-Spirit is a pan-Indigenous concept that describes a broad array of gender identities and sexual orientations (Vowel, 2016).
4 St. Francis Xavier University, in Antigonish, Nova Scotia.
5 Conrad Black is an exceptionally wealthy and influential man who ran numerous international newspapers, was a member of the Order of Canada, and is conferred as a Baron in the British House of Lords. In 2007, Black was convicted of fraud and obstruction of justice and served just over two years in an American prison. He was subsequently stripped of many of his titles and positions in business; however, in May 2019, President Donald Trump granted Black a full pardon.
6 Chico characterized individuals who are unilaterally driven by their addiction as animalistic in nature; he may also have been referring to the small, gated terrace adjacent to one of the shelters as the "cage" where people are "confined."
7 Given that Tom does not disclose his sexuality to other members of the homeless population, it is important to note that this distancing strategy is only available in certain contexts, such as with an "outsider" like myself, and is likely not very useful for him to negotiate his status among service providers or other people experiencing homelessness.
8 Chapter 6 looks closely at how the "seriously mentally ill," those who are at risk of hurting themselves or others and who have significant challenges meeting their basic needs, are regarded by the homelessness sector, in contrast with those other individuals who negotiate the mental illness identity more deliberately.

Chapter 5: Taking the Blame

1 Although the correct reference is the Christmas TV special *Rudolph the Red-Nosed Reindeer and the Island of Misfit Toys*, Max's reference to being "broken" is more in keeping with his and other participants' narratives of mental illness as having a biological etiology, where they feel their brains, synapses, and/or chemical makeup are maladaptive or broken (Ussher, 2005).

2 Valverde (2006) acknowledges the tension in AA between its Protestant history, its theory of addiction as a disease, and its focus on habit-based governing techniques and suggests that it is the hybridity between these theories and ideological positions that accounts for AA's longevity.
3 As mentioned in Chapter 3, the City of Ottawa has at least a five-year wait-list for social housing (Social Housing Registry of Ottawa, 2014). There are no statistics on the overall wait times for free or low-cost counselling services, but Melissa, a case worker who participated in the focus group, claims that the average wait time in Ottawa is three months.

Chapter 6: The Homeless Mental Health Consumer

1 Reith (2004) points out the ironic relationship between neoliberal conceptualizations of freedom that include self-control and a search for self-actualization and a consumerist framework that encourages hedonistic practices where people constantly consume, act on their desires, and aim for short-term happiness.
2 Federal and provincial correctional facilities lack adequate health, mental health, and harm reduction services, with provincial jails in particular having limited or no programming at all offered by the ministries (Dodge & McIntosh, 2014; van der Meulen et al., 2017).
3 The overall vacancy rate in Ottawa in 2019 was 1.8 percent, lower than the Canadian average of 2.2 percent (Canada Mortgage and Housing Corporation, 2020). Meanwhile, the lack of affordable housing in Ottawa and across Canada is staggering. Investment in affordable housing declined rapidly in the 1990s and even with a renewed investment in 2013, when adjusted for inflation, per capita spending on affordable housing is $55 less than it was in 1989 (Gaetz et al., 2014; Suttor, 2016). The federal government's National Housing Strategy, released in 2017, is set to create 100,000 new affordable housing units over ten years (Ministry of Families, Children and Social Development, 2017).
4 Donohue and Moore (2009) explain how the prisoner and the person experiencing homelessness can be constituted differently, despite the significant overlap in the populations: "We are careful here not to see offenders and clients as different people. Instead, we follow Foucault (1977), to see these characters as different subjectivities who exist in the same body and whose expressions are dependent on the relationships, locations and actions of the individual" (p. 320).
5 The City of Ottawa pays the shelters a per diem of $44 for every person who sleeps in their shelter on a given night. The province covers 20 percent of this cost. Shelters and service providers also receive grants and program-specific funding from other public agencies and private corporations. Organizations that serve the homeless, such as CMHA and community health centres, are generally funded through multiple levels of government.
6 While there is scant literature on the prescription rates for antipsychotic medication in the homeless population, because of the overlap between the homeless and prison populations (Fischer et al., 2008), the plethora of research on the subject of medication non-compliance among the homeless (Muir-Cochrane et al., 2006; Sajatovic et al., 2013), and the fact that 73 percent of this research sample had experience with

psychotropic medication, we can infer a high proportion of psychotropic medication prescriptions among those experiencing homelessness.

7 Effexor is a selective serotonin and norepinephrine reuptake inhibitor (SSNRI) used to treat depression and anxiety.

8 Although other mental health programmes, such as ACT and psychiatric outreach teams exist in Ottawa, none of the participants in this research project indicated that they had ever accessed these treatment methods.

9 Lenny's use of the term "prostitution" connotes sex work as an inherently negative, disreputable, and deviant occupation and identity marker. Valuable research and advocacy work across Canada have sought to break down the stigma associated with labour practices involving the skin trades (Bruckert, 2012; Raguparan, 2017).

10 Benzodiazepine is a drug classification referring to tranquilizers that are most often prescribed for anxiety. Clonazepam is a benzodiazepine.

11 Seamus's comment about physical dominance refers to a hyper-masculine concept of power (Beasley, 2008) that can be found in an all-male emergency shelter. Unfortunately, none of the women research participants discussed internal power dynamics in this way to allow for a comparative analysis.

12 In 2018, a single person on OW receives $733 a month. A single person on ODSP receives $1,169 a month. Those living in emergency shelters receive reduced rates (see the *Ontario Disability Support Program Act* and the *Ontario Works Act*). The Ford government recently announced cuts to the social assistance programs, making it more difficult for people to be eligible for ODSP.

13 Chuck uses the term *distress* differently than I do. Here, he is referring to the criteria for involuntary incapacitation in a psychiatric hospital – risk of harm to the self or others.

Chapter 7: Moving toward Inclusion

1 The Multnomah Community Ability Scale and Recovery Assessment Scale, respectively, contain these measures.

References

Abramovich, A. (2017). Understanding how policy and culture create oppressive conditions for LGBTQ2S youth in the shelter system. *Journal of Homosexuality, 64*(11), 1484–1501.

Adler, P. A., & Adler, P. (1987). *Membership roles in field research.* Thousand Oaks, CA: Sage.

Ahmed, S. (2010). *The promise of happiness.* Durham, NC: Duke University Press.

Ahmed, S. (2012). *On being included: Racism and diversity in institutional life.* Durham, NC: Duke University Press.

Alaazi, D. A., Masuda, J. R., Evans, J., & Distasio, J. (2015). Therapeutic landscapes of home: Exploring Indigenous peoples' experiences of a Housing First intervention in Winnipeg. *Social Science & Medicine, 147,* 30–37.

Allen, T. C. (2000). *Someone to talk to: Care and control of the homeless.* Black Point, NS: Fernwood Press.

Alliance to End Homelessness Ottawa. (2015). *Community debrief and call to action: Ottawa's participation in 20,000 homes.* Ottawa, ON: Alliance to End Homelessness Ottawa.

Alliance to End Homelessness Ottawa. (2016). *2016 progress report on ending homelessness in Ottawa.* Ottawa, ON: Alliance to End Homelessness Ottawa.

Allwood, C. M., & Berry, J. W. (2006). Origins and development of Indigenous psychologies: An international analysis. *International Journal of Psychology, 41*(4), 243–268.

American Psychiatric Association. (2013). *Diagnostic and Statistical Manual of Mental Disorders DSM-5.* Washington, DC: American Psychiatric Association.

Asberg, K., & Renk, K. (2015). Safer in jail? A comparison of victimization history and psychological adjustment between previously homeless and non-homeless incarcerated women. *Feminist Criminology, 10*(2), 165–187.

Aubry, T., Farrell, S. J., Hwang, S. W., & Calhoun, M. (2013). Identifying the patterns of emergency shelter stays of single individuals in Canadian cities of different sizes. *Housing Studies, 28*(6), 910–927.

Bahr, H. M. (1970). *Disaffiliated man: Essays and bibliography on Skid Row, vagrancy, and outsiders.* Toronto, ON: University of Toronto Press.

Baker, C. K., Billhardt, K. A., Warren, J., Rollins, C., & Glass, N. E. (2010). Domestic violence, housing instability, and homelessness: A review of housing policies and program practices for meeting the needs of survivors. *Aggression and Violent Behavior, 15*(6), 430–439.

Baldry, E., Dowse, L., & Clarence, M. (2012). *People with mental and cognitive disabilities: Pathways into prison* [background paper for Outlaws to Inclusion Conference]. School of Social Sciences and International Studies, The University of New South Wales.

Barker, S., Barron, N., McFarland, B. H., and Bigelow, D. A. (1993). *User's manual for the Multnomah Community Ability Scale.* Portland, OR: Network Behavioral Healthcare.

Bauman, Z. (1988). *Freedom.* London: Open University Press.

Bauman, Z. (1998). *Work, consumerism and the new poor.* London: Open University Press.

Bauman, Z. (2001a). *Community: Seeking safety in an insecure world.* Cambridge, UK: Polity Press.

Bauman, Z. (2001b). Consuming life. *Journal of Consumer Culture, 1*(1), 9–29.

Bauman, Z. (2004). *Wasted lives: Modernity and its outcasts.* Cambridge, UK: Polity Press.

Bauman, Z. (2007). *Consuming life.* Cambridge, UK: Polity Press.

Beasley, C. (2008). Rethinking hegemonic masculinity in a globalizing world. *Men and Masculinities, 11*(1), 86–103.

Beaudette, J. N., Power, J., & Stewart, L. 2015. *National prevalence of mental disorders among incoming federally-sentenced men offenders* (Research Report R-357). Ottawa, ON: Correctional Service Canada – Research Branch.

Becker, H. S. (1963). *Outsiders: Studies in the sociology of deviance.* London Free Press of Glencoe.

Becker, H. S. (1967). Whose side are we on? *Social Problems, 14*(3), 239–247.

Beckett, K., & Herbert, S. (2010). Penal boundaries: Banishment and the expansion of punishment. *Law & Social Inquiry, 35*(1), 1–38.

Beckett, K., & Murakawa, N. (2012). Mapping the shadow carceral state: Towards an institutionally capacious approach to punishment. *Theoretical Criminology, 16*(2), 221–244.

Beier, A. L. (2004). *The problem of the poor in Tudor and early Stuart England.* Oxfordshire, UK: Taylor & Francis.

Belanger, Y. D., Awosoga, O., & Weasel Head, G. (2013). Homelessness, urban Aboriginal people, and the need for a national enumeration. *Aboriginal Policy Studies, 2*(2), 4–33.

Ben-Moshe, L. (2017). Why prisons are not "the new asylums." *Punishment & Society, 19*(3), 272–289.

Berlant, L. (2011). *Cruel optimism.* Durham, NC: Duke University Press.

Bernier, D., Bellot, C., Sylvestre, M-E., & Chesnay, C. (2011). *La judiciarisation des personnes on situation d'itinérance à Québec: Point de vue des actors sociojudiciaires et analyse du phénomène*. Toronto, ON: Canadian Homelessness Research Network Press.

Bessenoff, G. R., & Snow, D. (2006). Absorbing society's influence: Body image self-discrepancy and internalized shame. *Sex Roles, 54*(9–10), 727–731.

Binch, J., Dej, E., & Ecker, J. (2018, November 6). *Rooming houses: Homeless or housed?* [Conference presentation]. Canadian Alliance to End Homelessness 2018: National Conference on Ending Homelessness, Hamilton, ON, Canada.

Blackstock, C. (2014). The Government of Canada: On trial for the racial discrimination of First Nations children. In S. Hessle (Ed.), *Environmental change and sustainable social development: Social work – social development* (pp. 7–12). Farnham, UK: Ashgate.

Blumer, H. (1969). *Symbolic interactionism: Perspectives and method*. Prentice-Hall.

Bosworth, M. (2007). Creating the responsible prisoner: Federal admission and orientation packs. *Punishment & Society, 9*(1), 67–85.

Bosworth, M., & Carrabine, E. (2001). Reassessing resistance: Race, gender and sexuality in prison. *Punishment & Society, 3*(4), 501–515.

Bourdieu, P. (1980). Le capital social. *Actes de la recherche en sciences sociales, 31*, 2–3.

Boydell, K. M., Goering, P., & Morrell-Bellai, T. L. (2000). Narratives of identity: Re-presentation of self in people who are homeless. *Qualitative Health Research, 10*(1), 26–38.

Brennan, S. (2011). Violent victimization of Aboriginal women in the Canadian provinces, 2009. *Juristat*, 85-002-X.

Bruckert, C. (2012). The mark of "disreputable" labour: Workin' it: Sex workers negotiate stigma. In S. Hannem & C. Bruckert (Eds.), *Stigma revisited: Implications of the mark* (pp. 55–78). Ottawa, ON: University of Ottawa Press.

Burstow, B. (2004). Progressive psychotherapists and the psychiatric survivor movement. *Journal of Humanistic Psychology, 44*(2), 141–154.

Burstow, B. (2005). Feminist antipsychiatry praxis – women and the movement(s): A Canadian perspective. In W. Chan, D. Chunn, & R. Menzies (Eds.), *Women, madness and the law: A feminist reader* (pp. 245–258). San Diego, CA: Glasshouse Press.

Burstow, B. (2013). A rose by any other name: Naming and the battle against psychiatry. In B. A. LeFrançois, R. Menzies, & G. Reaume (Eds.), *Mad matters: A critical reader in Canadian mad studies* (pp. 79–90). Toronto, ON: Canadian Scholars' Press.

Butera, J-A. (2013). *Home takeovers of vulnerable tenants: Perspectives from Ottawa*. Ottawa, ON: Crime Prevention Ottawa.

Butler, J. (1990). *Gender trouble: Feminism and the subversion of identity*. Abingdon, UK: Routledge.

Butler, J. (2004a). *Precarious life: The powers of mourning and violence*. London and New York: Verso.

Butler, J. (2004b). *Undoing gender*. Abingdon, UK: Routledge.

Canada Mortgage and Housing Corporation. (2019). *Incidence of urban households in core housing need (%) 2012–2017*. https://www.cmhc-schl.gc.ca/en/data-and-research/data-tables/incidence-urban-households-core-housing-need.

Canada Mortgage and Housing Corporation. (2020). *Rental market statistics summary by metropolitan areas, census agglomerations and cities, October 2019.* https://www03.cmhc-schl.gc.ca/hmip-pimh/en/TableMapChart/Table?TableId=2.1.31.2&GeographyId=35&GeographyTypeId=2&DisplayAs=Table&GeograghyName=Ontario.

Carlen, P., & Tombs, J. (2006). Reconfigurations in penality: The ongoing case of the women's imprisonment and reintegration industries. *Theoretical Criminology, 10*(3), 337–360.

Caron, C. (2014). A witness to loss. In R. Berman (Ed.), *Corridor talk: Canadian feminist scholars share stories of research partnerships* (pp. 141–159). Toronto, ON: Inanna Publications and Education.

Castel, R. (1988). *The regulation of madness: The origins of incarceration in France* (W. D. Halls, Trans.). Los Angeles, CA: University of California Press.

Castel, R. (2003). *From manual workers to wage laborers: Transformation of the social question* (R. Boyd, Trans.). Piscataway, NJ: Transaction.

Centre for Social Justice. (2017). *Housing First: Housing-led solutions to rough sleeping and homelessness.* London, UK: Centre for Social Justice.

Chamberlain, C., & Johnson, G. (2018). From long-term homelessness to stable housing: Investigating "liminality." *Housing Studies, 33*(8), 1246–1263.

Chan, W., Chunn, D. E., & Menzies, R. J. (2005). *Women, madness and the law: A feminist reader.* San Diego, CA: Glasshouse Press.

Chapple, A., Ziebland, S., & McPherson, A. (2004). Stigma, shame, and blame experienced by patients with lung cancer: Qualitative study. *British Medical Journal, 328*(7454), 1470–1475.

Christensen, J. (2016). Indigenous homelessness: Canadian context. In E. Peters & J. Christensen (Eds.), *Indigenous homelessness: Perspectives from Canada, Australia, and New Zealand* (pp. 15–23). Winnipeg, MB: University of Manitoba Press.

Chunn, D., & Gavigan, S. A. M. (2004). Welfare law, welfare fraud, and the moral regulation of the "never deserving" poor. *Social & Legal Studies, 13*(2), 219–243.

Church, K. (2013). Making madness matter in academic practice. In B. A. LeFrançois, R. Menzies, & G. Reaume (Eds.), *Mad matters: A critical reader in Canadian mad studies* (pp. 181–190). Toronto, ON: Canadian Scholars' Press.

City of Ottawa. (2018a). *Everyone counts: Ottawa 2018 homelessness PiT count presentation.* Ottawa, ON: City of Ottawa.

City of Ottawa. (2018b). *10 year housing and homelessness plan progress report 2014–2017.* Ottawa, ON: City of Ottawa.

Clapham, D. (2010). Happiness, well-being and housing policy. *Policy & Politics, 38*(2), 253–267.

Cockerham, W. C. (2003). *Sociology of mental disorder.* Upper Saddle River, NJ: Prentice Hall.

Cohen, S. (1979). The punitive city: Notes on the dispersal of social control. *Crime, Law and Social Change, 3*(4), 339–363.

Cohen, S. (1985). *Visions of social control: Crime, punishment and classification.* Cambridge, UK: Polity Press.

Cole, D. (2020). *The skin we're in: A year of resistance and power.* Toronto, ON: Doubleday Canada.

Conrad, P. (2007). *The medicalization of society: On the transformation of human conditions into treatable disorders.* Baltimore, MD: Johns Hopkins University Press.

Conrad, P., & Schneider, J. W. (1992). *Deviance and medicalization: From badness to sickness.* Philadelphia, PA: Temple University Press.

Cook, J. A., & Jonikas, J. A. (2002). Self-determination among mental health consumers/survivors: Using lessons from the past to guide the future. *Journal of Disability Policy Studies, 13*(2), 88–96.

Cooper, D. (1967). *Psychiatry and anti-psychiatry.* New York: Ballantine Books.

Corrigan, P. W., Salzer, M., Ralph, R. O., Sangster, Y., & Keck, L. (2004). Examining the factor structure of the Recovery Assessment Scale. *Schizophrenia Bulletin, 30*(4): 1035–1041.

Crook, R., & Wood, D. (2014). "The customer is always right"? Consumerism and the probation service. *European Journal of Probation, 6*(1), 57–66.

Crossley, M. L., & Crossley, N. (2001). "Patient" voices, social movements and the habitus; How psychiatric survivors "speak out." *Social Science and Medicine, 52*(10), 1477–1489.

Cruikshank, B. (1999). *The will to empower: Democratic citizens and other subjects.* Ithaca, NY: Cornell University Press.

Daley, A., & Mulé, N. J. (2014). LGBTQs and the DSM-5: A critical queer response. *Journal of Homosexuality, 61*(9), 1288–1312.

Davis, A. Y. (1998, September 10). *Masked racism: Reflections on the prison industrial complex.* Colorlines. https://www.colorlines.com/articles/masked-racism-reflections-prison-industrial-complex.

Dean, M. (1996). Foucault, government and the enfolding of authority. In A. Barry, T. Osborne, & N. Rose (Eds.), *Foucault and political reason: Liberalism, neo-liberalism, and rationalities of government* (pp. 209–229). Chicago, IL: University of Chicago Press.

Dear, M. J., & Wolch, J. R. (1987). *Landscapes of despair: From deinstitutionalization to homelessness.* Cambridge, UK: Polity Press.

Dej, E. (2015). Sanctionner les (non-) coupables: Préciser la disposition de non-responsabilité criminelle. *Criminologie, 48*(1), 37–58.

Dej, E. (2018). When a man's home isn't a castle: Hegemonic masculinity among men experiencing homelessness and mental illness. In J. Kilty, M. Jennifer, & E. Dej (Eds.), *Containing madness: Gender and "psy" in institutional contexts* (pp. 215–239). London: Palgrave Macmillan.

DeOllos, I. Y. (1997). *On becoming homeless: The shelterization process for homeless families.* Lanham, MD: University Press of America.

Derkzen, D., Barker, J., McMillan, K., & Stewart, L. (2017). *Rates of current mental disorders among women offenders in custody in CSC* (Research Report, ERR 16–23). Ottawa, ON: Correctional Service Canada – Research Branch.

Desjarlais, R. (1997). *Shelter blues: Sanity and selfhood among the homeless.* Philadelphia, PA: University of Philadelphia Press.

DeVerteuil, G., May, J., & von Mahs, J. (2009). Complexity not collapse: Recasting the geographies of homelessness in a "punitive" age. *Progress in Human Geography, 33*(5), 646–666.

DeWard, S. L., & Moe, A. M. (2010). "Like a prison!": Homeless women's narratives of surviving shelter. *Journal of Sociology & Social Welfare, 37*(1), 115–135.

Diamond, S. (2013). What makes us a community? Reflections on building solidarity in anti-sanist praxis. In B. A. LeFrançois, R. Menzies, & G. Reaume (Eds.), *Mad matters: A critical reader in Canadian mad studies* (pp. 64–78). Toronto, ON: Canadian Scholars' Press.

Dobchuk-Land, B. (2017). Resisting "progressive" carceral expansion: Lessons for abolitionists from anti-colonial resistance. *Contemporary Justice Review, 20*(4), 404–418.

Doberstein, C., & Smith, A. (2019). When political values and perceptions of deservingness collide: Evaluating public support for homelessness investments in Canada. *International Journal of Social Welfare, 28*(3), 282–292.

Dodge, B., & McIntosh, J. (2014, September 18). *Rehab programs feel the crunch: A four-part series about recidivism in Ontario.* Ottawa Community News. http://www.mapinc.org/drugnews/v14/n763/a03.html?136.

Dolbeare, C. (1996). Housing policy: A general consideration. In J. Baumohl (Ed.), *Homelessness in America* (pp. 34–45). Phoenix, AZ: Oryx Press.

Donaldson, J. (2017). *Point-in-time count toolkit.* Toronto, ON: Canadian Observatory on Homelessness Press.

Donohue, E., & Moore, D. (2009). When is an offender not an offender? Power, the client and shifting penal subjectivities. *Punishment & Society, 11*(3), 319–336.

Douglas, S. J., & Michaels, M. W. (2004). *The mommy myth: The idealization of motherhood and how it has undermined women.* New York: Free Press.

Drake, R. E., & Whitley, R. (2014). Recovery and severe mental illness: Description and analysis. *The Canadian Journal of Psychiatry, 59*(5), 236–242.

Dumm, T. L. (1996). *Michel Foucault and the politics of freedom.* Thousand Oaks, CA: Sage.

Ecker, J., Aubry, T., & Sylvestre, J. (2019). A review of the literature on LGBTQ adults who experience homelessness. *Journal of Homosexuality, 66*(3), 297–323.

Elbogen, E. B., & Johnson, S. C. (2009). The intricate link between violence and mental disorder. *Archives of General Psychiatry, 66*(2), 152–161.

Else-Quest, N. M., LoConte, N., Schiller, J. H., & Shibley Hyde, J. (2009). Perceived stigma, self-blame, and adjustment among lung, breast, and prostate cancer patients. *Psychology and Health, 24*(8), 949–964.

Esmonde, J. (2002). Criminalizing poverty: The criminal law power and the Safe Streets Act. *Journal of Law & Social Policy, 17,* 83–86.

Etter, G. W., Birzer, M. L., & Fields, J. (2008). The jail as a dumping ground: The incidental incarceration of mentally ill individuals. *Criminal justice Studies, 21*(1), 79–89.

Ewert v Canada, [2018] 2 SCR 165.

Fabris, E. (2011). *Tranquil prisons: Chemical incarceration under community treatment orders.* Toronto, ON: University of Toronto Press.

Fabris, E. (2013). Mad success: What could go wrong when psychiatry employs us as peers? In B. A. LeFrançois, R. Menzies, & G. Reaume (Eds.), *Mad matters: A critical reader in Canadian mad studies* (pp. 130–139). Toronto, ON: Canadian Scholars' Press.

Fahy, A. (2007). The unbearable fatigue of compassion: Notes from a substance abuse counselor who dreams of working at Starbucks. *Clinical Social Work Journal, 35*(3), 199–205.

Fairclough, N. (1985). Critical and descriptive goals in discourse analysis. *Journal of Pragmatics, 9*(6), 739–763.

Feldman, L. C. (2004). *Citizens without shelter: Homelessness, democracy, and political exclusion.* Ithaca, NY: Cornell University Press.

Fennell, D., & Boyd, M. (2014). Obsessive-compulsive disorder and the media. *Deviant Behavior, 35*(9), 669–686.

Fennell, M. J. V. (2004). Depression, low self-esteem and mindfulness. *Behaviour Research and Therapy, 42*(9), 1053–1067.

Finkler, L. (2013). "They should not be allowed to do this to the homeless and mentally ill": Minimum separation distance bylaws reconsidered. In B. A. LeFrancois, R. Menzies, & G. Reaume (Eds.), *Mad matters: A critical reader in Canadian mad studies* (pp. 221–238). Toronto, ON: Canadian Scholars' Press.

Firestone, M., Syrette, J., Jourdain, T., Recollet, V., & Smylie, J. (2019). "I feel safe just coming here because there are other Native brothers and sisters": Findings from a community-based evaluation of the Niiwin Wendaanimak Four Winds Wellness Program. *Canadian Journal of Public Health, 110*(4), 404–413.

Fischer, B., Turnbull, S., Poland, B., & Haydon, E. (2004). Drug use, risk and urban order: Examined supervised injection sites (SISs) as "governmentality." *International Journal of Drug Policy, 15*(5–6), 357–365.

Fischer, S., Shinn, M., Shrout, P., & Tsemberis, S. (2008). Homelessness, mental illness, and criminal activity: Examining patterns over time. *American Journal of Community Psychology, 42*(3), 251–265.

Fontana, A., & Frey, J. H. (2000). The interview: From structured questions to negotiated text. In N. K. Denzin & Y. S. Lincoln (Eds.), *Handbook of qualitative research* (2nd ed., pp. 645–672). Thousand Oaks, CA: Sage.

Food Banks Canada. (2016). *Hunger count 2016: A comprehensive report on hunger and food bank use in Canada, and recommendations for change.* Toronto, ON: Food Banks Canada.

Foop, R. (2002). Increasing the potential for gaze, surveillance and normalisation: The transformation of an Australian policy for people who are homeless. *Surveillance & Society, 1*(1), 48–65.

Foucault, M. (1976). *The birth of the clinic* (A. M. Sheridan Smith, Trans.). Abingdon, UK: Routledge.

Foucault, M. (1977). *Discipline & punish: The birth of the prison* (A. M. Sheridan Smith, Trans.). New York: Vintage.

Foucault, M. (1980a). *The history of sexuality*, Vol. I. New York: Vintage.

Foucault, M. (1980b). Two lectures. In C. Gordon (Ed.), *Power/knowledge: Selected interviews and other writings, 1972–1977* (pp. 79–108). New York: Pantheon.

Foucault, M. (1988). *Madness and civilization: A history of insanity in the age of reason* (R. Howard, Trans.). New York: Vintage.

Foucault, M. (1991). Governmentality. In G. Burchell, C. Gordon, & P. Miller (Eds.), *The Foucault effect: Studies in governmentality* (pp. 87–104). Chicago, IL: University of Chicago Press.

Foucault, M. (2005). *The hermeneutics of the subject: Lectures at the Collège de France 1981–82* (G. Burchell, Trans.). London: Palgrave Macmillan.

Frankish, C. J., Hwang, S. W., & Quantz, D. (2005). Homelessness and health in Canada: Research lessons and priorities. *Canadian Journal of Public Health, 96*, S23–S29.

Freistadt, J. (2016). No dumping: Indigenousness and the racialized police transport of the urban homeless. In E. Peters & J. Christensen (Eds.), *Indigenous homelessness: Perspectives from Canada, Australia, and New Zealand* (pp. 67–90). Winnipeg, MB: University of Manitoba Press.

Fukui, S., Starnino, V. R., Susana, M., Davidson, L. J., Cook, K., Rapp, C. A., Gowdy, E. A. (2011). Effect of wellness recovery action plan (WRAP) participation on psychiatric symptoms, sense of hope, and recovery. *Psychiatric Rehabilitation Journal, 34*(3), 214–222.

Gaetz, S. (2014). *A safe and decent place to live: Towards a Housing First framework for youth*. Toronto, ON: Homeless Hub Press.

Gaetz, S., Barr, C., Friesen, A., Harris, B., Hill, C., Kovacs-Burns, K., Pauly, B., Pearce, B., Turner, A., & Marsolais, A. (2017). *Canadian definition of homelessness*. Toronto, ON: Canadian Observatory on Homelessness Press.

Gaetz, S., & Dej, E. (2017). *A new direction: A framework for homelessness prevention*. Toronto, ON: Canadian Observatory on Homelessness Press.

Gaetz, S., Dej, E., Donaldson, J., & Ali, N. (2017). *Leading the way: Reimagining federal leadership on preventing homelessness*. Toronto, ON: Canadian Observatory on Homelessness Press.

Gaetz, S., Dej, E., Richter, T., & Redman, M. (2016). *The state of homelessness in Canada 2016*. Toronto, ON: Canadian Observatory on Homelessness Press.

Gaetz, S., Donaldson, J., Richter, T., & Gulliver, T. (2013). *The state of homelessness in Canada 2013*. Toronto, ON: Canadian Homelessness Research Network Press.

Gaetz, S., Gulliver, T., & Richter, T. (2014). *The state of homelessness in Canada 2014*. Toronto, ON: Homeless Hub Press.

Gaetz, S., & O'Grady, B. (2009). Homelessness, incarceration, and the challenge of effective discharge planning. In J. D. Hulchanski, P. Campsie, S. Chau, S. W. Hwang, & E. Paradis (Eds.), *Finding home: Policy options for addressing homelessness in Canada*. Toronto, ON: Canadian Homelessness Research Network.

Garland, D. (1990). *Punishment and modern society*. Chicago, IL: University of Chicago Press.

Garland, D. (1997). "Governmentality" and the problem of crime: Foucault, criminology, sociology. *Theoretical Criminology, 1*(2), 173–214.

Garland, D. (2001). *The culture of control: Crime and social order in contemporary society*. Chicago, IL: University of Chicago Press.

Gergen, K. J. (2000). *The saturated self: Dilemmas of identity in contemporary life*. New York: Basic Books.

Giddens, A. (1991). *Modernity and self-identity: Self and society in the late modern age*. Cambridge, UK: Polity Press.

Gilligan, C. (1982). *In a different voice: Psychological theory and women's development*. Cambridge, MA: Harvard University Press.

Goddard, T., & Myers, R. R. (2017). Against evidence-based oppression: Marginalized youth and the politics of risk-based assessment and intervention. *Theoretical Criminology, 21*(2), 151–167.

Goering, P., Veldhuizen, S., Watson, A., Adair, C., Kopp, B., Latimer, E., Aubry, T., Nelson, G., MacNaughton, E., Streiner, D., Rabouin, D., Ly, A., & Pow, G. (2014). *National At Home/Chez Soi final report*. Ottawa, ON: Mental Health Commission of Canada.

Goffman, E. (1959). *The presentation of self in everyday life*. New York: Doubleday.

Goffman, E. (1961). *Asylums. Essays on the social situation of mental patients and other inmates*. New York: Doubleday Anchor.

Goffman, E. (1963). *Stigma: Notes on the management of spoiled identity*. Upper Saddle River, NJ: Prentice-Hall.

Gordon, C. (1991). Governmental rationality: An introduction. In G. Burchell, C. Gordon, & P. Miller (Eds.), *The Foucault effect: Studies in governmentality* (pp. 1–51). Chicago, IL: University of Chicago Press.

Gounis, K. (1992). The manufacture of dependency: Shelterization revisited. *New England Journal of Public Policy, 8*, 685–693.

Greenberg, G. A., & Rosenheck, R. A. (2008). Jail incarceration, homelessness, and mental health: A national study. *Psychiatric Services, 59*(2), 170–177.

Hacking, I. (1995). The looping effects of human kinds. In D. Sperber, D. Premack, & A. J. Premack (Eds.), *Causal cognition: A multi-disciplinary debate* (pp. 351–383). Oxford, UK: Oxford University Press.

Hacking, I. (1999). *The social construction of what?* Ithaca, NY: Harvard University Press.

Hacking, I. (2004). Between Michel Foucault and Erving Goffman: Between discourse in the abstract and face-to-face interaction. *Economy and Society, 33*(3), 277–302.

Hannah-Moffat, K. (2000a). Prisons that empower: Neo-liberal governance in Canadian women's prisons. *British Journal of Criminology, 40*(3), 510–531.

Hannah-Moffat, K. (2000b). Re-forming the prison: Rethinking our ideals. In K. Hannah-Moffat & M. Shaw (Eds.), *An ideal prison? Critical essays on women's imprisonment in Canada* (pp. 30–40). Black Point, NS: Fernwood.

Hannah-Moffat, K. (2016). A conceptual kaleidoscope: Contemplating "dynamic structural risk" and an uncoupling of risk from need. *Psychology, Crime & Law, 22*(1–2), 33–46.

Hannem, S. (2014). Grappling with reflexivity and the role of emotion in criminological analysis. In J. M. Kilty, M. Felices-Luna, & S. C. Fabian (Eds.), *Demarginalizing voices: Commitment, emotion, and action in qualitative research* (pp. 267–285). Vancouver, BC: UBC Press.

Hansen, H., Bourgois, P., & Drucker, E. (2014). Pathologizing poverty: New forms of diagnosis, disability, and structural stigma under welfare reform. *Social Science & Medicine, 103*, 76–83.

Harding, R. (2006). Historical representations of Aboriginal people in the Canadian news media. *Discourse & Society, 17*(2), 205–235.

Harrington, Daniel W., Wilson, K., & Rosenberg, M. W. (2014). Waiting for a specialist consultation for a new condition in Ontario: Impacts on patients' lives. *Healthcare Policy, 9*(4), 90–103.

Hartwell, S. (2004). Triple stigma: Persons with mental illness and substance abuse problems in the criminal justice system. *Criminal Justice Policy Review, 15*(1), 84–99.

Hermer, J., & Mosher, J. (Eds.). (2002). *Disorderly people: Law and the politics of exclusion in Ontario*. Black Point, NS: Fernwood.

Hogan, B., & Berry, B. (2011). Racial and ethnic biases in rental housing: An audit study of online apartment listings. *City & Community, 10*(4), 351–372.

Holton, E., Gogosis, E., & Hwang, S. W. (2010). *Housing vulnerability and health: Canada's hidden emergency*. Vancouver, Toronto, Ottawa: Research Alliance for Canadian Homelessness, Housing, and Health.

Hook, D. D. (1984). First names and titles as solidarity and power semantics in English. *International Review of Applied Linguistics in Language Teaching, 22*(3), 183–190.

Huey, L. (2012). *Invisible victims: Homelessness and the growing security gap*. Toronto, ON: University of Toronto Press.

Huff, T. (2008). *Bent hope: A street journal*. Pickering, ON: Castle Quay Books.

Hughes, J. (Ed.). (2018). *Beyond shelters: Solutions to homelessness in Canada from the front lines*. Toronto, ON: James Lorimer.

Hwang, S. W., Aubry, T., Palepu, A., Farrell, S., Nisenbaum, R., Hubley, A. M., Klodawsky, F., Gogosis, E., Hay, E., Pidlubny, S., Dowbor, T. & Chambers, C. (2011). The health and housing in transition study: A longitudinal study of the health of homeless and vulnerably housed adults in three Canadian cities. *International Journal of Public Health, 56*, 609–623.

Indian Act, RSC 1985, c I-5.

Jacob, J. D., Holmes, D., Rioux, D., & Corneau, P. (2018). Patients' perspectives on mechanical restraints in acute and emergency psychiatric settings: A poststructural feminist analysis. In J. M. Kilty & E. Dej (Eds.), *Containing madness: Gender and "psy" in institutional contexts* (pp. 93–118). London: Palgrave Macmillan.

Jiwani, Y. (2001). The criminalization of "race," the racialization of crime. In W. Chan & K. Mirchandani (Eds.), *Crimes of colour: Racialization and the criminal justice system in Canada* (pp. 67–86). Peterborough, ON: Broadview Press.

John Howard Society of Toronto. (2010). *Homeless and jailed: Jailed and homeless*. Toronto, ON: John Howard Society of Toronto.

Johnsen, S., Fitzpatrick, S., & Watts, B. (2018). Homelessness and social control: A typology. *Housing Studies, 33*(7), 1106–1126.

Johnstone, M., Parsell, C., Jetten, J., Dingle, G., & Walter, Z. (2016). Breaking the cycle of homelessness: Housing stability and social support as predictors of long-term well-being. *Housing Studies, 31*(4), 410–426.

Jones, R. (2000). Digital rule: Punishment, control and technology. *Punishment & Society, 2*(1), 5–22.

Kaler, A., & Beres, M. (2010). *Essentials of field relationships*. Walnut Creek, CA: Left Coast Press.

Karabanow, J. (2006). Becoming a street kid: Exploring the stages of street life. *Journal of Human Behavior in the Social Environment*, 13(2), 49–72.

Katz, A. S., Zerger, S., & Hwang, S. W. (2017). Housing First the conversation: Discourse, policy and the limits of the possible." *Critical Public Health*, 27(1), 139–147.

Katz, M. B. (2013). *The undeserving poor: America's enduring confrontation with poverty*. Oxford, UK: Oxford University Press.

Kendall, J. (2001). Circles of disadvantage: Aboriginal poverty and underdevelopment in Canada. *American Review of Canadian Studies*, 31(1–2), 43–59.

Kendall, K. (2000). Psy-ence fiction: Inventing the mentally-disordered female prisoner. In K. Hannah-Moffat & M. Shaw (Eds.), *An ideal prison? Critical essays on women's imprisonment in Canada* (pp. 82–93). Black Point, NS: Fernwood.

Kennelly, J. (2018). Envisioning democracy: Participatory filmmaking with homeless youth. *Canadian Review of Sociology*, 55(2), 190–210.

Kerman, N., Sylvestre, J., Aubry, T., & Distasio, J. (2018). The effects of housing stability on service use among homeless adults with mental illness in a randomized controlled trial of housing first. *BMC Health Services Research*, 18(1), 190–204.

Kidd, S. A., Frederick, T., Karabanow, J., Hughes, J., Naylor, T., & Barbic, S. (2016). A mixed methods study of recently homeless youth efforts to sustain housing and stability. *Child and Adolescent Social Work Journal*, 33(3), 207–218.

Kilty, J. M. (2012). "It's like they don't want you to get better": Practicing "psy" in the carceral context. *Feminism & Psychology*, 22(2), 162–182.

Kilty, J. M., & Dej, E. (2012). Anchoring amongst the waves: Discursive constructions of motherhood and addiction. *Qualitative Sociology Review*, 8(3), 6–23.

Kirkup, K. (2018). Gender dysphoria and the medical gaze in Anglo-American carceral regimes. In J. M. Kilty & E. Dej (Eds.), *Containing madness: Gender and "psy" in institutional contexts* (pp. 145–165). London: Palgrave Macmillan.

Klassen, A. L. (2016). Spinning the revolving door: The governance of non-compliant psychiatric subjects on community treatment orders. *Theoretical Criminology*, 21(3), 361–379.

Kral, M. J., Idlout, L., Minore, J. B., Dyck, R. J., & Kirmayer, L. J. (2011). Unikkaartuit: Meanings of well-being, unhappiness, health, and community change among Inuit in Nunavut, Canada. *American Journal of Community Psychology*, 48(3), 426–438.

Kuehn, B. M. (2010). Integrated care key for patients with both addiction and mental illness. *Journal of the American Medical Association*, 303(19), 1905–1907.

Laing, R. D. (1960). *The divided self*. New York: Pantheon Books.

Laing, R. D. (1967). *The politics of experience*. New York: Ballantine Books.

Lamb, H. R., Weinberger, L., & Gross, B. (2004). Mentally ill persons in the criminal justice system: Some perspectives. *Psychiatric Quarterly*, 75(2), 107–126.

Landry, D. (2017). Survivor research in Canada: "Talking" recovery, resisting psychiatry, and reclaiming madness. *Disability & Society*, 32(9), 1437–1457.

Lebenbaum, M., Chiu, M., Vigod, S., & Kurdyak, P. (2018). Prevalence and predictors of involuntary psychiatric hospital admissions in Ontario, Canada: A population-based linked administrative database study. *BJPsych Open*, 4(2), 31–38.

Lee, S. J., Thomas, P., Doulis, C., Bowles, D., Henderson, K., Keppich-Arnold, S., Perez, E., & Stafrace, S. (2015). Outcomes achieved by and police and clinician perspectives on a joint police officer and mental health clinician mobile response unit. *International Journal of Mental Health Nursing, 24*(6), 538–646.

Lees, L. H. (1998). *The solidarities of strangers: The English Poor Laws and the people, 1700–1948*. Cambridge, UK: Cambridge University Press.

Lemert, E. M. (1979). Primary and secondary deviation. In J. E. Jacoby (Ed.), *Classics of criminology* (pp. 193–195). Long Grove, IL: Waveland.

Lofland, J., Snow, D. A., Anderson, L., & Lofland, L. H. (2006). *Analyzing social settings: A guide to qualitative observation and analysis* (4th ed.). Wadsworth/Thomson Learning.

Londerville, J., & M. Steele. 2014. *Housing policy targeting homelessness*. Toronto, ON: Canadian Observatory on Homelessness Press.

Lowman, J., Menzies, R. J., & Palys, T. S. (1987). Introduction: Transcarceration and the modern state of penality. In J. Lowman, R. J. Menzies, & T. S. Palys (Eds.), *Transcarceration: Essays in the sociology of social control* (pp. 1–15). Aldershot, UK: Gower.

Lupton, D. (1995). *The imperative of health: Public health and the regulated body*. Thousand Oaks, CA: Sage.

Lyon-Callo, V. (2000). Medicalizing homelessness: The production of self-blame and self-governing within homeless shelters. *Medical Anthropology Quarterly, 14*(3), 328–345.

Lyon-Callo, V. (2004). *Inequality, poverty, and neoliberal governance: Activist ethnography in the homeless sheltering industry*. Peterborough, ON: Broadview Press.

Lyons, T., Krusi, A., Pierre, L., Smith, A., Small, W., & Shannon, K. (2016). Experiences of trans women and two-spirit persons accessing women-specific health and housing services in a downtown neighborhood of Vancouver, Canada. *LGBT Health, 3*(5), 373–378.

Mack, T. (2014). The mad and the bad: The lethal use of force against mad people by Toronto police. *Critical Disability Discourse, 6*, 7–52.

Madden, D., & Marcuse, P. (2016). *In defense of housing*. London and New York: Verso.

Maidment, M. R. (2006). *Doing time on the outside: Deconstructing the benevolent community*. Toronto, ON: University of Toronto Press.

Marcus, A. (2003). Shelterization revisited: Some methodological dangers of institutional studies of the homeless. *Human Organization, 62*(2), 134–142.

Martel, J. (2006). To be, one has to be somewhere: Spatio-temporality in prison segregation. *British Journal of Criminology, 46*(4), 587–612.

Maruna, S. (2001). *Making good: How ex-convicts reform and rebuild their lives*. Washington, DC: American Psychological Association.

Maruna, S., & Ramsden, D. (2004). Living to tell the tale: Redemption narratives, shame management, and offender rehabilitation. In A. Lieblich, D. P. McAdams & R. Josselson (Eds.), *Healing plots: The narrative basis of psychotherapy* (pp. 129–149). Washington, DC: American Psychological Association.

Maté, G. *Scattered minds: A new look at the origins of healing attention deficit disorder*. Toronto, ON: Vintage Canada.

Maté, G. (2008). *In the realm of hungry ghosts: Close encounters with addiction.* Toronto, ON: Vintage Canada.

Matejkowski, J., & Draine, J. (2008). Investigating the impact of Housing First on ACT fidelity. *Community Mental Health Journal, 45*(1), 6–11.

Maynard, R. (2017). *Policing Black lives: State violence in Canada from slavery to the present.* Black Point, NS: Fernwood.

Mayock, P., Bretherton, J., & Baptista, J. (2016). Women's homelessness and domestic violence: (In)visible interactions. In P. Mayock & J. Bretherton (Eds.), *Women's homelessness in Europe* (pp. 127–154). London: Palgrave Macmillan.

Mayock, P., & Parker, S. (2019). Homeless young people "strategizing" a route to housing stability: Service fatigue, exiting attempts and living "off grid." *Housing Studies, 35*(3), 459–483.

McLean, A. (2000). From ex-patient alternatives to consumer options: Consequences of consumerism for psychiatric consumers and the ex-patient movement. *International Journal of Health Services, 30*(4), 821–847.

McLeod, M. N., Heller, D., Manze, M. G., & Echeverria, S. E. (2019). Police interactions and the mental health of Black Americans: A systematic review. *Journal of Racial and Ethnic Health Disparities, 7,* 10–27. https://doi.org/10.1007/s40615-019-00629-1.

Mental Health Commission of Canada. (2012). *Changing directions, changing lives: The mental health strategy for Canada.* Mental Health Commission of Canada.

Milaney, K., Williams, N., & Dutton, D. (2018). Falling through the cracks: How the community-based approach has failed Calgary's chronically homeless. *The School of Public Policy Publications, 11*(9), 1–17.

Miller, G. (2010). *Learning the language of addiction counseling.* Hoboken, NJ: John Wiley & Sons.

Miller, A. B., & Keys, C. B. (2001). Understanding dignity in the lives of homeless persons. *American Journal of Community Psychology, 29*(2), 331–354.

Miller, P. & Rose, N. (2008). *Governing the present: Administering economic, social and personal life.* Cambridge, UK: Polity Press.

Ministry of Families, Children and Social Development. (2017). *Canada's National Housing Strategy: A place to call home.* Ottawa, ON: Government of Canada.

Moore, D. (2007a). *Criminal artefacts: Governing drugs and users.* Vancouver, BC: UBC Press.

Moore, D. (2007b). Translating justice and therapy: The drug treatment court networks. *British Journal of Criminology, 47*(1), 42–60.

Moore, D. (2011). The benevolent watch: Therapeutic surveillance in drug treatment court. *Theoretical Criminology, 15*(3), 255–268.

Moore, D., & Hirai, H. (2014). Outcasts, performers and true believers: Responsibilized subjects of criminal justice. *Theoretical Criminology, 18*(1), 5–19.

Morrow, M. (2017). "Women and madness" revisited: The promise of intersectional and mad studies frameworks. In M. Morrow & L. Halinka Malcoe (Eds.), *Critical inquiries for social justice in mental health* (pp. 33–59). Toronto, ON: University of Toronto Press.

Morrow, M., & Weisser, J. (2012). Towards a social justice framework of mental health recovery. *Studies in Social Justice, 6*(1), 27–43.

Mosher, J. (2002). The shrinking of the public and private spaces of the poor. In J. Hermer & J. Mosher (Eds.), *Disorderly people: Law and the politics of exclusion in Ontario* (pp. 41–53). Black Point, NS: Fernwood.

Mosley, J. E. (2012). Keeping the lights on: How government funding concerns drive the advocacy agendas of nonprofit homeless service providers. *Journal of Public Administration Research and Theory, 22*(4), 841–866.

Muir-Cochrane, E., Fereday, J., Jureidini, J., Drummond, A., & Darbyshire, P. (2006). Self-management of medication for mental health problems by homeless young people. *International Journal of Mental Health Nursing, 15*(3), 163–170.

Munn, M., & Bruckert, C. (2010). Beyond conceptual ambiguity: Exemplifying the "resistance pyramid" through the reflections of (ex) prisoners' agency. *Qualitative Sociology Review, 6*(2), 137–149.

Munshi, S., & Willse, C. (2007). Foreword. In INCITE! Women of Color Against Violence (Ed.), *The revolution will not be funded: Beyond the non-profit industrial complex* (pp. xiii–xxii). Durham, NC: Duke University Press.

Myers, N. M. (2016). Eroding the presumption of innocence: Pre-trial detention and the use of conditional release on bail. *British Journal of Criminology, 57*(3), 664–683.

National Inquiry into Missing and Murdered Indigenous Women and Girls. (2019). *Reclaiming power and place: The final report of the National Inquiry into Missing and Murdered Indigenous Women and Girls*. Ottawa, ON: National Inquiry into Missing and Murdered Indigenous Women and Girls.

Nelson, G., Macnaughton, E., Curwood, S. E., Egalité, N., Voronka, J., Fleury, M.-J., Kirst, M., Flowers, L., Patterson, M., Dudley, M., Piat, M., & Goering, P. (2015). Collaboration and involvement of persons with lived experience in planning Canada's At Home/Chez Soi project. *Health & Social Care in the Community, 24*(2), 184–193.

Nettleton, S. (1997). Governing the risky self: How to become healthy, wealthy and wise. In A. Petersen & R. Bunton (Eds.), *Foucault, health and medicine* (pp. 207–222). Abingdon, UK: Routledge.

Nichols, N. (2014). *Youth work: An institutional ethnography of youth homelessness.* Toronto, ON: University of Toronto Press.

Nichols, N., & Braimoh, J. (2018). Community safety, housing precariousness and processes of exclusion: An institutional ethnography from the standpoints of youth in an "unsafe" urban neighbourhood. *Critical Sociology, 44*(1), 157–172.

Nikoo, M., Gadermann, A., To, M. J., Krausz, M., Hwang, S. W., & Palepu, A. (2017). Incidence and associated risk factors of traumatic brain injury in a cohort of homeless and vulnerably housed adults in 3 Canadian cities. *Journal of Head Trauma Rehabilitation, 32*(4), E19–26.

Novac, S., Hermer, J., Paradis, E., & Kellen, A. (2009). A revolving door? Homeless people and the justice system in Toronto. In J. D. Hulchanski, P. Campsie, S. Chau, S. W. Hwang, & E. Paradis (Eds.), *Finding home: Policy options for addressing homelessness in Canada.* Toronto, ON: Canadian Homelessness Research Network.

Novas, C. (2006). The political economy of hope: Patients' organizations, science and biovalue. *Biosocieties, 1*(3), 289–305.

Nussbaum, M. (2006). *Hiding from humanity: Disgust, shame, and the law.* Princeton, NJ: Princeton University Press.

O'Campo, P., Stergiopoulos, V., Nir, P., Levy, M., Misir, V., Chum, A., Bouchra, A., Nisenbaum, R., To, M. J., & Hwang, S. W. (2016). How did a Housing First intervention improve health and social outcomes among homeless adults with mental illness in Toronto? Two-year outcomes from a randomised trial. *BMJ Open, 6*(9), e010581. https://doi.org/10.1136/bmjopen-2015-010581.

Office of the Correctional Investigator. (2013). *A case study of diversity in corrections: The Black inmate experience in federal penitentiaries.* Ottawa, ON: Correctional Investigator Canada.

Office of the Correctional Investigator. (2020). Indigenous people in federal custody surpasses 30%: Correctional Investigator issues statement and challenge. Ottawa, ON: Correctional Investigator Canada. https://www.oci-bec.gc.ca/cnt/comm/press/press20200121-eng.aspx.

O'Grady, B., Gaetz, S., & Buccieri, K. (2011). *Can I see your ID? The policing of youth homelessness in Toronto.* Toronto, ON: JFCY & Homeless Hub.

Olin, J. S. (1966). "Skid row" syndrome: A medical profile of the chronic drunkenness offender. *Canadian Medical Association Journal, 95*(5), 205–214.

Omonira, R. (2014). Black and dangerous? Why are black people with mental health problems more likely to be heavily medicated, restrained and detained against their will? *Socialist Lawyer, 68,* 28–35.

Ontario Non-Profit Housing Association. (2016). *2016 waiting list survey report: ONPHA's final report on waiting lists statistics for Ontario.* Toronto, ON: Ontario Non-Profit Housing Association.

O'Reilly, M., Taylor, H. C., & Vostanis, P. (2009). "Nuts, schiz, psycho": An exploration of young homeless people's perceptions and dilemmas of defining mental health. *Social Science and Medicine, 68*(9), 1737–1744.

Osman, L. (2018, March 5). *ByWard Market petition compares shelters to "cancer."* CBC News. http://www.cbc.ca/news/canada/ottawa/byward-market-homeless-shelters-petition-1.4562771.

Padgett, D. K. (2007). There's no place like(a)home: Ontological security among persons with serious mental illness in the United States. *Social Science & Medicine, 64*(9), 1925–1936.

Pam, A. (1995). Biological psychiatry: Science or pseudoscience? In C. A. Ross & A. Pam (Eds.), *Pseudoscience in biological psychiatry: Blaming the body.* Hoboken, NJ: John Wiley & Sons.

Paradis, E. (2014). "I would like us to unite and fight for our rights together because we haven't been able to do it alone": Women's homelessness, disenfranchisement, and self-determination. In J. M. Kilty (Ed.), *Within the confines: Women and the law in Canada* (pp. 52–75). Toronto, ON: Women's Press.

Parsons, T. (1975). The sick role and the role of the physician reconsidered. *Milbank Quarterly, 53*(3), 257–278.

Partis, M. (2003). Hope in homeless people: A phenomenological study. *Primary Health Care Research & Development, 4*(1), 9–19.

Pearce, D. (1978). The feminization of poverty: Women, work, and welfare. *Urban & Social Change Review, 11*(1–2), 28–36.

Phillips, C. (2016). *The promises of Housing First and the realities of neoliberalism: Lessons from Toronto's Streets to Homes programme* [Doctoral dissertation,

Ryerson University]. Ryerson University Library Digital Repository. https://digital.library.ryerson.ca/islandora/object/RULA:4957.

Piat, M., Polvere, L., Kirst, M., Voronka, J., Zabkiewicz, D., Plante, M.-C., Isaak, C., Nolin, D., Nelson, G., & Goering, P. (2014). Pathways into homelessness: Understanding how both individual and structural factors contribute to and sustain homelessness in Canada. *Urban Studies, 52*(13), 2366–2382.

Pleace, N., & Bretherton, J. (2013). The case for Housing First in the European Union: A critical evaluation of concerns about effectiveness. *European Journal of Homelessness, 7*(2), 21–41.

Pollack, S. (2005). Taming the shrew: Regulating prisoners through women-centered mental health programming. *Critical Criminology, 13*(1), 71–87.

Pollack, S. (2006). Therapeutic programming as a regulatory practice in women's prisons. In G. Balfour & E. Comack (Eds.), *Criminalizing women: Gender and (in)justice in neoliberal times* (pp. 236–249). Black Point, NS: Fernwood.

Pollack, S. (2009). "You can't have it both ways": Punishment and treatment of imprisoned women. *Journal of Progressive Human Services, 20*(2), 112–128.

Pomeroy, S. (2017). *Why core housing need is a poor metric to measure outcomes of Canada's National Housing Strategy.* Ottawa, ON: Caledon Institute of Social Policy.

Priester, M. A., Browne, T., Iachini, A., Clone, S., DeHart, D., & Seay, K. D. (2016). Treatment access barriers and disparities among individuals with co-occurring mental health and substance use disorders: An integrative literature review. *Journal of Substance Abuse Treatment, 61,* 47–59.

Prince, M. J. (2015). Shelter and the street: Housing, homelessness, and social assistance in the Canadian provinces. In D. Béland & P-M. Daigneault (Eds.), *Welfare reform in Canada: provincial social assistance in comparative perspective* (pp. 353–366). Toronto, ON: University of Toronto Press.

Prior, S. (2011). Overcoming stigma: How young people position themselves as counselling service users. *Sociology of Health & Illness, 34*(5), 697–713.

Quilgars, D., & Pleace, N. (2016). Housing First and social integration: A realistic aim? *Social Inclusion, 4*(4), 5–15.

Quirouette, M. (2016). Managing multiple disadvantages: The regulation of complex needs in emergency shelters for the homeless. *Journal of Poverty, 20*(3), 316–339.

Quirouette, M. (2018). Community practitioners in criminal courts: Risk logics and multiply-disadvantaged individuals. *Theoretical Criminology, 22*(4), 582–602.

Raguparan, M. (2017). "If I'm gonna hack capitalism": Racialized and Indigenous Canadian sex workers' experiences within the neo-liberal market economy. *Women's Studies International Forum, 60*(1), 69–76.

Ranasinghe, P. (2013). Discourse, practice and the production of the polysemy of security. *Theoretical Criminology, 17*(1), 89–107.

Ranasinghe, P. (2014). The humdrum of legality and the ordering of an ethic of care. *Law and Society Review, 48*(4), 709–739.

Ranasinghe, P. (2017). *Helter shelter: Security, legality, and an ethic of care in an emergency shelter.* Toronto, ON: University of Toronto Press.

Rankin, B. H., & Quane, J. M. (2000). Neighborhood poverty and the social isolation of inner-city African American families. *Social Forces, 79*(1), 139–164.

Razack, S. H. (2015). *Dying from improvement: Inquests and inquiries into Indigenous deaths in custody*. Toronto, ON: University of Toronto Press.

Redlich, A. D., Steadman, H. J., Robbins, P., & Swanson, J. W. (2006). Use of the criminal justice system to leverage mental health treatment: Effects on treatment adherence and satisfaction. *Journal of the American Academy of Psychiatry and the Law, 34*(3), 292–299.

Reindal, S. M. (1999). Independence, dependence, interdependence: Some reflections on the subject and personal autonomy. *Disability and Society, 14*(3), 353–367.

Reisig, M. D., Holtfreter, K., & Morash, M. (2002). Social capital among women offenders: Examining the distribution of social networks and resources. *Journal of Contemporary Criminal Justice, 18*(2), 167–187.

Reith, G. (2004). Consumption and its discontents: Addiction, identity and the problems of freedom. *British Journal of Sociology, 55*(2), 283–300.

Rickford, R. (2015). Black Lives Matter: Toward a modern practice of mass struggle. *New Labor Forum, 25*(1), 34–42.

Rimke, H. M. (2000). Governing citizens through self-help literature. *Cultural Studies, 14*(1), 61–78.

Rimke, H. M. (2016). Mental and emotional distress as a social justice issue: Beyond psychocentrism. *Studies in Social Justice, 10*(1), 4–17.

Roca, P., Panadero, S., Rodríguez-Moreno, S., Martín, R. M., & Vázquez, J. J. (2019). The revolving door to homelessness: The influence of health, alcohol consumption and stressful life events on the number of episodes of homelessness. *Annals of Psychology, 35*(2), 175–180.

Rodríguez, D. (2007). The political logic of the non-profit industrial complex. In INCITE! Women of Color Against Violence (Ed.), *The revolution will not be funded: Beyond the non-profit industrial complex* (pp. 21–40). Durham, NC: Duke University Press.

Rogers, A., & Pilgrim, D. (2014). *A sociology of mental health and illness* (5th ed.). London: Open University Press.

Rose, N. (1988). Calculable minds and manageable individuals. *History of the Human Sciences, 1*(2), 179–200.

Rose, N. (1996). Governing "advanced" liberal democracies. In A. Barry, T. Osborne, & N. Rose (Eds.), *Foucault and political reason* (pp. 37–64). Cambridge, UK: University of Chicago Press.

Rose, N. (1998). *Inventing our selves: Psychology, power, and personhood*. Cambridge, UK: Cambridge University Press.

Rose, N. (1999). *Powers of freedom: Reframing political thought*. Cambridge, UK: Cambridge University Press.

Rose, N. (2000). Government and control. *British Journal of Criminology, 40*(2), 321–339.

Rose, N. (2007). *The politics of life itself: Biomedicine, power, and subjectivity in the twenty-first century*. Princeton, NJ: Princeton University Press.

Rose, N., & Novas, C. (2005). Biological citizenship. In A. Ong & S. Collier (Eds.), *Global assemblages: Technology, politics and ethics as anthropological problems* (pp. 439–463). Hoboken, NJ: Blackwell.

Roseneil, S., & Seymour, J. (1999). Practicing identities: Power and resistance. In S. Roseneil & J. Seymour (Eds.), *Practicing identities: Power and resistance* (pp. 1–10). London: Palgrave Macmillan.

Rosenthal, R. (2000). Imaging homelessness and homeless people: Visions and strategies within the movement(s). *Journal of Social Distress and Homelessness, 9*(2), 111–126.

Ruddick, S. (1996). From the politics of homelessness to the politics of the homeless. In R. Keil, G. R. Wekerle, & D. V. J. Bell (Eds.), *Local places in the age of the global city* (pp. 165–171). Montreal, QC: Black Rose Books.

Rugkåsa, J. (2016). Effectiveness of community treatment orders: The international evidence. *Canadian Journal of Psychiatry, 61*(1), 15–24.

Sajatovic, M., Levin, J., Ramirez, L. F., Hahn, D. Y., Tatsuoka, C., Bialko, C., Cassidy, K. A., Fuentes-Casiano, E., & Williams, T. D. (2013). Prospective trial of customized adherence enhancement plus long-acting injectable antipsychotic medication in homeless or recently homeless individuals with schizophrenia or schizoaffective disorder. *Journal of Clinical Psychiatry, 74*(12), 1249–1255.

Savage, L. (2019, January 10). *Female Offenders in Canada, 2017*. https://www150.statcan.gc.ca/n1/pub/85-002-x/2019001/article/00001-eng.htm.

Schilt, K., & Westbrook, L. (2009). Doing gender, doing heteronormativity: "Gender normals," transgender people, and the social maintenance of heterosexuality. *Gender & Society, 23*(4), 440–464.

Schmidt, R., Hrenchuk, C., Bopp, J., & Poole, N. (2015). Trajectories of women's homelessness in Canada's 3 northern territories. *International Journal of Circumpolar Health, 74*(1), 29778–29787.

Schneider, B. (2010). *Hearing (our) voices: Participatory research in mental health*. Toronto, ON: University of Toronto Press.

Schnittker, J. (2008). An uncertain revolution: Why the rise of a genetic model of mental illness has not increased tolerance. *Social Science & Medicine, 67*, 1370–1381.

Sealy, P., & Whitehead, P. C. (2004). Forty years of deinstitutionalization of psychiatric services in Canada: An empirical assessment. *Canadian Journal of Psychiatry, 49*(4), 249–257.

Sedgwick, P. (1982). *Psychopolitics: Laing, Foucault, Goffman, Szasz and the future of mass psychiatry*. New York: Harper & Row.

Seltser, B. J., & Miller, D. E. (1993). *Homeless families: The struggle for dignity*. Champaign County, IL: University of Illinois Press.

Shimrat, I. (1997). *Call me crazy: Stories from the mad movement*. Press Gang.

Shore, K., & Lavoie, J. A. A. (2018). Exploring mental health-related calls for police service: A Canadian study of police officers as "frontline mental health workers." *Policing: A Journal of Policy and Practice, 13*(2), 157–171.

Silver, H., & Miller, S. M. (2002). Social exclusion: The European approach to social disadvantage. *Poverty & Race, 11*(5), 1–11.

Smith, A. (2007). Introduction. In INCITE! Women of Color Against Violence (Ed.), *The revolution will not be funded: Beyond the non-profit industrial complex* (pp. 1–18). Durham, NC: Duke University Press.

Smith, J. M. (2014). Interrogating whiteness within criminology. *Sociology Compass, 8*(2), 107–118.

Snow, D. A., & Anderson, L. (1993). *Down on their luck: A study of homeless street people.* Los Angeles, CA: University of California Press.

Snow, D. A., Anderson, L., & Koegel, P. (1994). Distorting tendencies in research on the homeless. *American Behavioral Scientist, 37*(4), 461–475.

Snow, D. A., Baker, S. G., Leon, A., & Martin, M. (1986). The myth of pervasive mental illness among the homeless. *Social Problems, 33*(5), 407–423.

Social Housing Registry of Ottawa. (2014). FAQs. The Registry: The Social Housing Registry of Ottawa. http://www.housingregistry.ca/faqs/.

Spitzer, S. (1975). Toward a Marxian theory of deviance. *Social Problems, 22*(5), 638–651.

Spivak, G. C. (1988). Can the subaltern speak? In C. Nelson & L. Grossberg (Eds.), *Marxism and the interpretation of culture* (pp. 271–311). Champaign County, IL: Board of Trustees of the University of Illinois.

Stark, L. (1994). The shelter as "total institution": An organizational barrier to remedying homelessness. *American Behavioral Scientist, 37*(4), 553–562.

Steadman, H. J., Deane, M. W., Borum, R., & Morrissey, J. P. (2000). Comparing outcomes of major models of police responses to mental health emergencies. *Psychiatric Services, 51*(5), 645–649.

Stergiopoulos, V., Hwang, S. W., Gozdzik, A., Nisenbaum, R., Latimer, E., Rabouin, D., Adair, C. E., Bourque, J., Connelly, J., Frankish, J., Katz, L.Y., Mason, K., Misir, V., O'Brien, K., Sareen, J., Schütz, C. G., Singer, A., Streiner, D. L., Vasiliadis, H. M., Goering, P. N., & At Home/Chez Soi Investigators. (2015). Effect of scattered-site housing using rent supplements and intensive case management on housing stability among homeless adults with mental illness: A randomized trial. *JAMA, 313*(9), 905–915.

Strachan, B. (2018, September 12). *Penticton man pleads guilty to panhandling in case that cost city more than $25,000 in legal fees.* CBC News. https://www.cbc.ca/news/canada/british-columbia/penticton-man-pleads-guilty-to-panhandling-in-case-that-cost-city-more-than-25-000-in-legal-fees-1.4821272.

Stuart, F. (2016). *Down and out and under arrest: Policing and everyday life in Skid Row.* Chicago, IL: University of Chicago Press.

Suttor, G. (2016). *Still renovating: A history of Canadian social housing policy.* Ottawa and Montreal: McGill-Queen's University Press.

Sylvestre, M.-E. (2010a). Disorder and public spaces in Montreal: Repression (and resistance) through law, politics, and police discretion. *Urban Geography, 31*(6), 803–824.

Sylvestre, M.-E. (2010b). Policing the homeless in Montreal: Is this really what the population wants? *Policing and Society, 20*(4), 432–458.

Sylvestre, M.-E., Blomley, N., Damon, W., & Bellot, C. (2017). *Red zones and other spatial conditions of release imposed on marginalized people in Vancouver.* Ottawa, ON: Social Sciences and Humanities Research Council.

Szasz, T. (1974). *The myth of mental illness: Foundations of a theory of personal conduct* (Rev. ed.). New York: Harper & Row.

Szasz, T. (1989). *Law, liberty, and psychiatry: An inquiry into the social uses of mental health practices.* Syracuse, NY: Syracuse University Press.

Tam, L. (2013). Whither Indigenizing the mad movement? Theorizing the social relations of race and madness through conviviality. In B. A. LeFrançois, R. Menzies, & G. Reaume (Eds.), *Mad matters: A critical reader in Canadian mad studies* (pp. 281–297). Toronto, ON: Canadian Scholars' Press.

Tew, J. (2005). Core themes of social perspectives. In J. Tew (Ed.), *Social perspectives in mental health: Developing social models to understand and work with mental distress* (pp. 13–31). London: Jessica Kingsley.

Thistle, J. (2015). Hail Mary Pass. In Inclusion Working Group, Canadian Observatory on Homelessness (Ed.), *Homelessness is only one piece of my puzzle: Implications for policy and practice* (pp. 39–45). Toronto, ON: Canadian Observatory on Homelessness Press.

Thistle, J. (2017). *Definition of Indigenous homelessness in Canada*. Toronto, ON: Canadian Observatory on Homelessness Press.

To, M., Palepu, A., Matheson, F. I., Ecker, J., Farrell, S., Hwang, S. W., & Werb, D. (2016). The effect of incarceration on housing stability among homeless and vulnerably housed individuals in three Canadian cities: A prospective cohort study. *Canadian Journal of Public Health, 107*(6), 550–555.

Tomczak, P., & Thompson, D. (2019). Inclusionary control? Theorizing the effects of penal voluntary organizations' work. *Theoretical Criminology, 23*(1), 4–24.

Topolovec-Vranic, J., Schuler, A., Gozdzik, A., Somers, J., Bourque, P.-E., Frankish, C. J., Jbilou, J., Prakzad, S., Palma Lazgare, L. I., & Hwang, S. W. (2017). The high burden of traumatic brain injury and comorbidities amongst homeless adults with mental illness. *Journal of Psychiatric Research, 87*, 53–60.

Travis, T. (2009). *The language of the heart: A cultural history of the recovery movement from Alcoholics Anonymous to Oprah Winfrey*. Chapel Hill, NC: University of North Carolina Press.

Truth and Reconciliation Commission of Canada. (2015). *Honouring the truth, reconciling for the future*. Truth and Reconciliation Commission of Canada.

Tsemberis, S., & Eisenberg, R. F. (2000). Pathways to housing: Supported housing for street-dwelling homeless individuals with psychiatric disabilities. *Psychiatric Services, 51*(4), 487–493.

Turner, A., Albanese, T., & Pakeman, K. (2017). Discerning "functional and absolute zero": Defining and measuring an end to homelessness in Canada. *School of Public Policy SPP Research Papers, 10*(2), 1–41.

Ussher, J. M. (1991). *Women's madness: Misogyny or mental illness?* Harvester Wheatsheaf.

Ussher, J. M. (2003). The role of premenstrual dysphoric disorder in the subjectification of women. *Journal of Medical Humanities, 24*(1/2), 131–146.

Ussher, J. M. (2005). Unravelling women's madness: Beyond positivism and constructivism and towards a material-discursive-intrapsychic approach. In W. Chan, D. Chunn, & R. Menzies (Eds.), *Women, madness and the law: A feminist reader* (pp. 19–39). San Diego, CA: Glasshouse Press.

Ussher, J. M. (2010). Are we medicalizing women's misery? A critical review of women's higher rates of reported depression. *Feminism & Psychology, 20*(1), 9–35.

Valverde, M. (1998). *Diseases of the will: Alcohol and the dilemmas of freedom*. Cambridge, UK: Cambridge University Press.

Valverde, M. (2006). The power of powerlessness: Alcoholics Anonymous's techniques for governing the self. In A. Glasbeek (Ed.), *Moral regulation and governance in Canada: History, context, and critical issues* (pp. 299–326). Toronto, ON: Canadian Scholars' Press.

van der Meulen, E., Watson, T. M., & De Shalit, A. (2017). Insights on prison needle and syringe programs: Research with former prisoners in Canada. *Prison Journal, 97*(5), 628–643.

van Dijk, T. A. (1993). Principles of critical discourse analysis. *Discourse & Society, 4*(2), 249–283.

Van Veen, C., Ibrahim, M., & Morrow, M. (2018). Dangerous discourses: Masculinity, coercion and psychiatry. In J. M. Kilty & E. Dej (Eds.), *Containing madness: Gender and "psy" in institutional contexts* (pp. 241–266). London: Palgrave Macmillan.

Vaz, P., & Bruno, F. (2003). Types of self-surveillance: From abnormality to individuals "at-risk." *Surveillance & Society, 1*(3), 272–291.

Voronka, J. (2017). Turning mad knowledge into affective labor: The case of the peer support worker. *American Quarterly, 69*(2), 333–338.

Voronka, J., Wise Harris, D., Grant, J., Komaroff, J., Boyle, D., & Kennedy, A. (2014). Un/helpful help and its discontents: Peer researchers paying attention to street life narratives to inform social work policy and practice. *Social Work in Mental Health, 12*(3), 249–279.

Vorspan, F., Mehtelli, W., Dupuy, G., Bloch, V., & Lépine, J-P. (2015). Anxiety and substance use disorders: Co-occurrence and clinical issues. *Current Psychiatry Reports, 17*(2), 1–7.

Vowel, C. (2016). *Indigenous writes: A guide to First Nations, Métis & Inuit issues in Canada*. Winnipeg, MB: Highwater Press.

Wacquant, L. (2000). The new "peculiar institution": On the prison as surrogate ghetto. *Theoretical Criminology, 4*(3), 377–389.

Wacquant, L. (2002). From slavery to mass incarceration: Rethinking the "race question" in the US. *New Left Review, 13*(1), 41–60.

Wacquant, L. (2008). *Urban outcasts: A comparative sociology of advanced marginality*. Cambridge, UK: Polity Press.

Wacquant, L. (2009). *Prisons of poverty*. Minneapolis, MN: University of Minnesota Press.

Waegemakers Schiff, J., & Rook, J. (2012). *Housing First: Where's the evidence?* Toronto, ON: Canadian Observatory on Homelessness Press.

Wallace, B., Pauly, B., Perkin, K., & Cross, G. (2019). Where's the housing? Housing and income outcomes of a transitional program to end homelessness. *Journal of Poverty, 23*(2), 161–178.

Walsh, C. A., Hanley, J., Ives, N., & Hordyk, S. R. (2016). Exploring the experiences of newcomer women with insecure housing in Montréal Canada. *Journal of International Migration and Integration, 17*(3), 887–904.

Werth, R. (2012). I do what I'm told, sort of: Reformed subjects, unruly citizens, and parole. *Theoretical Criminology, 16*(3), 329–346.

West, C., & Zimmerman, D. H. (1987). Doing gender. *Gender & Society, 1*(2), 125–151.

White, C. (2015). Incarcerating youth with mental health problems: A focus on the intersection of race, ethnicity, and mental illness. *Youth Violence and Juvenile Justice, 14*(4), 426–447.

Whiting, D. (2009). Does decision-making capacity require the absence of pathological values? *Philosophy, Psychiatry, & Psychology, 16*(4), 341–344.

Williams, D. T. (2009). Grounding the regime of precarious employment: Homeless day laborers' negotiation of the job queue. *Work and Occupations, 36*(3), 209–246.

Wilson, D., & Macdonald, D. (2010). *The income gap between Aboriginal peoples and the rest of Canada.* Ottawa, ON: Canadian Centre for Policy Alternatives.

Wilson Gilmore, R. (2007). In the shadow of the shadow state. In INCITE! Women of Color Against Violence (Ed.), *The revolution will not be funded: Beyond the non-profit industrial complex* (pp. 41–52). Durham, NC: Duke University Press.

Woolford, A., & Curran, A. (2011). Neoliberal restructuring, limited autonomy, and relational distance in Manitoba's nonprofit field. *Critical Social Policy, 31*(4), 583–606.

Wynn, R. (2006). Coercion in psychiatric care: Clinical, legal, and ethical controversies. *International Journal of Psychiatry in Clinical Practice, 10*(4), 247–251.

Yalnizyan, A. (2010). *The rise of Canada's richest 1%.* Ottawa, ON: Canadian Centre for Policy Alternatives.

Young, J. (1999). *The exclusive society: Social exclusion, crime and difference in late modernity.* Thousand Oaks, CA: Sage.

Zinger, I. (2012). Mental health in federal corrections: Reflections and future directions. *Health Law Review, 20*(2), 22–25.

Zinger, I. (2020). Indigenous People in federal custody surpasses 30%: Correctional Investigator issues statement and challenge. Office of the Correctional Investigator of Canada. https://oci-bec.gc.ca/cnt/comm/press/press20200121-eng.aspx?texthighlight=indigenization.

Index

Abdi, Abdirahman, 44, 199*n*8
activism: about, 195–96; historical background, 3, 37–38; homelessness prevention, 53, 190–92, 194–95; human rights, 183, 190–91, 195–96; recommendations for change, 194–96; TRC recommendations, 187–88, 194. *See also* Housing First (HF); mad movement and anti-psychiatry
addiction: about, 41–42, 103–5, 122; biological determinism, 115–21; biopsychology, 129–34, 143; breaking of social norms, 42; concurrent disorders, 41–42, 103–5, 119–20, 158–59; harm reduction, 42, 122, 130–31; interviewees, demographics, 7(t), 103; medical model, 41–42, 117–22, 136; self-medication model, 103; statistics, 41; structural and systemic context, 122–23; substance-induced model, 103. *See also* individualization of social problems; medical model; structural and systemic context; substance use
addiction treatments: consumers/clients, 145–51, 158–59, 161–62; diagnosis, 4, 100–1, 154–56, 159; drug courts, 21, 142; freedom and choice, 136, 166–67; identity performance, 24; lack of needed resources, 58, 103–5, 150, 165–66, 175–76, 201*n*2 (ch. 6); medical model, 117–22; ongoing identity, 26, 153–54, 161–63, 166; psy-language, 41–42, 101, 103; responsibilization, 120, 122, 129–30, 139–40, 143–44; self-blame, 14–15, 26, 115–17, 126–27, 133–35; talk therapy, 103–5; true and untrue selves, 116, 124–27, 173; twelve-step programs (AA/NA), 120, 122, 130, 162, 173, 201*n*2 (ch. 5)
ADHD (attention deficit hyperactivity disorder), 100, 103, 130, 159, 161, 200*n*2
affordable housing: about, 32, 159–60, 191–92; historical background, 32–33, 95, 191, 201*n*3; lack of support services, 142, 160, 191–92; National Housing Strategy (2017), 32, 191, 201*n*3; Ottawa registry, 65,

67, 201*n*3; quality of life, 159–60; recommendations for change, 194–96; rooming houses, 66–67, 160, 192; safety and security, 66–67, 99–100, 160; shortages and waitlists, 65, 67, 152, 201*n*3; statistics, 30. *See also* Housing First (HF); housing and homes; structural and systemic context
Ahmed, Sara, 21, 146
Alcoholics Anonymous (AA), 120, 122, 130, 162, 173, 201*n*2 (ch. 5)
alcoholism: concurrent disorders, 41–42, 103–5, 119–20, 158–59; identity management, 110, 173; inclusion among the excluded, 173; Indigenous Peoples, 103–4; medical model, 41–42, 119–20, 122; stereotypes, 103–4. *See also* addiction; addiction treatments; substance use
allergy model, 120. *See also* medical model
Anderson, Leon, 33–34, 174
Anthony (shelter manager), 56, 127, 175, 178
anti-Black and anti-Brown racism, 44, 199*n*7
anti-citizens, 17, 19, 137.
anti-psychiatry, 37–39. *See also* mad movement and anti-psychiatry; psychiatry and psychology
anti-social people, 19–20, 199*n*4. *See also* social exclusion and the irredeemable
anxiety, 39–40, 100–1, 159, 202*n*10
Assertive Community Treatment (ACT) team, 41, 202*n*8
assistance, social. *See* welfare and social assistance
Asylums (Goffman), 54, 74
At Home/Chez Soi, 40–41, 190–93. *See also* Housing First (HF)
authentic and true self, 111–14, 116, 124–27, 183. *See also* identity performance

autonomy. *See* freedom, autonomy, and choice

Bauman, Zygmunt, 11, 95, 140–41, 146–47, 172, 175–76, 180, 184
Beckett, Katherine, 54
Ben-Moshe, Liat, 43
Berlant, Lauren, cruel optimism, 21–22, 153, 157–58, 161, 183–84
biological determinism, 115–21, 124–30, 143–44. *See also* medical model
bipolar disorder, 39–40, 100, 103, 124–25, 198*n*3, 200*n*10
Black people: Black Lives Matter, 44, 123; criminal justice system, 44, 45, 123, 199*n*8; historical background, 2; interviewees, demographics, 7(t); systemic racism, 2, 123–24. *See also* racialized people
brain: biopsychology and changes in, 129–34, 143–44; injuries, 40. *See also* medical model
Butler, Judith, 88, 109, 112, 183

Canadian Alliance to End Homelessness, 53
Canadian Definition of Homelessness, 28
Canadian Observatory on Homelessness (COH), 28, 41, 190
Canadian Shelter Transformation Network, 53
capitalism, 18, 48, 49, 51–52, 145–46. *See also* consumers and clients; neoliberalism
chemical imbalances. *See* medical model
choice. *See* freedom, autonomy, and choice
CMHA (Canadian Mental Health Association), 58, 105, 142, 158, 165, 201*n*5
Cohen, Stanley, 47, 54, 66
concurrent disorders, 41–42, 103–5, 119–20, 158–59. *See also* addiction; dual diagnosis; mental illness

consumers and clients: about, 15–16, 145–51, 158–59, 167, 180–81; employment, 12, 91, 170–71, 186; flawed consumers, 15–16, 147–51, 165–67, 180–81; freedom and choice, 145–46, 148–51, 154–56, 163, 164, 201*n*1; homelessness industrial complex, 23, 147–51, 156–59; inclusion of the excluded, 173; lack of needed services, 150, 155–57, 165–66, 175–76, 201*n*2 (ch. 6); mental health system, 154–59, 161, 170–71, 180–81; neoliberalism, 15–16, 145–51, 180, 201*n*1; as ongoing and unfinished, 26, 147, 153–54, 161–63; political economy of hope, 23, 147, 156–64; poverty, 147–48; project of the self, 147–49, 154–59; redeemability/ irredeemability, 145–51, 175, 188–89; social control, 15–16. *See also* neoliberalism

correctional facilities. *See* jails and detention centres; prison industrial complex

criminal justice system: about, 43–49; consumers/clients, 145–51; CTOs (community treatment orders), 36; drug courts, 21, 142; freedom and choice, 150–51; historical background, 32, 43–44; interviewees, demographics, 7(t), 167–68; minor offences, 15, 44, 47–49, 58–59; people experiencing homelessness, 15, 27–28, 43–49; people identified as mentally ill, 27–28, 39, 43–46, 48–49; project of the self, 150–51; recommendations for change, 194–96; redeemability/ irredeemability, 19–20, 24–26, 178–81, 199*n*4; social construction of identities, 27–28; social junk and social dynamite categories, 18–19, 24, 199*n*4; statistics, 2, 20, 46–47; transcarceration, 52, 55. *See also* police

Crossroads men's emergency shelter (pseudonym): about, 6–7, 56–57; funding, 9–10, 87, 157, 199*n*2, 201*n*5; hierarchies of residents, 168–70; loss of dignity, 87; spatial restrictions, 61; staff, 7, 56–57, 76; statistics, 6. *See also* emergency shelters; research project

cruel optimism, Berlant's, 21–22, 153, 157–58, 161, 183–84

demographics: food insecurity, 30; homelessness, 1, 29, 32, 191; Indigenous Peoples, 30, 98; interviewees, 7–8, 7(t), 100, 105

DeOllos, Ione Y., 86

dependency, 71–75, 81. *See also* emergency shelters, residents

depression, 39–40, 100–1, 103, 119, 121–22, 171, 198*n*3. *See also* mental illness

deservingness, 88–89, 96–99, 133–34, 156, 168–72. *See also* redeemability

detention centres. *See* jails

Diagnostic and Statistical Manual of Mental Disorders (DSM-V), 42, 115

dignity, 87–88

disabilities, people with, 171–72, 194, 202*n*12

disciplinary strategies. *See* social control and discipline

distress: alternatives to medical model, 37–39; criminalization of, 43–49; diagnoses, 39–40, 100–1; historical background, 32–35, 95; individualization of social problems, 33–34, 116–17, 126; irredeemability, 174–75; medical model, 34–37, 117–21, 126; as term, 197*n*3. *See also* individualization of social problems; mad movement and anti-psychiatry; medical model; mental illness; psychiatry and psychology

Dolbeare, Cushing, 191

Donohue, Erin, 150, 154, 201*n*4

drugs and alcohol. *See* addiction; addiction treatments; alcoholism; psychotropic medications; substance use

DSM-V *(Diagnostic and Statistical Manual of Mental Disorders)*, 42, 115

dual diagnosis (concurrent disorders), 41–42, 103–5, 119–20, 158–59. *See also* addiction; mental illness

emergency shelters: about, 25, 50–55, 80–81; average stay, 200*n*7; care and compassion, 6, 50, 74–78, 172, 186; funding, 9–10, 87, 157, 199*n*2, 201*n*5; historical background, 32, 51; lack of needed resources, 176–77; neoliberal total institution, 51–55, 60, 65, 68–72, 80–81; police, 178–80; power relations, 55–57, 60; recommendations for change, 194–96; safety and security, 7, 55–57, 70–71, 76–80, 99–100, 138, 178–80; social supports, 51, 55, 69; spatial restrictions, 56–57, 60–67; transcarceration, 52, 55. *See also* consumers and clients; Crossroads men's emergency shelter (pseudonym); emergency shelters, residents; emergency shelters, staff; Haven men's and women's shelter (pseudonym)

emergency shelters, residents: case files, 57–58; categories of, 59–60; daily activities, 54, 60, 63, 68–74; dependency, 71–75, 81; dignity, 87–88; employment of residents, 91, 170–71, 186; families and friends, 61–62, 86, 90; freedom, 52–53, 55, 58, 60–67, 71, 81, 150–51; gender separation, 62; hierarchies of residents, 168–70; meanings of home, 71, 99–100; mortification, 59, 65–66, 78, 81; names and identities, 59–60; normalization, 56–57, 102, 106; positive attitudes, 70, 75–76; power relations, 53, 55–56; privacy, 59–60; privileges, 11, 24, 77–80, 168–73, 180, 189; responsibilization, 60, 135; social control, 52, 54–60, 66–75, 89–95; social exclusion, 73–74, 81, 92–95; social housing, 55, 64–67, 201*n*3. *See also* consumers and clients; identity; identity performance; people experiencing homelessness; redeemability; shame

emergency shelters, staff: about, 57–58, 74–80; balance of security and care, 186; as case managers, 57–58; flexibility of rules, 77–80; frontline staff ("the bubble"), 156–57, 170; as mental health workers, 57–58, 176–79; as police, 76–77, 179; power relations, 53, 74–80, 156–57, 170, 176–78; redeemability/ irredeemability of residents, 77–80, 168–70, 174–78; residents' positive attitudes toward, 70, 75–76; social control, 56–60, 176, 179

employment, 12, 91, 170–71, 186

enriched environments, 130–31, 132–33

exclusion. *See* social exclusion; social exclusion and the irredeemable; social inclusion

families and friends, 12, 61–62, 86, 90
Feldman, Leonard C., 55–56
Finkler, Lilith, 39
First Nations. *See* Indigenous Peoples
food insecurity, 30. *See also* poverty
Forcillo, James, 44, 199*n*8
Foucault, Michel: discipline, 68; governmentality, 13, 15, 55; medicine of the mind, 117; power, 13–14, 34–35, 168; subjectivities, 201*n*4
freedom, autonomy, and choice: about, 13–16, 51, 63–67, 133, 150–51, 182–83; autonomy, 13–15, 51, 81, 133; choice vs biological determinism, 115–21, 126–30,

143–44; choice narratives, 130, 136, 141–42, 154; consumers/clients, 15–16, 145–51, 154–56, 163–64, 201*n*1; empowerment by restraints on, 140–42; identity performance, 83; neoliberalism, 63, 150–51, 201*n*1; power relations, 13–14; privileges in shelters, 172–73; project of the self, 14–15, 150–51; psychotropic medications, 166–67; redeemability, 145–46, 150–51, 154, 188–89; self-blame, 26, 115–17, 126–27, 133–37, 186; social mobility, 172, 183. *See also* project of the self; responsibilization; social control and discipline
frontline staff. *See* emergency shelters, staff

Gaetz, Stephen, 41, 190
gender: gender differences, 97, 137–38; hyper-masculinity, 202*n*11; identity performance, 84; interviewees, demographics, 7(t); shame, 87–88; Two-Spirit, 200*n*3. *See also* LGBTQ2S+ people; women
genetics and distress. *See* medical model
Gergen, Kenneth J., 111
Giddens, Anthony, 111
girls and women. *See* women
Goffman, Erving: *Asylums*, 54, 74; identity performance, 82–84, 102, 107, 109–10, 112–13, 183; moral career of mental patient, 59–60, 74, 81, 158, 199*n*5; names and identities, 59; power relations, 74; total institutions, 52–55, 59, 63–67, 78, 80–81, 182–83
Gounis, Kostas, 61, 71

Hacking, Ian, 101, 131
happiness industry, 146–47. *See also* consumers and clients
harm reduction, 6, 122, 130–31

Haven men's and women's shelter (pseudonym): about, 6–7, 56–57; gender separation, 62; harm reduction, 6–7; hierarchies of residents, 168–69; power relations, 56–57, 76; residents' positive attitudes toward, 75–76; safety and security, 7, 56–57, 70–71; staff, 7, 56–57; statistics, 6. *See also* emergency shelters; research project
HF. *See* Housing First (HF)
Hirai, Hideyuki, 142, 162
homeless shelters. *See* emergency shelters
homelessness: about, 27–34, 49; "anti-homelessness" legislation, 47–48; causes, 29–34; classifications, 28–30; critical scholarship, 32–34, 39; defined, 28–31; historical background, 31–32; as identity marker, 27; Indigenous experiences, 28–29, 31–32, 198*n*8; individualization of social problems, 33–34; measurements, 28–34; mental illness as factor, 39–42; prevention programs, 53, 190–92, 194–95; recommendations for change, 194–96; short terms, 29, 66, 191; social construction of identities, 27–28; statistics, 1, 29–30, 32, 39, 47, 191; structural and systemic context, 30, 33–34. *See also* individualization of social problems; people experiencing homelessness; people identified as mentally ill; stereotypes; structural and systemic context
homelessness industrial complex: about, 9–11, 25–26, 49–51, 182–87; consumers/clients, 23, 145–51, 156–57; dependency, 71–75, 81; exclusionary practices, 25, 185–87; freedom and choice, 150–51, 154–56; funding, 9–10, 87, 157, 199*n*2, 201*n*5; individualization of social problems, 9–13, 33–34; medical

model, 115–17; pathologization of homelessness, 3, 10–11, 41, 156, 173; political economy of hope, 23, 129, 147, 159–60, 162–63, 174; power relations and knowledge, 168–69; recommendations for change, 194–96; redeemability/irredeemability, 11–12, 25–26, 77–80, 94, 145–46, 174–76, 199*n*4; responsibilization, 25, 115–17, 135; services, 94; social control, 15, 25; state downloading to non-state actors, 53, 77; structural limitations, 10–11, 13, 33–34; transcarceration, 52, 55. *See also* emergency shelters; homelessness; individualization of social problems; people experiencing homelessness; structural and systemic context

homes. *See* affordable and social housing; housing and homes

hope and hopelessness: about, 22–23, 129–33, 156–59, 180–81, 183–84; biopsychology, 129–34, 143; consumers/clients, 23, 147, 156–58, 162; cruel optimism, 21–22, 153, 157–58, 161, 183–84; hopelessness, 12–13, 174–75, 179–81; inclusion among the excluded, 22–25, 172–73, 183; inclusion goals, 22–23, 85, 151–59, 183; political economy of hope, 23, 129, 147, 159–63, 174; redeemability/irredeemability, 11–12, 132, 151, 174–75, 179–81, 188–89, 199*n*4; structural and systemic context, 22. *See also* redeemability; social exclusion; social inclusion

Housing First (HF): about, 40–41, 190–93; eligibility and assessment, 41, 175, 198*n*8; prevention programs, 53; program supports, 40, 192–93; recommendations for change, 194; redeemability/irredeemability, 94, 172, 175, 193; social exclusion, 94, 160, 192–93; vs treatment first, 40, 104. *See also* affordable and social housing

housing and homes: about, 191–92; assumption of social inclusion, 12, 191–93; critical scholarship, 32–34, 39; historical background, 32–33; home takeovers, 67, 192; homelessness prevention, 53, 190–92, 194–95; human rights, 183, 190–91, 195–96; as insufficient to end homelessness, 191–93; National Housing Strategy (2017), 191, 201*n*3; quality of life, 159–60; safety and security, 66–67, 100; symbolic significance, 28–29, 71, 99–100. *See also* affordable housing; emergency shelters; homelessness; Housing First (HF)

Hughes, James, 53

human rights: criminalization of mentally ill, 44; housing rights, 183, 190–91, 195–96; of shelter residents, 58

identity: about, 82–85, 113–14; consumers/clients, 145–51, 180; employment, 12, 91, 170–71, 186; families and friends, 61–62, 86, 90; fluidity of, 20, 84, 101, 106–8, 131, 162; heterogeneous identities, 96–100; before homeless identity, 74, 93, 106–7; homelessness, 62, 84–85, 99–100; "imposters," 107–8; loss of, 59, 65–66, 81; markers, 11–12, 84–85; materiality, 83; mental illness, 84–85; moral career of homeless person, 59–60, 74, 81, 158, 199*n*5; mortification in total institutions, 59, 65–66, 78, 81; names and identities, 59–60, 108–9; sense of self, 82–83; social construction, 27–28, 82–85, 105–8. *See also* people experiencing homelessness; people identified as mentally ill, identities; project of the self; redeemability; shame; social exclusion; social inclusion identity performance: about, 25–26, 82–85, 105–9, 113–14, 183; distancing, 109–11, 200*n*7; facades, 111–14; gender differences, 97; heterogeneous identities, 96–101; idealized self, 109–11; impression management, 109–14; inclusion among the excluded, 22–25, 102, 172–73, 183; labels as descriptors, 82, 100–1; limitations, 106–9; management of, 83–85, 100–1, 105–9; mental illness, 82–83, 84–85, 100–6, 162; motherhood, 110–11; redeemability/irredeemability, 11–12, 83, 95, 109, 114, 126, 135, 160, 168–70; resistance to homeless identity, 99–100, 106–8, 163–64; situated identity, 83–84, 108; stereotypes, 83, 105–6; true and untrue selves, 111–14, 116, 124–27, 173, 183. *See also* consumers and clients; people experiencing homelessness; people identified as mentally ill, identities; project of the self; redeemability

immigrants and refugees, 98, 122–23, 194. *See also* newcomers

impression management, 109–14. *See also* identity performance

included among the excluded. *See* social exclusion

inclusion. *See* social inclusion

Indigenous Peoples: about, 2–3, 28–29, 187–88; homelessness, 28–29, 198*n*8; intergenerational trauma, 71, 118; interviewees, demographics, 7(t); missing and murdered women (NIMMIWG), 31–32, 138–39, 194; poverty, 2–3, 97–99; prison system, 2, 45, 47, 198*n*8; racism, 98–99; recommendations for change, 194–96; settler-colonialism, 2–3, 31–32, 95, 118, 130, 138–39; Sixties Scoop, 103–4; statistics, 2, 29, 30, 98; stereotypes, 103–4, 199*n*6; TRC recommendations, 187–88, 194; Two-Spirit, 200*n*3; women, 2, 45, 138–39. *See also* marginalized people

individualization of social problems: about, 1, 9–11, 13, 33–34, 49, 149, 190; consumers/clients, 149, 152; criminalization of mental illness, 43–44; cruel optimism, 153; dependency, 71–75, 81; failure of state vs individual, 183; historical background, 32–35, 95; homelessness industrial complex, 146, 149; Indigenous Peoples, 118; medical model and treatments, 128–29, 143–44, 152, 183; pathologization of homelessness, 3, 10–11, 32–33, 41, 156, 173; project of the self, 149, 153; recommendations for change, 194–96; vs structural context, 9–11, 13, 21, 33–34, 152–53, 183, 190; VI-SPDAT screening tool, 198*n*8. *See also* medical model; project of the self; responsibilization; self-help programs; structural and systemic context

Intensive Case Management (ICM), 41

interdependence vs dependency, 72. *See also* emergency shelters, residents

interviewees. *See* research project, participants

Inuit: demographics, 30, 98; homelessness, 28–29; racism, 98–99; stereotypes, 103–4. *See also* Indigenous Peoples

irredeemability. *See* redeemability; social exclusion and the irredeemable

jails and detention centres: about, 47–49, 198*n*10; the irredeemable, 24–25; lack of needed services, 46–47, 201*n*2 (ch. 6); mental health, 44–49; short custody, 25, 45; statistics, 2, 46; terminology, 198*n*10;

transcarceration, 52, 55. *See also* prison industrial complex
Johnsen, Sarah, 56, 187

Kathy (public health nurse), 58, 120–21, 126–27, 157, 167

Laing, Ronald David, 37–38, 123
legislation: "anti-homelessness," 47–48; mental health, 36–37
Lemert, Edwin, 83
LGBTQ2S+ people: about, 90–91; distancing strategies, 90–91, 200*n*7; gay actor, 91, 111, 200*n*7; identity management, 108–9, 111; interviewees, demographics, 7(t); recommendations for change, 194; safety in housing, 100; statistics on homelessness, 29; trans people, 108–9; Two-Spirit, 200*n*3

mad movement and anti-psychiatry: about, 3, 37–39, 49, 121–24; anti-psychiatry, 3, 37–38; consumers/clients, 121–22, 148–49, 164–66; critical scholarship, 3, 37–39, 49; historical background, 3, 37–38, 198*n*6; lack of needed resources, 38, 176; mad movement, 3, 37–39, 121, 148–49, 198*n*4; peer support, 3, 176, 185, 195, 198*n*4; resistance to medical model, 3–4, 37–39, 121–24, 163–64, 198*n*4. *See also* medical model; psychiatry and psychology; psy-language
Marcus, Anthony, 65, 200*n*7
marginalized people: about, 1–3, 16–20, 49; categories and stereotypes, 16–22, 24; consumers/clients, 145–51; otherness, 89–90; power relations, 168–69; social control, 2–3, 89–90; systemic discrimination, 41. *See also* Black people; Indigenous Peoples; people experiencing homelessness; people identified as mentally ill; racialized people; social control and discipline
Maruna, Shadd, 133, 135
Maté, Gabor, 129–33, 136
medical model: about, 1, 34–37, 49, 115–21, 143–44; addiction, 41–42, 115; allergy model, 120; assumption in scholarship, 27–28; biological determinism, 115–21, 124–30, 143–44; biopsychology, 129–34, 143; cure vs symptom management, 36, 120–21; diagnosis, 4, 100–1, 154–56, 159; of distress, 115–16, 197*n*3; historical background, 34–35; individualization of social problems, 116; legitimacy of medical profession, 35; pathologization, 3, 10–11, 26, 41, 156, 173; power relations, 34–36; resistance to, 3–4, 37–39, 116–17, 121–24, 155–56, 163–64, 198*n*4; responsibilization, 115–17, 119, 126–28, 143–44; self-blame, 26, 115–17, 119, 126–27, 133–35, 143, 186; structural and systemic context, 128; triggers, 117, 131; true and untrue selves, 116, 124–27. *See also* mad movement and anti-psychiatry; psychiatry and psychology; psychiatric hospitals; psychotropic medications; psy-language; responsibilization
medications. *See* psychotropic medications
Melissa (case worker), 176, 178, 201*n*3
men: hyper-masculinity, 202*n*11; interviewees, demographics, 7(t). *See also* gender
mental health system: about, 34–42, 49; Assertive Community Treatment (ACT), 41, 202*n*8; assessments, 174–78; care and compassion, 164–65; consumers/clients, 23, 145–54, 156–59, 163–65, 170–71, 180–81; and criminal justice system, 43–49; diagnosis, 4, 100–1, 154–56,

159; flawed consumers, 15–16, 147–51, 165–67, 180–81; freedom and choice, 150–51, 154–56; historical background, 43, 198*n*6; identity performance, 152–54; inclusion goals, 151–59; lack of needed resources, 38, 58, 103–5, 150, 155–59, 165–66, 175–76, 198*n*6, 201*n*2 (ch. 6); programs, 94, 105, 152, 158–59; project of the self, 150–54; public vs for-profit services, 165–66; recommendations for change, 194–96; resistance to, 3, 37–39, 49, 121–24, 198*n*4. *See also* medical model; psychiatry and psychology; psychiatric hospitals; psychotropic medications; psy-language

mental illness: about, 49; biological determinism, 115–21; biopsychology, 129–34, 143; breaking of social norms, 42; community programs, 41, 43, 199*n*7; concurrent disorders, 41–42, 103–5, 119–20, 158–59; CTOs (community treatment orders), 36, 154; diagnosis, 4, 39–40, 100–1, 154–56, 159; medical model, 120–21, 128–29; normalization, 56–57, 102, 106; responsibilization, 128–30; social construction of identities, 27–28; statistics, 39; stigma, 101–2. *See also* medical model; people identified as mentally ill; people identified as mentally ill, identities

mental illnesses, specific. *See* anxiety; bipolar disorder; depression; OCD (obsessive-compulsive disorder); PTSD (post-traumatic stress disorder); schizophrenia

mental illnesses, treatments for. *See* addiction treatments; mad movement and anti-psychiatry; project of the self; psychiatry and psychology; psychiatric hospitals; psychotropic medications; psy-language; self-help programs

Métis, 28–30, 124. *See also* Indigenous Peoples

migrants. *See* newcomers

missing and murdered Indigenous women and girls, 31–32, 138–39, 194. *See also* Indigenous Peoples

Montsion, Daniel, 44, 199*n*8

Moore, Dawn, 24, 36, 142, 150, 154, 162, 186, 201*n*4

Morrow, Marina, 39

National At Home/Chez Soi, 40, 190–93. *See also* Housing First (HF)

National Housing Strategy (2017), 32, 191, 201*n*3

National Inquiry into Missing and Murdered Indigenous Women and Girls (NIMMIWG), 31–32, 138–39, 194

neoliberal total institutions: compared with total institutions, 52–55, 60, 65, 68, 70–71, 80–81. *See also* emergency shelters; total institutions

neoliberalism: about, 32, 51–53, 81; capitalism, 18, 48, 49, 51–52, 145–46; choice vs biological determinism, 115–21, 126–30, 143–44; consumers/clients, 15–16, 23, 145–51, 180, 201*n*1; dismantling of social welfare, 32, 51, 96–97; downloading to non-state actors, 51–53, 77; emergency shelters, 51–55, 80–81; freedom and choice, 51, 63, 145–46, 150–51, 201*n*1; historical background, 32; identity performance, 83–84; inclusion goals, 22, 85; project of the self, 51, 83–84, 147–49; responsibilization vs dependency, 71–75, 81, 135, 143–44; transcarceration, 52. *See also* consumers and clients; emergency shelters; freedom, autonomy, and choice; individualization of social problems; project of the self; responsibilization

newcomers, 98, 122–23, 194. *See also* immigrants and refugees
NIMMIWG (National Inquiry into Missing and Murdered Indigenous Women and Girls), 138–39, 194
non-profit industrial complex, 9–10. *See also* homelessness industrial complex
norms. *See* social norms
Novas, Carlos, 23, 129

OCD (obsessive-compulsive disorder), 100–1, 129–30, 155
Ontario Disability Support Payments (ODSP), 171–72, 202*n*12
Ontario Works (OW), 171–72, 202*n*12
Otherness, defined, 89
Ottawa: demographics, 30, 46, 98; detention centre, 46–47, 76; emergency shelters, 30, 93, 200*n*7, 201*n*5; Indigenous Peoples, 30, 98–99; mental health centre (ROH), 76, 158, 200*n*9; safety concerns, 179; social housing, 65, 67, 201*n*3 (ch. 5), 201*n*3 (ch. 6); women's poverty, 96–97. *See also* Crossroads men's emergency shelter (pseudonym); Haven men's and women's shelter (pseudonym); research project
Ottawa-Carleton Detention Centre (OCDC), 46–47, 76

panhandling legislation, 47–48
participants in research project. *See* research project, participants
pathologization of homelessness, 3, 10–11, 32–33, 41, 156, 173. *See also* homelessness industrial complex; individualization of social problems
peer support, 176, 185, 195, 198*n*4
people, Indigenous. *See* Indigenous Peoples
people of colour. *See* Black people; racialized people

people with disabilities, 171–72, 194, 202*n*12
people experiencing homelessness: about, 16–20, 27–28, 188–89; "anti-homelessness" legislation, 47–48; categories and stereotypes, 16–22, 24, 199*n*4; consumers/clients, 147–51; dehumanization, 16–19, 88, 197*n*4; future research needed, 187; gender differences, 97; heterogeneous identities, 96–100; historical background, 95–97; hopelessness, 12–13; identities, 25–28; lived experience, 34, 183–84, 194, 197*n*3; meaning-making, 96; mental illness, 39–42; social construction of identities, 27–28; social junk and social dynamite categories, 18–19, 24, 199*n*4; statistics, 1, 29–30, 32, 39, 191; strength and perseverance, 188–89; women, 96–97. *See also* consumers and clients; homelessness; hope and hopelessness; identity; identity performance; people identified as mentally ill; redeemability; research project; social control and discipline; social exclusion; stereotypes
people identified as mentally ill: about, 26–28, 49; consumers/clients, 145–51; criminalization, 39; homelessness, 39–42, 49; interviewees, demographics, 7(t), 100; the irredeemable, 24–25, 178–80, 199*n*4; lack of needed services, 38, 58, 103–5, 150, 155–57, 165–66, 175–76, 201*n*2 (ch. 6); psychotropic medications, 100, 103; redeemability/irredeemability, 11–12, 24–26, 174–81, 188–89, 199*n*4; responsibilization, 102, 115, 120, 122; self-blame, 26, 115–17, 126–27, 133–35, 186; social control, 58–59, 199*n*4. *See also* consumers and clients; mad movement and

anti-psychiatry; medical model; mental health system; mental illness; redeemability; responsibilization
people identified as mentally ill, identities: about, 27–28, 100–2; identity performance, 100–2; inclusion among the excluded, 22–25, 102, 173; normalization, 56–57, 102, 106; psy-language, 37, 41–42, 101, 167, 172; resistance, 163–64; self-diagnoses, 100–1; social construction, 27–28, 82–83, 105–8; true and untrue selves, 116, 124–27. *See also* identity; identity performance; social exclusion
personas. *See* identity performance
Phillips, Colin Robert, 94
police: about, 43–44, 123; the irredeemable, 24–25, 178–80, 199*n*4; police-mental health units, 43–44, 199*n*7; practices, 25, 44, 48–49, 58–59, 109, 170, 199*n*8; racialized people, 44, 123, 199*n*8. *See also* criminal justice system
political economy of hope, 23, 129, 147, 159–63, 174. *See also* hope and hopelessness
poverty: "anti-homelessness" legislation, 47–48; core housing need, 30; criminal justice system, 47, 178; deservingness, 88–89, 172, 179; disability payments, 171–72, 202*n*12; flawed consumers, 15–16, 147–48, 165–67, 180–81; food insecurity, 30; medicalization of, 171–72; racialized people, 98–99; recommendations for change, 194–96; shame, 85–89, 93, 95; social control, 15; statistics, 2, 29–30; women, 29, 96–98. *See also* affordable and social housing; people experiencing homelessness; welfare and social assistance
power relations: about, 13–14, 53, 74–76; changes in, 56–57; freedom and choice, 14–15; hierarchies of shelter residents, 168–70; historical background, 34–35; hypermasculinity, 202*n*11; marginalized people, 168–69; medical model, 34–36; redeemability/irredeemability, 174; social constructionism, 5; staff-resident relations, 53, 74–80, 156–57, 176; truth claims, 5, 13. *See also* freedom, autonomy, and choice; social control and discipline
precarious employment, 12, 91, 170–71, 186
precarious housing. *See* affordable and social housing; housing and homes
prison industrial complex: about, 9–10, 46–49; homelessness after prison, 46–47, 176; Indigenous prisoners, 2, 47, 198*n*8; individualization of social problems, 44–46; the irredeemable, 24–25, 178–80, 199*n*4; lack of needed services, 46–47, 150, 176, 201*n*2 (ch. 6); mental health, 44–46; racialized prisoners, 2, 45, 47, 123–24; redeemability/irredeemability, 24–26, 126–27, 140–41, 178–81, 199*n*4; responsibilization, 126–27, 135, 140–41; social control, 47–49, 140–41; statistics, 2, 44–47; terminology, 198*n*10; total institutions, 53–54; transcarceration, 52, 55; true and untrue selves, 126–27; women prisoners, 44–45. *See also* criminal justice system; jails and detention centres; total institutions
project, research. *See* research project
project of the self: about, 14, 51, 147, 152–54; consumers/clients, 23, 147–51, 153–54, 158–59, 201*n*1; cruel optimism, 21–22, 153, 157–58, 161, 183–84; dependency, 71–75, 81; inclusion goals, 85, 151–59, 183; moral career of homeless person, 59–60, 74, 81, 158, 199*n*5; neoliberalism, 51; as ongoing and unfinished, 26, 147,

153–54, 161–63; redeemability/
irredeemability, 11–12, 149–52,
168, 174–75; schedules and
routines, 69–70; self-blame, 14,
26, 115–17, 126–27, 133–35, 140,
186; self-objectification, 140, 158.
See also freedom, autonomy, and
choice; hope and hopelessness;
redeemability; self-help programs
psychiatry and psychology: about,
3–4, 49; consumers/clients, 23, 147,
159, 163–64; historical background,
35–36, 198*n*6; internal vs external
causes of distress, 35; legitimacy of
medical profession, 35, 152; medical
model, 34–37; resistance to, 3–4,
37–39, 163–64, 198*n*4. *See also* mad
movement and anti-psychiatry;
medical model; psychiatric
hospitals; psychotropic medications;
psy-language
psychiatric hospitals: consumers/
clients, 145–51; historical
background, 43, 198*n*6; involuntary
detention ("form"), 36–37, 58, 154,
175; the irredeemable, 24–25, 175,
178–80, 199*n*4; total institutions,
53–54; transcarceration, 52, 55.
See also total institutions
psychotropic medications: about,
35–36, 120–21; antipsychotics,
200*n*10, 201*n*6; benzodiazepines,
155, 166–67, 202*n*10; Big Pharma,
35–36, 164, 166; compliance, 36,
120–21, 155–56, 201*n*6; consumers
and clients, 23, 156–59, 201*n*6; CTOs
(community treatment orders), 36,
154; cure vs symptom management,
36, 120–21; freedom and choice,
166–67; historical background,
35–36; interviewees, demographics,
7(t), 100, 103, 105, 201*n*6; political
economy of hope, 23; prescriptions
without diagnoses, 100–1; resistance
to, 37–39, 163–64, 175, 198*n*4; social

control, 121, 163–64; sole method of
treatment, 103, 157
psy-language: about, 3–4, 100–2;
consumers/clients, 147, 159; distress,
as term, 197*n*3; identity performance,
101–2, 134, 172; subjugated
knowledges, 5, 167; widespread use
of, 37, 41–42,
100–1, 159
PTSD (post-traumatic stress disorder),
39–40, 103, 159
public spaces: about, 16, 61–63, 186;
"anti-homelessness" legislation,
47–48; policing practices, 123; safety
concerns, 64; social exclusion, 3, 16,
61–63, 186, 198*n*9

racialized people: about, 2, 98–99;
interviewees, demographics, 7(t);
over-policing, 44, 123, 199*n*8; poverty,
98–99; prisoners, 2, 45, 123–24; racism
and discrimination, 41, 123–24. *See also*
Black people; Indigenous Peoples;
marginalized people
Ranasinghe, Prashan, 55, 77–78
recovery industry, 142, 161–64, 184,
198*n*5. *See also* homelessness
industrial complex; mental health
system; project of the self
redeemability: about, 9, 11–12,
19–20, 145–46, 167–70, 180–81,
188–89; adoption of social norms,
11–12, 21–22, 168–70, 184; care
and compassion, 77–78, 172;
consumers/clients, 145–46, 149–51,
158–59, 180–81; continuum, 11–12,
16–26, 89, 121, 151, 172–73; cruel
optimism, 21–22, 153, 157–58,
161, 183–84; deservingness,
24, 88–89, 96–99, 133–34, 156,
168–72; distancing strategies,
109; freedom and choice, 150–51,
154–56; identity performance, 11,
83, 95, 109, 114, 126, 135, 160, 168;
inclusion among the excluded,

22–25, 102, 172–73, 183; inclusion goals, 12–13, 21, 73, 85, 151–62, 183–84; interviewees, 19–20, 167–68; as ongoing and unfinished, 26, 89, 147, 153–54, 161–63, 193; pathologization of homelessness, 3, 10–11, 26, 41, 156, 173; power relations, 19, 168–70; privileges and perks, 11, 24, 77–80, 168–73, 180, 189; responsibilization, 20, 132–35, 142–44; schedules and routines, 69–70; self-blame, 26, 115–17, 126–27, 133–35, 137, 143; shame, 85, 89, 94–95, 133; social control, 19–20, 140, 142; working homeless, 170–71. *See also* hope and hopelessness; identity performance; responsibilization; social exclusion; social exclusion and the irredeemable; social inclusion
refugees and immigrants, 98, 122–23, 194
Reith, Gerda, 148, 201*n*1
research project: about, 3–9; author's background, 3–8, 50, 92–93, 185, 186–87; critical discourse analysis, 8–9; data collection, 6, 7; focus group, 5, 57–58; future research needed, 187; interviews, 5, 7–8, 7(t), 75; key messages, 12–13; methodology, 5, 7–9; participant observation, 5, 7; power relations, 4–5; recommendations for change, 193–96; site (Ottawa), 4, 6–7, 30; social constructionism, 4–5, 9, 27–28; symbolic interactionism, 4–5
research project, participants: about, 7–8, 7(t); addiction, 103; chronic homelessness, 30; disability payments, 171–72, 202*n*12; focus group, 8; homelessness, length of time, 96; interviews, 7–8, 7(t), 197*n*6; lack of employment, 171; newcomers, 98; professionals and para-professionals, 8; psychotropic medications, 100, 105; racialized people, 98; recruitment, 8; redeemability/irredeemability, 19–20, 167–68; specific populations, 7(t)
residents of emergency shelters. *See* emergency shelters, residents
resistance to psy-disciplines. *See* mad movement and anti-psychiatry
responsibilization: about, 13–15, 26, 115–17, 127–33, 139–44; vs biological determinism, 115–21, 126–30, 143–44; biopsychology, 129–34, 143; vs dependency, 71–75, 81; empowerment by, 139–44; enriched environments, 130–33; freedom and choice, 13–15, 130, 136–37, 140; medical model, 115–17, 119, 126–31, 143–44; neoliberal values, 130, 135, 142; psy-language, 101, 134; redeemability/irredeemability, 11–12, 24, 137, 140–41, 143–44, 168, 175, 188–89; schedules, 69–70; self-blame, 26, 115–17, 126–27, 137, 139–40, 143, 186; social control, 140, 142; treatment discourses, 128–33, 139–44. *See also* individualization of social problems; redeemability
Rick (support worker), 96, 98, 106
rights. *See* human rights
Rimke, Heidi Marie, 35, 37, 158
rooming houses, 66–67, 160, 192. *See also* affordable and social housing; housing and homes
Rose, Nikolas, 11, 14, 17, 19–20, 22, 23, 137, 157
Rosenthal, Rob, 97
Royal Ottawa Hospital (ROH), 76, 105, 158, 200*n*9
Ruddick, Sue, 93

schizophrenia, 36, 39–40, 101, 122–23, 128, 198*n*5
Schneider, Barbara, 39
screening tools, 41, 198*n*8

self-governance. *See* freedom, autonomy, and choice; project of the self; responsibilization
self-help programs: about, 14–15, 69; consumers/clients, 147, 152–54; medical model, 70, 152; perpetual dissatisfaction, 147, 153–54; schedules and routines, 69–70; twelve-step programs (AA/NA), 120, 122, 130, 162, 173, 201*n*2 (ch. 5). *See also* project of the self; redeemability; responsibilization
self-responsibilization. *See* responsibilization
Seroquel, 75, 79, 157, 158, 200*n*10, 201*n*6
sex work, 202*n*9
sexual orientation. *See* LGBTQ2S+ people
shame: about, 85–95, 186; dependency, 94; deservingness of assistance, 88–89, 96–98; gendered shame, 87–88; loss of dignity, 87–88, 186; poverty, 85–89, 93–95; redeemability, 85, 89, 94–95, 133; sexuality, 90–92; social construction, 200*n*1; as social control, 88. *See also* identity; identity performance; poverty; responsibilization
shelters. *See* emergency shelters
Smith, Ashley, 44
Snow, David A., 33–34, 174
social assistance. *See* welfare and social assistance
social context for homelessness. *See* structural and systemic context
social control and discipline: about, 2–4, 15–20, 49, 145–46; consumers/clients, 15–16, 147–48, 201*n*1; dehumanization, 16, 88; dependency, 71–75, 81; discipline, defined, 15; excluded status, 142; governmentality, 13; mental health system, 37–39; otherness, 89–90; recovery industry, 163–64;
redeemability/irredeemability, 11–12, 19–20, 24–26, 145–46, 199*n*4; resistance to, 37–39; risk management, 19–20; social junk and social dynamite categories, 18–19, 24–25, 199*n*4; surveillance, 20; typology, 187. *See also* emergency shelters, residents; freedom, autonomy, and choice; power relations; project of the self; redeemability; social exclusion
social exclusion: about, 11–13, 16–20, 22–25, 49, 173–81, 182–87, 192–96; characteristics, 24, 151, 173–74; continuum, 11–12, 16–25, 151, 172–73; criminalization of excluded, 24–25, 178–81; cruel optimism, 21–22, 153, 157–58, 161, 183–84; hope and hopelessness, 12–13, 16, 174–75, 179–81; inclusion among the excluded, 22–25, 102, 167–73, 183; inclusion goals, 85, 151–59, 183–85; lived experience, 34, 73–74, 183–84, 194, 197*n*3; management of, 176–78; mental illness, 174–75, 179–81; negative effects of exclusion, 12–13, 28; pathologization of homelessness, 3, 10–11, 26, 32–33, 41, 156, 173, 184; political economy of hope, 23, 129, 159–60, 162–63, 172–74; public spaces, 3, 16, 61–63, 186; recommendations for change, 194–96; social junk and social dynamite categories, 18–19, 24–25, 199*n*4. *See also* hope and hopelessness; people experiencing homelessness; people identified as mentally ill; project of the self; redeemability; shame; social control and discipline; social exclusion and the irredeemable; social inclusion
social exclusion and the irredeemable: about, 11–12, 19–20, 24–26, 173–81; assessment of, 174–77; characteristics, 19–20, 24, 173–75,

199n4; continuum of redeemability, 11–12, 16–26, 121, 151, 172–73, 199n4; defined, 19, 199n4; distancing from, 20, 109, 134; exclusion from the excluded, 24, 94–95, 174, 180–81; hopelessness, 174–75, 179–81, 199n4; incarceration, 24–25, 175, 178–81, 199n4; not included as interviewees, 19–20; social control, 19–20, 24–25, 174–78, 199n4; social dynamite, 18–19, 24; worthiness, 88–89

social inclusion: about, 11–12, 20–22, 191–96; adoption of social norms, 11–12, 21–22; assumption of housing as, 191–92; belonging, 189, 191–92; characteristics, 11–12, 142, 151, 162–63; continuum, 11–12, 16–25, 151, 172–73; employment, 12, 91, 170–71, 186; families and friends, 12, 86, 90; recommendations for change, 194–96; variation in, 20–22. *See also* redeemability; social exclusion

social justice. *See* activism; human rights

social norms: as comparisons, 74; happiness, 91–92; HF programs, 192–93; human and social capital, 92, 106–7; identity performance, 82–83; otherness, defined, 89; power relations, 14; redeemability as adoption of, 11–12, 21–22; resistance to, 91–92; sense of self, 82–83. *See also* consumers and clients; identity; social control and discipline

Spitzer, Steven, 11, 18–19, 24

staff. *See* emergency shelters, staff

Stark, Louisa R., 55

stereotypes: about, 16–18, 29–30, 96; critical scholarship, 33–34; deservingness of assistance, 88–89, 96–98, 134, 156, 172; false dichotomies, 16–18; gender differences, 97; historical background, 32; identity construction, 83, 105–6; Indigenous Peoples, 103–4, 199n6; skid row character, 32, 96

stigma: about, 101–2, 109, 185–86; employment of shelter residents, 170–71, 186; homelessness, 86, 185–86; management of, 101–2, 109–14, 120–21, 128; self-blame, 127–28; of skin trades, 202n9. *See also* social exclusion; social exclusion and the irredeemable

structural and systemic context: about, 1–3, 10–11, 13, 33–34, 49, 149, 152–53, 190; affordable housing shortages, 65, 67, 152, 201n3; criminalization of mental illness, 43–44; enriched environments, 130–31, 132–33; examples of, 10, 30, 123–24, 152, 161; failure of state, 152, 183, 190; funding for individual vs structural model, 9–10, 116, 157; gender differences, 137–39; historical background, 32–33, 95–96; homelessness prevention, 53, 190–92, 194–95; vs individualization, 9–11, 13, 21, 33–34, 152, 183, 190; lack of needed mental health resources, 38, 58, 103–5, 150, 155–59, 165–66, 175–76, 198n6, 201n2 (ch. 6); over-policing, 123–24; pathologization of homelessness, 3, 10–11, 32–33, 41, 156, 173; political economy of hope, 23, 160–61; recommendations for change, 194–96; self-blame, 26, 126–27, 137–39, 186. *See also* individualization of social problems

Stuart, Forrest, 58, 109, 170

subsidized housing. *See* affordable and social housing

substance use: about, 41–42; concurrent disorders, 41–42, 103–5, 119–20, 158–59; criminal justice system, 130–31; harm reduction, 42, 122, 130–31; identity management, 110. *See also* addiction; addiction treatments; alcoholism

Sylvestre, Marie-Eve, 48
symbolic interactionism, 4–5
systemic challenges. *See* structural and systemic context
Szasz, Thomas, 37–38, 117

Thistle, Jesse, 28, 31–32, 118, 128
total institutions: about, 25, 52–55, 80–81; balance of security and care, 76–77; compared with neoliberal total institutions, 52–55, 60, 65, 68, 70–71, 80–81; defined, 53–54; freedom to leave, 60–63, 64–67, 81; mortification, 59, 65–66, 78, 81; power relations, 74; social control, 55–60, 80–81. *See also* emergency shelters
transcarceration, 52, 55. *See also* emergency shelters; homelessness industrial complex; prison industrial complex
transgender people, 29, 108–9. *See also* LGBTQ2S+ people
TRC (Truth and Reconciliation Commission), 187–88, 194. *See also* Indigenous Peoples
"treatment first," 40, 104. *See also* Housing First (HF)
true and untrue selves, 111–14, 116, 124–27, 173, 183. *See also* identity performance
truth regimes, 5, 13
twelve-step programs (AA/NA), 120, 122, 130, 162, 173, 201*n*2 (ch. 5)

unsalveagable, 19–20, 199*n*4. *See also* social exclusion and the irredeemable

violence: home takeovers, 67, 192; intimate partner violence, 156; sexual violence, 138–39
VI-SPDAT (Vulnerability Index-Service Prioritization Decision Assistance Tool), 41, 198*n*8
Voronka, Jijian, 39, 193

vulnerable people. *See* Indigenous Peoples; marginalized people; racialized people

Wacquant, Loïc, 91
wealth inequality, 30
welfare and social assistance: about, 85; deservingness, 88–89, 96–99, 133–34, 156, 172; disabled people, 171–72, 194, 202*n*12; flawed consumers, 147–49, 156; historical dismantling of, 32, 51, 95–97; inclusion goals, 85, 159; responsibilization, 134; self-blame, 149; shame, 85, 87; social junk category, 18–19. *See also* Ontario Disability Support Payments (ODSP); Ontario Works (OW); people with disabilities; people experiencing homelessness; people identified as mentally ill; poverty
women: criminal justice system, 44–45; deservingness, 97–98; ethic of care, 138–39; gender differences, 97, 137–38; gendered shame, 87–88; historical background, 32, 96–97; identity performance, 110–14; Indigenous women, 31–32, 138–39, 194; interviewees, demographics, 7(t); motherhood, 110–11, 138; poverty, 29, 96–98; responsibilization, 137–38; safety and security, 100; statistics, 29, 44–45; victims of violence, 138, 156. *See also* gender; Haven men's and women's shelter (pseudonym)
work and employment, 12, 91, 170–71, 186

Yatim, Sammy, 44, 199*n*8
Young, Jock, 11, 16, 17, 109, 173, 184
youth: critical scholarship, 34; demographics, 7(t), 29; historical background, 32, 96; marginalized youth, 47–48

Zinger, Ivan, 44